THE LICHEN FACTOR

The Quest
for
Community Development
in
Canada

Jim Lotz

The University College of Cape Breton Press acknowledges the support received from the Canada Council for the Arts for our publishing program.

Cover design by Ryan Astle

Book design by Joseph E. MacEachern
Printed and bound in Canada by City Printers

Canadian Cataloguing in Publication Data

Main entry under title

The lichen factor

Includes bibliographical references.
ISBN 0-920336-62-2

1. Community development -- Canada. I. Title.

HN110.Z9C6 1998   307.1'47'0971   C98-950115-9

UCCB Press
Box 5300
Sydney, Nova Scotia
B1P 6L2
CANADA

This one's for Peter, my grandson

Books by the author:

Community and Regional Development
Northern Realities
Understanding Canada
Cape Breton Island (with Pat Lotz)
Head, Heart and Hands: Craftspeople of Nova Scotia
Sharing a Lifetime of Experience: The CESO Story
Father Jimmy: The Life and Times of Father Jimmy Tompkins
(with Michael Welton)

Canadian History
A History of Canada
Canadian Pacific
The Mounties
Prime Ministers of Canada
Canadians at War

Murder Mysteries/Thrillers
Death in Dawson
Murder on the Mackenzie
Killing in Kulane
The Sixth of December

Other
Discover Canada: Nova Scotia
(Ed.) Pilot Not Commander: Essays in Memory of Dr. Diamond Jenness (with Pat Lotz)
(Ed.) Nova Scotia Small Business Year Book, 1987-88

CONTENTS

ACKNOWLEDGEMENTS

This book has been a long time in the making, and I cannot begin to thank all those whose ideas, suggestions, comments and corrections have helped me to understand the myths and realities of community development. They range from those I met in Christian communities to a number of Canadian academics who have been supportive of the views and eccentricities of an independent researcher.

I owe much to Alex Sim, pioneer Canadian adult educator, and to Dr. Michael Welton who is following in his footsteps. Pat Dunphy and Angus MacIntyre shared their experiences on the front lines of community development with me. George Melnyk's work on co-ops and co-operation has been a constant inspiration. I learned a lot about community life in Nova Scotia from the late Brad Finigan and his wife Muriel. Dr. Jim McNiven's ideas on the broader context of community development in today's world have been very helpful.

To Dr. Gertrude MacIntyre and her husband Carl, I owe a special debt of gratitude for hospitality and inspiration during visits to Cape Breton. Mike Robinson, Executive Director of the Arctic Institute of North America, has sent me his papers on community development and generously shared his ideas and experiences in this field. Bill Pardy's idealism and belief in the wisdom of ordinary people and their ability to solve their own problems with their own resources have been a guiding light in recent years, as has Dr. Desmond Connor's continuing search for sane and effective ways of encouraging public participation in decision making. Estelle and Mario Carota have shown how effective individuals can be in the struggle for social justice and have shared their stories with me. I thank them both. Frank Thompson of Stornoway on the island of Lewis has been a faithful friend and correspondent, and the information he has given me on what is happening on the edges of Scotland has helped me to make sense of what is happening on the edges of Canada. Dr. Desmond Morton offered some valuable criticisms of earlier drafts of the book and helped me to focus my rather scattered thoughts and words. Arnold Edinborough also receives my thanks for his early involvement in this book.

Hank Woods and Leo Deveau, in their very different ways, enhanced the ways I learned about Canada, as did Dr. Colin Dodds of Saint Mary's University, Halifax. Numerous other individuals have added their wisdom to this process, including Narindar Singh, Dr. D.S. Chahal, Karen Casselman, Allan Andrews, Dr. Roger Pearson, Catherine Umland (née Campbell), Peter O'Brien, Dr. Joe Bogen, André Carrel (Rossland), Karl Schutz (Chemainus), Juan Tellez, John Burbridge, Sandra Hayes, Professor John Fairley, Hywel Griffiths, Sheila Bailey.... The list of those who shared their ideas and knowledge with me seems endless.

I am, as ever, deeply indebted to my wife Pat. Her good sense, objectivity and skilled editorial eye helped immensely in a difficult task.

In 1989, I received a grant for my research from the Social Sciences and Humanities Research Council as a private scholar. This category of support no long exists, unfortunately, but this funding allowed me to step back and look at my work with a fresh eye. In 1992, I received a senior Canada Council Arts grant to write this book. The two grants allowed me to concentrate my random thoughts at a rather hectic time of scrambling for a living.

Needless to say, any errors, omissions or plain old fashioned mistakes and misinterpretations in the book are entirely my own responsibility. I have ever been open to correction. One theme of *The Lichen Factor* has always had special relevance to my life and thought: Nobody's perfect!

PROLOGUE

"Old men ought to be explorers."
T.S. Eliot, *East Coker*

This book forms the last part of a trilogy on Canada. I came to this country in 1954, and have been struggling since then to understand its complexity and potential.

After carrying out research in the north between 1955 and 1966, I wrote *Northern Realities*, published in 1970. It outlined the history of northern development, and looked at the ways in which Canadians viewed that vast and desolate land beyond the country's settled, southern belt. Some Canadians see the north as a place to clean up and clear out, make money, then beat a hasty retreat to kinder climes. Others view the north as a pure and pristine wilderness, a primeval, untainted land, free of all the ills of industrial society. To most Canadians, the north is simply there, part of the national identity, a land of ice and snow, Inuit and Mounties, expensive to visit and a difficult place in which to survive.

After research in a wide variety of settings, I wrote *Understanding Canada*, published in 1977. It examined the relationships between citizens and the state in Canada. To some people, government served as a source of benefits, a sure and stable point of reference in their lives. To other Canadians, the state represented an oppressive force, limiting their freedom, liberty and right to do their own thing. Increasingly, however, we have begun to experience a high degree of ambiguity about our governments at every level. We no longer trust them to do the right thing as once we did, and the gaps in society between "Us" and "Them" keep widening. And life does not seem to be as good these days as it used to be in the past.

The *Lichen Factor* addresses these concerns. It seeks to explain the roots of the discontents of our time, to determine why the gaps between government and people are widening, and to suggest some ways of narrowing the divisions that have emerged in Canada by using the approach to change known as community development. In the past, governments have promoted too many private fantasies at public expense. Now the climate has changed, and the eye of everyone is on the bottom line and value for money.

I'm not an objective observer of life in Canada. I have a deep and passionate concern for a country that has given me lots of opportunities and experiences about which I could never have dreamed while growing up in working-class Liverpool, England. James Thurber writes of sketching what he saw through a microscope, and being told by his instructor that he'd drawn his own eye. Taking weather observations in the Arctic I often wondered whether I was measuring objective realities. Or was I, by installing instruments on the surface of glaciers, creating a microclimate and simply measuring *that*? In 1960 I moved from the physical to the social sciences. Most of my research since then has been on outsiders and those living on the edges of Canadian society—northerners, Maritimers, squatters, unemployed youth, Indian women. Here, as in my research in the physical sciences, I had difficulty with the concept of objectivity, of being a mere observer of human interactions. Whatever I studied touched chords in my own being. My probings into the lives of individuals and communities proved to be a mirror to myself—and a window on a large and complex world shot through with mystery and ambiguity.

Since leaving university life in 1973, I've continued my research as an independent scholar, while making a living in diverse ways. Thus I have been freed from the necessity to promote certain theories to please my peers. And I have not had to adhere to one ideology or school of thought that explains everything, everywhere. I have borrowed theories, devised a few of my own, and watched them dissolve in the acid tests of reality. The mystery of the world, its complexity, its sheer unknowingness, its pervasive ambiguity and wonder continually baffled me—and baffles me still. During the Sixties, social scientists began to influence government policies, plans and actions through their theoretical work. I wondered how they knew so much about everything while I seemed to know so little about anything. I watched in awe as some individuals complicated and fouled up simple tasks while others did great things with limited resources.

I was trained in the pragmatic British tradition of learning through the soles of your feet, by going out, seeing what was happening on the ground and talking to those involved. Walter Fitzgerald, my first professor, told of going to a conference on Africa in London. One of the experts present stated that mangroves did not grow in a certain part of the continent. Fitzgerald said: "I've been there and I've seen them." Herodotus also played a part in my early education. In his histories, he always told the reader what he had seen—and what he had heard from others.

The Lichen Factor attempts to summarize what I've learned about community development since 1960. The word "community" has become a mantra for our troubled times. Slapped on any and every initiative from the local to the national, the word, and the concept behind it, offers warmth, comfort, a sense of belonging to solitary souls adrift in an uncaring world. But the reasons we crave community are rooted in complex historical forces. Creating community is no easy matter, and the process is much prone to failure. In demythologizing community, I have sought to replace it with the idea of mutual aid, of interdependence between humans that mirrors the symbiosis found in the lichen. In bringing the concept of community down to earth, I have drawn upon the history of how humans have attempted to create better societies through co-operation. In examining mutual aid, interdependence and symbiosis in human relationships I have tried to identify the forces and factors that make them work. Canada has a long history of effective community development. The excessive individualism and brute materialism of the United States makes the creation of new communities there difficult. In the older societies of Europe and the rest of the world, conformity to past ways, ancient fears and hatreds, the struggle for survival limit what can be done to create better societies. Canada strongly resembles Bernard Shaw's definition of marriage: He claimed that it combined the maximum of temptation with the maximum of opportunity. We are still making a new kind of nation in a huge, harsh and difficult land. How we deal with our temptations and opportunities will mould our common future—and offer direction and ideas to other countries struggling with divisive forces.

The Lichen Factor offers no more than a rough path through the thickets of change that entangle our lives and limit our hopes for a better future. I have walked this path of community, blazed a trail, indicating its promise and perils, and now erect a few signposts to guide those seeking to follow it. The book is offered to all who love this strange and bewildering land of Canada and who are working towards the future of its many communities. It shows what is possible, even in the hardest times, for those who seek to encourage the Lichen Factor, that mysterious process underlying all forms of human co-operation and mutual aid.

Jim Lotz,

Halifax, Nova Scotia.

September, 1997.

INTRODUCTION

"We shall not cease from exploration
And the end of all our exploring
Will be to arrive where we started
And know the place for the first time."

T.S. Eliot, *Little Gidding*

Little Gidding, in Huntingdon, England, came into being in 1625, a troubled time in English history. Its founder, Nicholas Ferrar, a wealthy man, turned his back on power and privilege to live a simple, religious life. This intentional Christian community fell into decline after his death in 1637. In 1981, the Community of Christ the Sower, with an international membership, was founded here.

CARIBOU, MUSK-OXEN, LICHEN

"Science cannot solve the ultimate mystery of
nature. And that is because...
we ourselves are part of nature and therefore of the
mystery we are trying to solve."
Max Planck, formulator of the quantum theory.

In Canada's Arctic, you encounter three responses to the challenges of survival in this harsh land.

When caribou fight, they sometimes lock horns. Rushing frantically backwards and forwards, trying desperately to untangle themselves, they eventually collapse and die. Across the north you find small heaps of bones and interlocked antlers, silent witness to the folly of mutually assured destruction.

Musk-oxen, great, shaggy beasts, wander the tundra, browsing on its scanty vegetation. When attacked by wolves, the males form a defensive circle, putting their mates and young in the middle, pointing their horns outwards. Any wolf coming too close risks being hooked and hurled into the air. Along the shores of Lake Hazen in northern Ellesmere Island, we found heaps of bones and the bullet shattered skulls of long-dead musk-oxen. The animals had been shot by Peary and his hunters in the early years of this century. When the musk-oxen formed circles to defend themselves against these new intruders, their stance simply made it easier for these meat-hungry men to kill them.

The Canadian north also harbours over a thousand separate species of lichen. They are symbioses between two different forms of life, algae and fungi: One cannot live without the other. Because they are dual organisms, lichen do not fit into a single plant kingdom. The alga makes food for itself and the fungus, synthesizing carbohydrates from the air with the help of the sun's energy. The fungus draws minerals from the rocks and supplies them to its partner. Some lichens are over two thousand years old. Others survive on glaciers. Certain species can lie dormant for decades, awaiting the right moment to grow, expand and colonize new areas. If an environment becomes too rich, or too polluted, lichens die. In Antarctica, black lichens have survived for centuries in dry valleys with average annual temperatures of -45 C.[1]

This simple life form splashes boulders, trees, buildings in diverse forms, shapes and colours. No law demands this diversity. No government agency forces lichens to do what they do. No human agency insists that they conform to a preset, standard pattern.

Caribou sustained some Inuit groups, and musk-oxen provided them—and intruders into their land—with meat and clothing. Lichens have many more uses. They play a vital role in the web of new life in barren places, providing food for bugs, and cover for mites, wood lice and caterpillars as the process of soil formation begins. Lichens have been a boon to humans too. The ancient Egyptians made flour from them. As the Israelites struggled towards the Promised Land, they may have fed on the manna lichen, a desert species. Inuit in Canada and Greenland snacked on lichens, a source of Vitamin C and starch. Sir John Franklin claimed that *tripe de roche* saved his party from starvation in 1829. In the fourteenth century, a Florentine discovered a way of making dyes from lichens, founding a family fortune. Makers of Harris Tweed coloured their cloth with lichen-dyes to ensure its durability and to resist moths. Karen Casselman, a Nova Scotia weaver, carries on this tradition and teaches its techniques to others.[2] Lichens contain usnic acid, which has been found to be more effective than penicillin in healing certain kinds of wounds, burns and infections. In recent years, as environmental pollution increases, lichens have begun to serve as useful indicators of its levels.

As Bland puts it:

"Lichens are notably inconspicuous—hiding in plain sight... Thriving on neglect, they are far more competent to hold their own in the struggle for existence than most higher plants."[3]

Lichens show how mutual aid and interdependence enable two different life forms to survive in extreme conditions. But they still puzzle scientists and offer mysteries that have yet to be unravelled. Is the symbiosis found in lichen based on mutuality—or parasitism? Are the algae taking advantage of the fungi—or *vice versa*? How did this unique life form come into being? There is no trace of lichens in the fossil record. And why does this symbiosis colonize the harshest, most difficult and most challenging edges of the earth, the hot and cold deserts, the high mountains?

Interest in symbiosis, mutualism and cooperation between different life forms has increased in recent years. Carolus Linnaeus (1707-78) noted certain birds alerting others to the presence of hawks. A crab acts as guardian of larger conches, protecting them from predators. In Houston, Texas, a species of beetle prunes old branches from mimosa trees, keeping them healthy. *Polygonium* flourishes on Saint Pierre and Miquelon and elsewhere. The ornamental bush enriches and purifies soil through its roots. You can uproot it, poison it, cover the plant in concrete. It will still survive and grow because of its symbiotic and mutually beneficial relationship with the soil.

Caribou, musk-oxen and lichen are natural phenomena.

They also serve as symbols, showing the choices that humans can adopt in dealing with challenges and change: Conflict, Confrontation, Co-operation. Symbols reflect our ideals and our fears, move us beyond ourselves. They point the way to deeper, more mysterious realities than the everyday ones with which we have to cope. Symbols touch our heads and our hearts, bring alive hidden yearnings. Symbols like the Christian cross can inspire and uplift. Others, such as the Nazi swastika, exude threat and malevolence.

What I have called the Lichen Factor is elusive and mysterious. It offers a way of restructuring human relationships, providing a basis for mutual aid and co-operation, indicating the potential for generating harmony among diverse peoples. The Lichen Factor is not a prescriptive remedy for human ills, an instant solution for all the problems that afflict individuals and communities. Gabriel Marcel (1889-1973), the French existentialist Christian philosopher, distinguished between problems and mysteries.[4] A problem is outside you, in the external world. It can be solved, depending on the available social or mechanical technology. A mystery cannot be dealt with in the same way, for it is within you. In your daily interactions with others and the external world, you explore this mystery as you work through issues, complexities, concerns. This journey into the heart of the mystery within the self is not linear, rational or easy. Rather, it is winding, discursive, cyclical, moving you into the future, as you recall what you learned in the past. Most of our life consists of circling, doing more or less the same thing, in the same way, again and again. As Northrop Frye puts it: "Every circle is a failed cycle." During times of rapid change, there are opportunities to break out of traditional circles and to explore the depths of the self and the wonders of life beyond it.

The humble lichen points the way to doing this, its symbiotic form illustrating the benefits of mutual aid and co-operation in difficult places and times. Lichen are not intellectual constructs, theories, concepts, hypotheses, paradigms. They do not exist to teach or preach about better ways of surviving and thriving in harsh environments. They simply *are*, integral parts of nature. Their symbiotic form breaks through the entrenched "either/or" mindset that divides people and communities. Algae and fungi retain their separate identities while creating something different through co-operation. Most of the dialogues of our time are cast in terms of conflict: profits or people, centralization or decentralization, private enterprise or state control, "Us" versus "Them." This way of looking at the world has been strengthened by the spread of digital devices. The numbers in them are either one or zero, the switch always "on" or "off." Humans also learn from analogies, comparing what they do with what they see. Lichens serve as an analogy for a better kind of human community, at the local and the international levels. And the Lichen Factor is apparent everywhere, inconspicuous, not shouting its name, thriving on the margins of society, ignored and misunderstood, especially by the powerful and the media. This strange, mysterious factor does not fit easily into the categories they use to classify, describe and control people. Instead, the term "community" is thrown around and applied to a wide range of activities that may or may not demonstrate the Lichen Factor.

The presence of the Lichen Factor has to be seen in historical context. It is linked to an ongoing quest for the ideal community, the good society, utopia, and very hard to describe in words. Like sex, it's better enjoyed than analyzed. The Northern Lights flicker across the night sky, a wondrous and awesome phenomenon. They can be explained scientifically as the bombardment of the earth's atmosphere by ions. But knowing that does not diminish your sense of awe as you gaze at these lovely shimmering, ever-changing sheets of lights in the northern skies.

Words fail as you try to describe this kind of experience.

Which brings us to...

A WORD ABOUT WORDS

"Words strain
Crack and sometimes break, under the burden,
Under the tension, slip, slide, perish,
Decay with imprecision, will not stay in place,
Will not stay in place."

T.S. Eliot *Burnt Norton*

Every writer recognizes the truth of Eliot's observation, as they struggle to describe internal and external worlds with symbols that have meaning for others. Einstein claimed that he rarely thought in words at all. His formula, $E = MC^2$, reduced complex processes in nature to a few symbols, reshaping the way we look at the world.

The current enthusiasm for the Internet and the World Wide Web, with its huge outpourings of words, reflects what happened at the end of the nineteenth century. As people became increasingly literate, newspaper barons created the modern mass media to meet their hunger for news and information. In those days, you needed millions to enter the media world. Today, with modern electronic technology, anyone can be his or her own publisher with a few thousand dollars.

The excess of words in our world has deflated their meaning and power. While there is much talk these days about the "Information Revolution," our time has been one during which more nonsense and irrelevant material has been spewed out than ever before. As Gertrude Stein put it: "Everybody gets so much information all day that they lose their common sense."

The increase in the quantity of words has led to a demand for a better quality of them, and for more precision in communication. The English and the Americans have been described as a people divided by a common language. During the Korean War—euphemistically called a "police action" by politicians—ten thousand Chinese troops attacked a hill overlooking the Imjin River in April,1951. It was held by eight hundred men of the Gloucester Regimen, who fought desperately to defend it. The sensible thing would have been to withdraw the soldiers:

> "A British officer at Brigade HQ believed that the Americans did not understand until much too late how desperate was the predicament of 29 Brigade. When Tom [the brigadier] told Corps that his position was 'a bit sticky,' they simply did not grasp that in British Army parlance, that meant 'critical.'"[5]

Only forty-three soldiers escaped from what became known as Gloucester Hill. One hundred died, and the rest, including two hundred wounded, became captives of the Chinese. This disaster stemmed from a misunderstanding about the meaning of three words.

George Orwell sought to write prose as clear as a window pane. His observations on language are more relevant today than when he made them:

> "The great enemy of clear language is insincerity. [When there] is a gap between one's real and one's declared aims, one turns instinctively to long words and exhausted idioms, like a cuttlefish squirting ink."[6]

In our day when the personal is political, the world is awash with cuttlefish ink. Words that once had power, majesty and meaning—community, development, democracy, compassion, concern—have been drained of mystery and their ability to touch and animate people.

> "In our time, political speech and writing are largely the defence of the indefensible...Thus political language has to consist largely of euphemism, question-begging and sheer cloudy vagueness."[7]

Orwell wrote these words in 1946. He notes that the English language "becomes ugly and inaccurate because our thoughts are foolish, but the slovenliness of our language makes it easier for us to have foolish thoughts."[8]

The same problems that Orwell identified over fifty years ago still plague the English language: dying metaphors, verbal false limbs, pretentious diction, meaningless words. There are ways of cutting through the clutter of words, of transcending the endless nonsense spewed out by the media and politicians, of simplifying the complexities of the world and making them more understandable. Northrop Frye has pointed the way to do this. He distinguishes between anxiety and concern. Anxiety is a reaction to the daily deluge of bad news about tensions and crises poured out by the mainstream media. Concern is the calm, reflective response to genuine problems of real people. From concern, properly articulated, can come opportunities for mutual aid and co-operation with others. From anxiety comes guilt and feelings of powerlessness.

To operate effectively, all societies develop and nurture founding myths. For the Americans, the founding myth rests on the belief that every one is entitled to "Life, liberty and the pursuit of happiness." If these values are not visible every day, and in every way, Americans feel cheated. Canadians settled for, "Peace, Order and Good Government" as one of this nation's founding myths. These myths, however removed they are from reality, enable us to get through the day and give us standards by which we can judge how well or how ill the country fares. As Frye puts it:

> "Society attaches an immense importance to saying the right thing at the right time. In this conception of the 'right thing,' there are two factors involved one moral, one aesthetic. They are inseparable, and equally important."[9]

He identifies three levels of language:

> "Ordinary speech is largely concerned with registering our reactions to what goes on outside us. In all such reactions

there's a large automatic or mechanical element. And if our only aim is to say what gets by in society, our reactions will become almost completely mechanical."[10]

And so we have the mouthing of endless clichés that pass for conversation and serve as a way of numbing our capacity for original thought and expression. Any defence of the free-market is derided by left wingers as "neo-conservative." Any demand for more state intervention by radicals will be mocked by conservatives as a step on the road to serfdom. Both the free market and statism rest on mythical foundations. As John Bulloch, founding president of the Canadian Federation of Independent Business, put it: "No business person believes in competition, except between his or her suppliers."

Another kind of language emerges from governments and professions—"federal prose, the gabble of abstractions and vague words which avoids any simple or direct statement."[11] This renders "objective" and "impersonal" any official utterances "to suggest that the social machine...usually a government agency, is running smoothly, and that no human factors are going to disturb it."[12]

In 1997, two reports—that of the Royal Commission on Canada's Aboriginal Peoples and the Somalia enquiry one—overloaded the public consciousness with immense torrents of words showing that the machinery of government is not running smoothly. In defending their actions, senior military officers squirted out gallons of cuttlefish ink, obscuring what had really happened in Somalia and Canada. In 1997, I attended a meeting at which Indian dancers demonstrated how they celebrated their culture and how they dealt with intruders. Without words, they summarized dramatically the outcome of these encounters.

Which brings us to Frye's third level of language, that of the imagination, of personal visions and fantasies that describe castles in the air and dungeons beneath the earth: "It is the language of human nature, the language that makes both Shakespeare and Pushkin authentic poets, that gives social vision to both Lincoln and Gandhi."[13]

Frye points out that we all live in two worlds—that of reality and that of personal and collective visions. He ends his plea for an "Educated Imagination" with an image of how idealism and realism can come together in "the language of human nature." It:

> "...never speaks unless we take the time to listen in leisure, and it speaks only in a voice too quiet for panic to hear. And then all it has to tell us, when we look over the edge of our leaning tower, is that we are not getting any nearer heaven, and that it is time to return to earth."[14]

In exploring the myths surrounding the concept of community and examining the realities of mutual aid and co-operation, I have been greatly enlightened by the words of poets, playwrights and philosophers, and by the work of painters, dancers, craftspeople. Their imaginative expressions speak more clearly to ordinary people than do the masses of academic studies, the enormous piles of commission and enquiry reports, and the endless publications of government agencies and experts claiming to describe what is happening in the world today. The silent languages of art in particular, reflecting contemporary reality and anticipating future trends, is particularly useful in deciphering the codes by which people strive to communicate.

During the nineteenth century in France, most painters worked in their studios. As the Industrial Revolution darkened the skies over Europe, the Impressionists went into the countryside and splashed their canvases with light and colour. Technology, often presented as the polar opposite of art, assisted this process. New manufacturing methods offered artists brighter, sharper colours—and the tubes to contain them while they worked outdoors.

The Impressionists presented the world as a wash of colour and light.

Then came Cézanne—"the father of us all."

He combined opposites in his work, severity with a new way of painting light, structure with an underlying exuberance. Cézanne saw beyond the blazes of light and colour in the work of other painters to the elementary forms of artistic creation, the bare bones of landscapes, objects, human figures and faces. For Cézanne, everything was based on cylinders, spheres and cones. His work led the way for the cubists as the world began to disintegrate in the twentieth century.

In seeking to make sense of what I've seen and read about in the vast and expanding field of community development, I have attempted to reduce the forces and factors involved to a few symbols that have transcendental meaning—the cross, the spiral, the hourglass, the bell curve. Two dimensional paper limits what anyone can do in this respect. At Expo 67, Buckminster Fuller asked his audience to tell him the number of degrees in a right-angle triangle. Someone shouted: "180." Fuller nodded. Then he shaped a ball in his hands, pointing out that if you draw a right-angle triangle on it, each angle will subtend ninety degrees, making 270 in all. You cannot, for example, represent a spiral on a flat sheet of paper.

The symbols I have used indicate how mutual aid can flourish. For the past three hundred years, people in industrial societies have been obsessed with change. Using the lichen and its symbiotic form as a guide and a symbol, I have sought to determine what has assisted humans to create stable and secure relationships through co-operative action.

But first, we have to explore the sources of our present discontents.

THE SOURCES OF OUR DISCONTENTS

"As Canadians stand on the threshold of the 70s
they see on the horizon the outline of many brilliant
changes and developments...marking us as a community capable of realizing the full promise of the
post industrial era—developments which single us
out as one of the world's most affluent peoples
with a spiralling gross national product
and a rising standard of living."

White Paper on Unemployment (1970)

"Nation won't make it into 2000, a third believe.
Pollster calls Canadians' views
grimmest in 20 years."

Headline, Front Page, *Globe and Mail*, 18 December,1995.

THE BIRTH OF THE MODERN WORLD

"'Tis all in peeces, all cohaerence gone;
All just supply, and all Relation:
Prince, Subject, Father, Sonne, are things forgot,
For every man alone thinkes he hath got
To be a Phoenix, and that then can bee
None of that kinde, of which he is, but hee."

John Donne wrote those words in 1611, as the old ties of kin and community began to loosen in England. In 1517, Martin Luther protested against corruption in his church. The assault on centralized, hierarchical, authoritarian institutions accelerated as kings and leaders in northern Europe saw how breaking away from Catholicism could benefit them. Calvin's doctrine of predestination assured successful people that they were the elect of God. As R.H. Tawney pointed out in *Religion and the Rise of Capitalism*, this belief generated the "Protestant ethic" that equated success in business with God's approval of the ways of ruthless industrialists. The essence of the revolution they led can be summed up in three words: Cheapness, Quantity, Uniformity. Into the dark satanic mills of Britain moved the displaced land dwellers as the Agriculture Revolution, led by "improvers," showed how new crops, machines and techniques could produce more food with fewer hands. In rural areas, workers paced their lives by the seasons, wind and weather. In the new factories, they lived by clock time. In rural societies, individuals depended on each other in complex networks of relationships and responsibilities. Factories ran on standard, uniform, impersonal schedules.

As the Industrial Revolution speeded up, and the new middle class gained power, its members sought to overthrow the old, ossified, aristocratic social order that prevented progress. This concept, invented by French philosophers in the eighteenth century to sell their books, rested on the assumption that tomorrow could be made much better than today by the application of reason and technology to human affairs. The Democratic Revolution began in the American colonies. Chafing against the restraints upon their freedom imposed by the British, wealthy planters, merchants and others borrowed some ideas from the French philosophers and revolted. When Cornwallis surrendered to the American rebels at Yorktown in 1781, his army band played a popular tune: "The World Turned Upside Down." Suspicious of the ways of old Europe, the leaders of the Thirteen Colonies set up a government system to ensure that no single part of it would have supreme power. This notion of countervailing forces to check political and bureaucratic excess had little appeal in Canada. The United Empire Loyalists fled here to remain under the British crown and a unitary system of government.

The new United States and Canada had a singular advantage— plenty of space and lots of what looked like empty land. The energetic, ambitious and discontented could head to the frontier if they could not find a place in settled society.

When the French Revolution broke out in 1789, its leaders sought to replace tradition with the rule of reason, and to create new men and women dedicated to the pursuit of Liberty, Equality and Fraternity.

On 9 October, 1789, Dr. Joseph Ignace Guillotin, the former professor of anatomy at the medical faculty of Paris, put forward a proposition that combined ideas of progress and equality:

> "I. Crimes of the same kind shall be punished by the same kind of punishment, whatever the rank of the criminal
> II. In all cases...of capital punishment, it shall be executed by means of a machine..."

Guillotin defended his new device:

> "Now, with my machine, I strike off your head in a twinkling of an eye, and you never feel it."

At first, viewers of the new machine expressed disappointment with this new technology. It lacked the spectacle of the old way of killing people—it was too modern, too fast, an industrial machine, unlike the traditional hand-done executions by real professionals who knew how to prolong agonies.

The French Revolution plunged the country into turmoil.

And yet, life went on normally for many people. A Scottish gardener looking after the palace garden in Paris kept a diary. He made no mention of political events, except on 10 August, 1793:

> "...when he noted that crowds had trampled on the flower beds of the Tuileries. This was in fact the armed rising which led to the fall of the French monarchy."[15]

The Industrial and Democratic Revolutions swept over Europe during the nineteenth century as the new nations there extended their power over indigenous peoples in Africa and Asia. Life began to improve for ordinary people in Europe and North America. At the end of the nineteenth century, working men and women could look forward to a life free of daily drudgery. Their children lived longer, their diets improved, while universal education offered the promise of a more leisured and creative existence. Interest in how governments and powerful people organized society rose as workers questioned the divine right of others to rule their lives. As Julien Benda put it:

> "An apostle of the modern world clamors for 'politics first'... Coming to the man of the people, we can measure the increase of his political passions in modern times by considering, as Stendhal puts it, how long his whole passion was limited to (a) Not to be killed (b) For a good warm coat."[16]

The belief that reason, technology and the more efficient organization of society would usher in a better world pervaded the thinking of the leaders of nineteenth century. Richard Gatling (1818-1903) invented the rapid-fire gun named after him. It could fire 1,200 shots a minute. Its inventor believed that such killing power would make war impossible.

Superior military technology and disciplined armies enabled Europeans and North Americans to take possession of the lands of indigenous peoples: "We have got the Maxim gun. / And they have not." *Sanders of the River*, a British movie made in 1935 that turns up once in a while on late-night TV, shows how the colonial powers kept the natives in check. The locals sing: "Sandy the good, Sandy the wise, righter of wrongs, hater of lies." When a chief misbehaves, Sandy, ever the unflapable colonial administrator sends a boat up the river. Loyal African *askaris* spray the chief's village with machine-gun fire, then land and restore order with their rifles.

A plaque on a mansion on a Jamaica sugar plantation expresses the imperial British ethic, reflecting its arrogant ways whereby local people were kept in awe of empire:

> "His Majesty the King Emperor is personified in every Englishman abroad, and orders must be given in suitably imperious tone. Shout if necessary. God is your authority."[17]

The Edwardian era in Europe, a time of optimism and the blind belief in progress, took place as the imperial powers moved into their twilight. A quarter of the globe, coloured red, formed the British Empire upon which the sun never set. Germany and other powers had seized large chunks of Africa and Asia, and China had been humiliated. On 14-15 April, 1912, the *Titanic* sank after hitting an iceberg. That event haunts us still, the image of the mighty, modern ship slipping into the icy sea with a loss of over 1,500 lives.

Two years later, the world descended into the chaos of the First World War. Britain declared war on Germany and Austria on 4 August, 1914, without asking her colonies for their consent. Despite the euphoria and optimism of the pre-war days, underlying tensions had begun to surface. To many young men, the war offered a chance for adventure, for nations it promised a testing time of sacrifice and struggle. Churchill claimed that the rulers of Europe had fallen into "a kind of dull cataleptic trance." Franz Joseph, emperor of Austria and king of Hungary, sighed as he signed the declaration of war against Russia: "Well, if we must perish at least we will do it decently and in good order."

Canada had no quarrel with the European powers. But in the First World War, this "whelp of the English lion" suffered 232,494 casualties, including almost sixty thousand dead. The last words of former prime minister Wilfrid Laurier, dying on 18 February, 1919, could serve as an epitaph for his optimistic era: *"C'est fini."*

In the year that Laurier died, W.B. Yeats wrote *The Second Coming*. Its words echo through our troubled times:

"Things fall apart; the centre cannot hold;
Mere anarchy is loosed upon the world...
The best lack all conviction, while the worst
Are full of passionate intensity."

At the peace conference at Versailles, Canada took its place at the table as an equal partner because of this country's superb war record. President Wilson preached the gospel of the self-determination of nations, sowing the seeds for future conflicts. The peacemakers excluded revolutionary Russia from their deliberations, and crippled Germany with heavy reparations to pay for the conflict. An epidemic of Spanish flu in 1918 killed as many people as warfare had done. The post war years brought mild prosperity to Europe and North America, until the Great Depression began in 1929. The capitalist democracies seemed unable to cope with widespread unemployment. In Italy, Germany and Russia, dictators took power creating totalitarian states ruled by fear and bound together by fanatical nationalism. In Britain, John Maynard Keynes recommended that democratic government intervene in the market when it could not generate jobs for all. In the United States, President Roosevelt launched the New Deal through measures that the Supreme Court found to be outside the jurisdiction of his administration. But by the time the judges decided this, the world had plunged into war. The Canadian House of Commons delayed declaring war on Germany for a week after the British did so in September 1939. We had no quarrel with the Germans or ambitions in Europe. Often poorly trained, ill-equipped and badly led, Canadian men and women performed well under the worst conditions. About one in ten Canadians enlisted during the Second World War, and forty-two thousand of them died on foreign fields, in alien skies and distant oceans.

During both wars, Canadians showed a peculiar penchant for adhering to discipline *and* showing initiative when the occasion demanded it. The late "Robbie" Robinson, a Nova Scotian who served in both wars, summarized the difference between the two conflicts: "In the first one, you could drive a man. In the second, you had to ask him if he would do something."[18]

The Allies won the Second World War through superior technology, better organization, the industrial might of the United States, and the overwhelming number of men at the disposal of their commanders. Wartime propaganda presented the long struggle as a fight against totalitarianism and evil for the preservation of democracy and freedom. The crew of one Canadian warship took this rhetoric at face value. On 4 April, 1945, Prime Minister Mackenzie King announced that only volunteers would be sent to fight against Japan. *HMCS Uganda* supported the American invasion of Okinawa. Her crew voted on whether to stay in battle, or return home as many were not volunteers. Of the nine hundred men on the cruiser, two thirds "elected not to serve." *HMCS Uganda* headed home to Esquimault, arriving there a week before Japan surrendered. A retired Canadian naval officer referred to this incident as a "dreadful business."[19] Others might view it as a unique expression of democracy.

The Welfare Revolution, the third one whose impact has been felt throughout the world in this century, began in 1945. During the war, everyone in Britain had suffered equally—at least in theory. So, everyone should share the benefits of peace. "Fair shares for all" sums up the essence of the Welfare Revolution. The modern state should look after all the needs of its citizens and no one should ever want for the basic necessities of life. If the private sector could not generate jobs, then the state would create them. During the war, democratic governments acquired huge and dictatorial powers over their people. The British believed that the end of the war would bring an era of unparalled prosperity and ease after six years of shortages, sacrifices and stress. Members of the armed forces voted overwhelmingly for the British Labour Party which took power in 1945 and set about making life easier for everyone, especially the poor. Men like Aneurin Bevan, who had grown up in the depressed Welsh valleys, had first-hand experience of the ravages of industrial capitalism. Bevan became Minister of Health and set about establishing the "free" health system that many countries have today. No longer would anyone go without care because they lacked the money to pay for it. A strong, centralized state would ensure this—and full employment.

The concept of the welfare state had been formulated by a group of bureaucrats in London in 1940, when Britain had its back against the wall. Whitehall mandarins, headed by Sir William Beveridge, discussed the requirements of a prosperous and caring society while German aircraft did their best to level London. Beveridge's people did not originate the idea of the welfare state. It had been invented by Otto von Bismarck (1815-98), the iron chancellor who created the German nation, for very practical political purposes. He introduced into Germany a comprehensive scheme of social security, offering workers insurance against accident, sickness and old age. Bismarck's version of "socialism" owed nothing to altruism. He simply wanted to cut the ground out from under the Social Democrats and keep them out of power by ensuring that workers had some degree of security. Bismarck's scheme, widely admired, showed the rulers of Europe how they could retain power—and keep their people content.

The British Labour government, bent on creating a new Jerusalem in England's green and pleasant land, and in her drab and grimy cities, had a genuine idealistic thrust as it sought to rescue people from the arbitrary forces that shortened their lives and stunted their potential. Beveridge and his team offered neat, practical, bureaucratic ways of eliminating all the ills of Britain. The legacy of their thoughts are with us still, reflecting a lost tradition of Christian socialism based on *agape* (loving kindness).

The New Welfare State

"The art of leadership is making common men do
uncommon things."
Unpublished report, quoted on the title page of
The Pillars of Security by Sir William Beveridge (1943).

In contrast to Bismarck's opportunistic approach to making life better for workers, Beveridge and his team proposed a comprehensive program to offer security to everyone in Britain, without regard to income. Wearied by war, the British saw in the Beveridge Report (*Report on Social Insurance and Allied Services*) published in 1942, at the very nadir of the country's fortunes, a vision of a new earth and the promise of heaven upon it.

Beveridge's model of the welfare state has been widely copied. But his warnings about its limitations have not been heeded. Beveridge outlined three assumptions "without which no satisfactory scheme of social security can be devised." Children's allowances would ensure that their parents would feed and clothe them adequately. Comprehensive health and rehabilitation services would make Britons of all classes fit and able to enjoy their leisure. The third assumption was the crucial one: "If after the war mass unemployment returns, the stability of British institutions may be in peril. Vital political freedoms may be sacrificed by a despairing democracy in the hope of economic security."[20]

The aim of Britain's Welfare Revolution was to generate social stability by offering security to all. The planners proposed a middle way into the future, "a move neither towards Socialism nor towards Capitalism. It goes straight down the middle to a practical end."[21] When asked: "Will such a plan sap individuality and adventure?" Beveridge replied: "No, for the adventurous are those who have been well fed...there is no ceiling to human enterprise and needs...Man is spirit, not an animal."[22]

During the war, power in Britain had been centralized and the government exercised total control over the economy. London had also motivated people to serve and fight while smothering discontent. Beveridge favoured decentralization of power, and saw unemployment insurance simply as a short-term approach for workers between jobs or idled for other reasons. Underneath the visionary planner, however, lurked an evangelical reformer. In an address to a religious conference in 1942, Beveridge set out five propositions to test economic assumptions. They have a surprisingly modern ring:

1. Extreme inequality in wealth and possessions should be avoided.
2. Every child, regardless of race or class, should have equal opportunity for education, suitable for the development of his peculiar capabilities.
3. The family as a social unit must be safeguarded.
4. The sense of Divine Vocation must be restored to man's daily work.
5. The resources of the earth should be used as God's gifts to the whole human race and used with due consideration for the needs of present and future generations.[23]

In some ways, life in Britain became grimmer after the war in Britain. Bread rationing continued until July, 1948. In April, 1949, sweets and chocolates came off the ration, but disappeared so quickly that rationing had to be reimposed in August. Although onerous, rationing ensured that everyone received the same basic foods and clothing. Britain's currency reserves had been drained by war, and the country was in debt to the United States. But conditions slowly improved. A survey in York in 1936 estimated that 31.5 per cent of the working class lived in poverty. By 1950, the figure had dropped to 2.8 per cent.[24]

Lord Annan, an historian and member of the ruling class, claimed that he and his kind "radiated effortless confidence" in the 1950s: "Full employment had been achieved, growth assured, life was becoming easier, more interesting and rewarding and poverty receding. All that was required was to spread the benefits wider still."[25]

Total unemployment in post-war Britain never rose above half a million. Pent-up demand for goods and services ensured jobs aplenty for anyone willing to work. By 1948, however, Labour leaders began to wonder whether the social security system they had created could be sustained. Government intervention in the lives of its citizens had rescued many from the forces that made their existence miserable and sorrowful. But it also removed others from the consequences of their own folly and stupidity. As the extended family began to disintegrate and the nuclear family followed suit, the state moved in to take care of more and more people and to regulate their lives. As rational idealists, Labour politicians expected everyone to behave decently and sensibly in the British tradition, and not exploit the system they had set up to ensure equality and democracy. They did not reckon with bureaucratization, professionalism, careerism, individualism, specialization and the many other ways whereby people seek to advance their interests at the expense of the common good. As George Bernard Shaw observed: "All professions are conspiracies against the laity."

In 1951, Prime Minister Clement Attlee still retained his socialist idealism:

"We know the kind of society we want. We want a society of free men and women. Free from poverty, free from fear, able to develop their faculties in co-operation with their fellows; everyone giving, and having the opportunity to give, service to the community...a society bound together by rights and obligations."[26]

This language reflects the civilizing mission of the upper middle class, the idea of an organic society dedicated to service rather than competition for wealth. In *The Listener* of 3 January, 1952, William Beveridge, living in a town mainly populated by young married couples of the skilled working class, hoped that common activities would grow "with more than usual speed."

"...organisation of libraries, community drama, debating societies, voluntary services of all kinds—everything that calls for use of leisure in doing things rather than passively enjoying things."[27]

But now the workers had television and cars, and instead of resenting the upper middle classes, they began to ape them. After all the state would look after the unfortunates in society while workers acquired the trappings of middle class life. The Welfare Revolution and the expanded role of the state swept away many of the volunteer organizations and mutual aid systems woven into the web of British life.

In 1942, William Temple, then Archbishop of York, had warned against this possibility. *Christianity and Social Order*, which sold 139,000 copies, stressed the community context of British life:

"No man is fitted for an isolated life; every one has needs which he cannot supply for himself; but he needs not only what his neighbours contribute to the equipment of his life but their actual selves as the complement to his own. Man is naturally and incurably social."[28]

The family, schools, colleges, trade unions, professional associations, churches, voluntary groups and other non-governmental organizations offer spaces and places where people with shared interests can work together for their own personal development and that of their community. Here neither the profit motive nor the imperatives of government bureaucracies hold sway. This third presence in society, fertile field for the Lichen Factor and symbioses between divergent peoples and interests, plays a vital role in ensuring social stability and individual identity. Temple pointed out:

"It is a common failing of revolutionary politics to ignore or attempt to destroy these lesser associations. They are nearly always the product of historical growth and do not quite fit any theoretical pattern. So the revolutionary, who is of necessity a theorist, is impatient of them."[29]

This concept of Temple's, under the rubric of "civil society," has gained a great deal of attention in recent years as governments have run out of money and cut back on social security programmes. It runs counter to the entrenched bureaucratic culture that dominates the provision of social and economic services in our time. The style of the Welfare Revolution, the belief that the state must care for all its peoples, proved irresistible to the leaders of Britain's colonies, many of whom were educated in London and at provincial universities. In Canada, the Liberals borrowed the Bismarckian model of the welfare state, concerned more about the threat of socialism than the woes of Canadians. The proponents of the Social Gospel sought to create Jerusalem in Canada's empty spaces, and eventually many of them joined the Co-operative Commonwealth Federation (CCF). The Liberals took its platform, broke it apart, and used some of the planks to prop up the foundations of their power. William Beveridge's ideas, many of them unsuited to a boom and bust economy undergoing rapid growth, reached Canada through the work of Leonard Marsh. He had studied under Beveridge at the London School of Economics, and in 1943 produced his *Report on Social Security in Canada.* But Marsh lacked the clout, status and resources of Beveridge, so Ottawa paid little attention to his report. The Beveridge Report sold 630,000 copies. An abbreviated edition circulated among resistance groups in occupied Europe, with fifty thousand copies of the full report going to United States. Marsh's report did not receive anything like this distribution. Canada's social security net was put together, one strand at a time, in our typical cautious, gradual way. And it is being taken apart in the same way.

When the CCF took power in Saskatchewan in 1944, Premier Tommy Douglas introduced free medical care for everyone in the province, against the opposition of most of the doctors. In those days, medical care was equated with the presence of hospitals, and Douglas built scores of them in Saskatchewan's small communities. Eventually, the federal government adopted Medicare, which has become a sacred trust in Canada—and still associated with the services provided by doctors and hospitals. Meanwhile patterns of illness in western societies have changed. The old diseases, tuberculosis, diphtheria, polio, influenza, have been largely wiped out. Lifestyle illnesses such as cancer, stroke, AIDS, and heart attack and the problems associated with aging require costly and specialized medical services and new technology. While more and more Canadians are taking personal responsibility for their health, many others still believe that it is the responsibility of the state to keep them fit and functioning.

As in Britain, bureaucracy in Canada burgeoned with the introduction of the welfare state, and this country had plenty of money to support and extend it. Between 1965 and 1974, Canada's rate of growth exceeded interest rates by more than six per cent. The oil shock of 1972, and the depressions that hit the country in the 1980s forced everyone to examine the basic assumptions behind the welfare state.

REDEFINING HUMANS

"One must be very careful about coming to any
conclusions about the way we are,
or what can be expected of us."
- Václav Havel, "History of a Public Enemy,"
New York Review of Books, 31 May, 1990.

Václav Havel went from being described as an enemy of the public to the presidency of his country after the Velvet Revolution in Czechoslovakia in 1989. The overthrow of communism in central and eastern Europe represents but one chapter in the history of the Democratic Revolution. This revolution, and the Industrial and Welfare ones, changed the way people looked at the world and how they were defined.

In traditional societies and small communities residents make clear distinctions between insiders ("Us") and those who do not belong there ("Them"). In such places, everyone knows his or her place and role, ensuring a high degree of social stability: "Bless the squire and his relations...And always know our proper stations." In certain North American Indian tribes, homosexuals undertook the tasks of women. Women became chiefs in some aboriginal communities in Canada, while in others they were little better than slaves.

Traditional societies, often slighted by Westerners as "primitive" ones, operated with an enormously complex system of checks and balances. Tradition, rituals, taboos, ceremonies, symbols ensured order and survival. What came from outside, from away, was viewed with suspicion, for experience had shown that contact with strangers could be disastrous. Among some tribes, strangers, warmly welcomed, quickly learned how to adapt to local ways. In other places they ended up on the menu. If what entered the closed world of the small community could be fitted into its culture, defined as "the way we do things around here," then it might be adopted, adapted and accepted. Change and exchange also took place in traditional society. And ambitious men and women in tribal societies sought power and dominion over others. Others, discontented or driven by personal demons, left their homes and sought out new places. As Braudel and the members of the *Annales* school of history have shown, life before the Democratic and Industrial Revolutions was not confined by collectivity and local boundaries.[30] Dumb barter took place where the grasslands met the forests in Africa, as dwellers in these different environments exchanged their surpluses without seeing each other. A friend hunting with Indians in northern Ontario crossed a stream while running down a moose. After securing the animal, his companions quickly retreated back across the stream, very conscious that they had "invaded" the territory of another group. In 1771, Samuel Hearne journeyed north with a band of Chipewyans. Near the mouth of the Coppermine River, they came across an Inuit camp. The Indians killed everyone there, at the spot now known as Bloody Falls. The Inuit Land Occupancy project, and research on Indian land claims, have shown that these people had a very precise understanding of the territories occupied by their ancestors. These people did not seek to "conquer" and "own" the land in the way of westerners, but harvested it, taking what it yielded. The names strewn over the Canadian North by Europeans are possessives (Voisey's Bay) or those of individuals or other places (Baffin Island, Cambridge Bay). Inuit names describe these places (Aklavik—"where there are bears").

During the French Revolution, its leaders invented the idea of the nation. Before it, a French man or woman's country was simply the part of it in which he or she was born. To create the new nation of France, the revolutionaries developed new symbols, rituals and ceremonies. In his *Essay on the Origin of Language* (1772) Johan Herder (1744-1803), a German poet and critic, set out the basis of romantic nationalism. A nation (*Volk*) was a dynamic entity, not a static one, with its own language that distinguished it from other entities. And the intellectual, the manipulator of symbols, had to play the leading role in bringing into being this new form of society. In France, the old figures of saints were swept away and statues of the goddess

Reason set up in prominent places. A new national anthem, the *Marseillaises*, roused the population. Every French man and women could become a *citoyen* of the new republic, the *res publica*, the things of the public. An essential part of nationalism involves finding a common enemy to hate. If the newly-defined *citoyens* had rights, they also had responsibilities, including offering their lives in defence of the new order against the old and corrupt ones that threatened it. Thus the *levée en masse* came into being through universal conscription that raised citizen armies to fight the professional soldiers of the other European powers. Hobsbawn points out how difficult it is to define a nation, describing it as "a very recent newcomer in human history, and the product of particular, and inevitably localized or regional historical conjunctures."[31]

The concepts of nation and of community are inextricably intertwined, for they give new identities to people struggling to cope with change. In resisting efforts to integrate them into the Canadian mainstream, Canada's Indians have redefined themselves as members of this country's "First Nations."

The Industrial Revolution changed the way people saw themselves. No longer did they have to tip their hats to the squire and his relations. Now they owed their survival to factory owners and managers. Adam Smith, the father of the free market, and Karl Marx, the prophet of communism, both saw human beings simply as forms of "productive labour." In factories, workers became "hands," the only part of their body the owners needed. Henry Ford grumbled: "Why is that I always get a whole person when what I really want is a pair of hands?" Workers these days are called "human resources," the term implying that they simply serve as factors of production like capital and inanimate materials.

In their private lives, people are defined as "consumers" and the business world makes strenuous efforts to separate them from their money. If they are poor, and lack money, then they become the "clients" of agencies that operate on the assumptions of the Welfare Revolution, and try to treat everyone equally.

The power to define people carries with it the power to control them. Underneath the labels stuck on people are complex human beings, seeking to assert their own uniqueness and invidualities, re-fusing to be treated simply as members of abstract categories. The ideas of Gabriel Marcel make increasing sense in our time. He made a prescient observation: "The ticket collector is not the ticket col-lector." Even the simplest human being, doing a simple job, has dimensions about which we know little. Each has a life history, memories of the past, influences upon them that they only half un-derstand, untapped abilities. A civil servant who constantly sought advice and direction from his boss at work turned into a tiger when he led an office softball team, cajoling, animating, encouraging the players to do their best. Senior SS officers in Nazi Germany who planned mass killings held doctorate degrees and loved the music of Bach and Beethoven.

In addition to the demands generated by the Democratic, In-dustrial and Welfare Revolutions, everyone these days, from American billionaires to residents of remote Inuit communities, must learn to cope with the bureaucracies brought into being to deal with mass society.

THE BUREAUCRATIZATION OF THE WORLD

> "If you are going to sin, sin against God, not the
> bureaucracy. God will forgive you,
> but the bureaucracy won't."
> Admiral Hyman G. Rickover, nuclear submarine pioneer.

In its original definition, sin merely meant "missing the mark." Traditional and religious societies devise rituals to cope with human failings. The European Enlightenment spawned the notions of progress and human fallibility while society became increasingly secularized. To ensure that people behaved themselves, avoided mistakes and adhered to certain standards and rules, governments created bureaucracies to provide stability, security and continuity. There is a persistent belief in Canada that governments are interested in development. They are not. The name of their game is control, and they impose it through bureaucracies offering rewards for those who conform to their standards and punishing those who do not.

Bureaucracies are not a modern phenomenon for controlling people. The palaces of the Ancient Middle East contained storehouses of records of what the rulers owned. To control anything, you must be able to count it. Otherwise, how do you know how many sheep, slaves, jars of wine you possess? You must define and list these things, turn them into abstract symbols, figures inscribed on clay and stone. Milan Kundera described bureaucracy as "a world of abstractions...where actions have become mechanical and people do not know the meaning of what they do." An Ottawa civil servant, visiting an outport in Newfoundland, expressed amazement at the way in which people there adapted to a difficult land and a cruel sea: "They are just statistics to us."

Max Weber (1864-1920) studied and analyzed bureaucracies, concluding that the future belonged to these large, impersonal structures. As mass society came into being, their objective, relentless routinization and regularization of life would ensure stability, continuity and equality. Bureaucracies would smooth out the irregularities of life and keep in check the wilder schemes of politicians by using rational methods to assess the costs and impacts of proposed actions. Large corporate structures reject the irrational, the personal, the mysterious—anything that does not fit into the categories they establish to ensure the smooth running of society and to cut down risks and control change. Bureaucracies demonstrate characteristics of both caribou and musk-oxen. They continually fight off those who would invade their territory. When threatened by outsiders, they form a circle, horns outwards, charging at any threat to their community cohesion. Bureaucracies develop a number of ways to rationalize their existence and protect themselves. Secrecy is one way of doing this. As Bismarck put it: "Never believe anything until it is officially denied."

Many of the discontents in Canada, and throughout the world, stem from the blind, mindless way in which bureaucracies fail to respond to change. Despite freedom of information legislation and the probings of the mass media, it is still very difficult to determine why government agencies behave the way they do.

If those outside the bureaucracies are frustrated, so are those inside them. Many civil servants joined the government with high ideals, impelled by a sense of duty and commitment. In recent years, senior officials have quit when they have seen the gap between their ideals and the performance of their agencies becoming too wide to bear. Instead of being accountable to the public, or even to their minister, they find that serving the system becomes all-consuming. Paul Tellier, Clerk of the Privy Council and Secretary to the Cabinet in the Mulroney government, broke the code of silence when he left government and joined Canadian National. He noted:

> "In my 13 years as deputy minister, I spent far too much time having to justify my decisions to comptrollers of comptrollers. The problem was...at the lower ranks when I had to

answer irrelevant questions from individuals who were just trying to justify their existence."[32]

An ambitious plan to "re-engineer" and "re-invent" government, PS 2000, resulted in very modest changes:

"And today we still have a system where senior managers hire consultants to write ten-page job descriptions that nobody reads."[33]

Senior government officials can retire on pension or start new careers in the private sector. But many excellent, committed civil servants remain trapped in the lower levels of the bureaucracy, endlessly frustrated in their efforts to make their systems more open, accountable and responsive to the public. The Royal Commission on Employment and Unemployment in Newfoundland and Labrador reported that the vocational school system showed "inflexibility and inability to respond to local and regional needs." School staff struggled hard to serve students. But they complained that "central provincial authority has bottlenecked innovative ideas from local regions...the administrative territory has become unmanageable."[34] One of the iron laws of bureaucracy states: Nothing should ever be done for the first time. The Royal Commission report noted what happens when innovation is thwarted: "...local administrators disillusioned by their attempts to acquire more control in their administrative capacities, have become apathetic in accepting the status quo."[35]

Bureaucracies have to struggle with the demands by those inside and outside their boundaries for change *and* stability. Despite the talk of re-engineering and re-inventing large organizations to make them more innovative and accountable, the idea of bureaucracies made up entirely of creative, energetic individuals set on doing everything in different ways might create more frustration than the present system.

The impact of large bureaucracies on small societies and communities has been disastrous. In the past, Canada's Inuit lived in small nomadic groups, surviving by taking advantage of every possible source of food and sharing whatever its members caught or collected. The traditional law was informal, flexible, and relied on social pressure to ensure that people acted properly.

The Inuit have had to cope with the demands of the three world revolutions in less than fifty years. Like many traditional societies they did not have the resources to sustain hierarchical structures through which priests, kings and others held power over others. On 7 September, 1992, the *Globe and Mail* ran an advertisement for a senior administrator for the hamlet of Sachs Harbour on Banks Island. The salary was set at $40-50,000 for a settlement with 125 residents in 1991. Many of the problems of northern development in Canada relate to the way in which large, unresponsive, desk-bound bureaucracies impose their ways on people who once prided themselves on their ability to be self-reliant. The individual bureaucrats are not to blame, for most are decent, dedicated people. But they serve a system, and must abide by its impersonal dictates. The new Territory of Nunavut will come into being in April 1999. It will be largely populated by civil servants, and may come to resemble that fabled town where people earned their living by taking in each other's laundry. The government of the Northwest Territories launched a "Community Empowerment" programme in the mid-1990s, but its main aim appears to be to download government programmes and services to community groups.

An Inuk from Pangnirtung expressed the concern of many of his people about Nunavut and the bureaucratization of the North: "But just because we don't have Grade 12, that doesn't mean there are not a lot of us who are pretty smart...There are a lot of people sitting around, good qualified people."[36]

One of the people responsible for training northerners stated: "It's a nine-to-five world and we'll have to adjust."[37] Major-General Lewis Mackenzie, striving to keep peace in Bosnia while commanding Canadian soldiers assigned to the United Nations, expressed his frustration with the bureaucratic ways of the international organizational. Troops had to be on the alert twenty-four hours a day, seven days a week. But in New York, UN officials worked from nine to five, five days a week. Mackenzie had great difficult contacting any-one there for direction outside this bureaucratic time frame.

Bureaucracy is all pervasive, and its iron grip has stifled development, initiative and enterprise all over the world. In Uruguay, at one time, the national airline had one thousand people on staff—and one functioning airplane. At the government oil company, workers made an effort to arrive at their offices as early as possible: The agency had more employees than chairs. In Lima, Peru, Hernando de Soto's students set up a dummy company to determine how much it would cost and how long it would take to start a small business. The bureaucrats processing the applications for the company never realized they were dealing with a phantom. It took ten months, and $1,231—thirty two times the monthly minimum living wage in Lima—to create this imaginary venture.

In bureaucracies, process and procedure are all—content seldom matters. Senior bureaucrats have very little knowledge of exactly what they are dealing with in the real world. Very often they find out about it by reading the newspapers—or the letters to the editor in them. Hernando de Soto notes how successful "informals" set up by community groups have been in meeting housing needs, building markets and setting up and running transportation systems. In the developing world, many bureaucracies are corrupt and inefficient. But the bureaucrats devise ways to ensure that no single individual can be blamed for errors. In the Karachi Development Agency in 1991, up to 174 individuals handled a request to issue a single cheque.

A survey of 150 local organizations revealed that, in countries such as Kenya and Tanzania, the bureaucracy tries to curtail self-help organizations because their style of operation, using mutual aid and horizontal linkages, threatens the bureaucracy's management function, ideology and survival. After all, if people can solve their own problems with their own resources, why do they need bureaucrats?[38] Or, for that matter, politicians?

Bureaucracy is also pervasive in the large corporations of the private sector, especially those that have monopolies in certain areas.[39] Bell Canada once had no competitors of note in the telephone business, and created a huge bureaucracy. Its administration department managed management itself, controlled the organization and disseminated the values of the company. The utility had a manual of procedures made up of circulars on every conceivable detail of Bell's business. The manual ran to more than twenty volumes, one of which contained a circular on general circulars.[40]

To paraphrase Gabriel Marcel, however, the bureaucrat is not the bureaucrat. They have lives outside their closed world. And bureaucracies can be bypassed, penetrated, subverted, given time and chance, to make them more responsive to the needs of those they were set up to serve. As Saul Alinsky put it: "The only way to upset the power structure is to goad them, confuse them and, most of all, make them live by their own rules."

In the past, bureaucracies offered stability to those they served and security to those who staffed them. But many of them are mere ghosts from a past time, set up to meet certain needs that no longer exist. If you don't like the car you bought or the service you receive from the maker, you can switch to another company or model next time you shop for a vehicle. But if the government you elect starts to do foolish things and stupid actions, you have to wait until the next election.

So what can governments do to control their people when they become aware of the widening gaps in society between promise and performance? What can ordinary citizens do when their expectations cannot be matched by what governments and other large institutions offer? Bureaucracies deal with the norms of society, the mass of people, through inventing categories, symbols and abstractions—not with individual human beings. Anything out of the ordinary, anything that does not fit within their routines and their systems of administration, disturbs them. The rational world of the bureaucrat operates in a linear manner derived from the assumptions of Newtonian physics. You do *this*—and then automatically *that* will happen. Every action has an equal and opposite reaction. Learn the certainties, follow the rules, understand the reactions, and all will be well. The world of quantum mechanics has replaced the Newtonian one. Here, if you do *this*, there are varying degrees of *that* happening. Uncertainty, ambiguity and improbability have dominion here. Matter can behave like a particle or a wave, depending on the conditions under which it is studied and the instruments you use. Objectivity, which Pierre Vallières claimed was "the ideology of the *status quo,*" no longer exists. Every observation affects the phenomenon observed, every observer is a participant in the process he or she studies. We live in a world of changing relationships, not of fixed and static interactions.

What are the alternatives to our present bureaucracies?

Bigger, better bureaucracies—or anarchy?

Figure 1 illustrates the basic source of our discontents—the dualistic world where the middle ground between extremes continues to vanish.

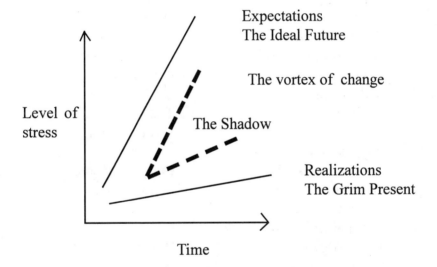

Figure 1: The Sources of Our Discontent

"Between the idea
And the reality
Between the notion
And the act
Falls the Shadow."
T.S. Eliot, *The Hollow Men*

Note on Figure 1

Other gaps that are widening in our society include those between:

Government	The Governed
"The Right"	"The Left"
The Community/Nation	The Individual
Autocracy	Democracy
Rich	Poor
Powerful	Powerless
Theory	Practice
Thought	Deed
Reason	Superstition
Unity	Diversity
Centres of Power	Edges of Society
Top down planning	Bottom up initiatives
Products	Processes
Radicalism	Conservatism
Modernity	Tradition
Generalities	Particularities
Bureaucracy	Anarchy
Abstract ideas	Concrete actions
Promise	Performance
Idealism	Materialism
External Demands	Inner Needs
Technology	Humanity
Hope	Despair
Order	Chaos
Concord	Discord
Rhetoric	Reality
"Them"	"Us"

And, in Canada...

Federalism	Separatism

THE CHOICES OF THE POWERFUL

"The crisis consists precisely in this fact that the old
is dying and that the new cannot be born;
in this interregnum, a great variety
of morbid symptoms appear."
Antonio Gramsci (1891-1937), Italian socialist

Antonio Gramsci, born in poverty, organized workers councils in Italian factories, became disenchanted with the reformist approach of socialism, and joined the communist party. Mussolini imprisoned him in 1926 and he died in jail. Gramsci's ideas, outlined in his prison notebooks, have become popular with left-wing intellectuals because they appear to offer an alternative to traditional, materialistic communism. Like all radicals, Gramsci had a vision of a more perfect world that could be achieved by human effort. This utopian ideal ignores an observation by Kant: "Out of the crooked timber of humanity no straight thing was ever made." Traditional quilt makers in Nova Scotia always made one deliberate mistake in their work, for they believed that perfection belonged only to God.

Among the legacies of the three revolutions is the ongoing quest for perfection in human beings and their institutions. As Robert Browning put it: "...a man's reach must exceed his grasp/Or what's a heaven for?" The widening gaps in Canadian and world society disturb many people. Some study the gaps, others set out to close them. Increasingly, their intellectual formulations and their actions seem inadequate.

But to bridge the widening gaps, you have to understand how the world really works, the source of the Shadow, and where possibilities for meaningful action can be found. The new science of chaos can help in this. Around zero, water behaves oddly. Sometimes it freezes, at other times remaining liquid. When water does freeze, it takes on a wide variety of different shapes and forms, depending on the conditions. What looks like a chaotic transition has its own logic. When a river flows over a waterfall, its form and energy change. You can tell nothing about what happens at a waterfall by examining a river before it goes over it. Nor can you see in a butterfly any resemblance to a caterpillar, or the tadpole in the frog. You have to examine the processes through which these forms of life pass as they change from one shape to the other. Scientists studying chaos come from the margins, the edges of their own disciplines. Science has become compartmentalized and specialized, and most scientists work in disciplinary boxes. But some are drawn to the boundaries of life and the interaction between different kinds of matter, the places of seeming chaos. You cannot impose *order* on chaos. You have to determine why it is happening, and recognize the regularities, the patterns that appear in transitional places.[41]

Governments and bureaucracies have a great deal of difficulty dealing with chaos. As things appear to fall apart and the centre seems increasingly unable to hold, the powerful people in society have espoused policies and plans that encourage three responses to change. They can be summed up as fascism, revolution and community development/co-operation/mutual aid. These responses to change reflect the three northern realities of the musk-oxen, the caribou and the lichen.

The Fascist Response

"Against individualism, the fascist concept is for the state; and it is for the individual in so far as he coincides with the state, which is the conscience and universal will of man in his historical existence."

Benito Mussolini

Fascism arose after the First World War, offering the promise of perfection imposed by the state. Mussolini ensured that Italian trains left the station exactly on time—"From now on, everything must function to perfection." He saw himself as embodying all the desirable qualities of the Italian people, breaking the power of the Mafia, working side by side in the fields with labourers, setting off on colonial adventures to recapture the lost glory of Imperial Rome. The Germans, tired of the divisions in their society and the inability of the democratically elected Weimar Republic to curb inflation and create employment, gave Hitler and his National Socialist (Nazi) party three million votes in 1930. Three years later, the strong man became chancellor of Germany and set about ridding the country of undesirable elements who blighted its Aryan purity.

After the Russian Revolution and the death of Lenin in 1924, Stalin took power and turned Russia into a police state.

The goal of fascism is to create a sheep's paradise. Every aspect of life is subject to official scrutiny to ensure that it conforms to the norms of the state. Citizens, treated like dumb animals, are fed, housed and worked by their keepers. No one questions the wisdom of the state or dreams of a better, more fuller life. Extensive systems of surveillance ensure that any disturbing voices, any form of opposition, is stifled and suppressed. Terror and fear keep people in their places. The Soviet constitution guaranteed freedom of speech. Russians joked that it did not guarantee freedom *after* speech.

Fascism still flourishes today, fifty years after the war that saved democracy. The rulers of Myanmar, North Korea and other countries practice fascism, keeping tight control over their people, avoiding change, ensuring everyone conforms to official norms.

Bertram Gross, an American academic concerned about the increasing power that corporations exercised over consumers and the political system coined the term "friendly fascism" to describe how democracies fall prey to control by large entities.[42] Instead of coercion, powerful bodies use advertising, public relations and a wide range of techniques of persuasion to prevent people from thinking for themselves and questioning the wisdom of the capitalist way of life. Acting together, the government and corporate elites pass legislation restricting individual freedom and imposing certain norms on people. A student challenged Gross one day, asking him if he was not a friendly fascist. She pointed out that he had helped to write and implement an act in 1946 that strengthened the power of the president, the government and the private sector over the lives of Americans. This question had a curious outcome. Gross dreamed that he was seeking friendly fascists in a large, rambling, many-roomed house. He opened door after door, finding nothing beyond them. Then he came to a half-lit room with many doors opening off it. Flinging one open, he saw himself. The desire to control others—especially for their own good—appears to be a part of human nature. We all have a bit of the fascist in us as we seek perfection, inside and outside ourselves.

Increasingly, under the pressures of industrialization, urbanization and change, even the most extreme fascist governments have to contend with demands for liberty, equality and fraternity. They have to learn how to deal with the disturbers of society, the rebels, revolutionaries and reformers while maintaining their grip on the mass of their people.

Rebels attack the existing order, but offer no constructive alternatives to it. Revolutionaries seek to sweep away all present forms of government and replace them with more democratic, open, efficient, responsive and accountable ways of running a country or an enterprise. Revolutions are, among other things, about jobs. An out group claims that it can do a better job than the present holders of power. Reformers seek to synthesize aspects of the past and the present to achieve the same goals as revolutionaries. Rebellion, revolution and reform are not separate categories, and can merge into each other. In 1789 and 1830, advisers to the French kings told them, as mobs filled the streets of Paris: "Sire, this is not a riot, it is a revolution."[43] Louis Auguste Blanqui, a French revolutionary, claimed: "It takes twenty-four hours to make a revolution."

The Revolutionary Option

"The Revolution must not mean that the new class rules, governs, through the *old* state machinery, but that this class *smashes* that machinery, and rules, governs through new machinery."

V.I. Lenin, 16 April, 1917, on arrival at Petrograd.

Lenin's metaphor for the state reveals the mechanistic image of the world that dominates so much thinking about social change. Government is a machine. If broken, it must be replaced by a new and more efficient device. In the business world, the need to make ventures more profitable and competitive has brought into being a plethora of mechanics to tell owners how to fix their machines. Stephen Covey, Peter Senge, Tom Peters and others all offer expensive tool kits for mending enterprises that are falling apart.

Revolutions in the political sphere occur when conditions in a country are improving—but not fast enough to satisfy the majority of the people. The Shadow, the gap between human expectations and the ability of people to realize them, becomes too large. Quite suddenly, as the centres of power lose touch with the ambitions and desires of ordinary people, something happens and a revolution breaks out.

In Europe during the nineteenth century, the rising middle class took to the barricades and led revolutions. In the developing world, it is inevitably university students who spearhead revolutions, not the peasants. It is the intellectuals who dream of more perfect worlds, and seek to turn their visions into realities. The British avoided revolution after 1688 by reforming their system of government, making Parliament supreme and slowly widening the franchise. Marx, who took part in the 1848 revolution in Paris, recognized that the middle class had taken power from the aristocracy. Soon the proletariat, as its members realized that they had power in numbers, would wrest power from the bourgeoisie and usher in a time of peace, prosperity and equality. Alas, as the English radical R.H. Tawney put it: "Revolutions, as long and bitter experience reveals, are apt to take their colour from the regime they overthrow."[43a] The Tsarist government in 1917 had a million civil servants running the country in a sluggish manner. By 1921, two and a half million bureaucrats ruled Russia. They formed a new class oppressing the very people the 1917 revolution had set out to liberate. In March, 1921, the sailors of Kronstadt, who had played a leading role in overthrowing the old order, rebelled, shouting: "Give us back our revolution." Trotsky led his soldiers across the ice to the Kronstadt naval base to crush the "counter revolutionaries."[44]

Canadians have never been very good at organizing revolutions. The rebellions in Upper and Lower Canada in 1837 had a feeble, at times farcical, tone to them. The Riel Rebellions, sparked by threats to the Métis way of life, ended in the defeat of those who took up arms against the central government.

Most change in Canada has come about through reform, in keeping with our mild, deferential, middle-of-the-road way of doing things. On 8 May, 1945, VE-Day, a horde of happy men and women streamed down Yonge Street in Toronto, celebrating the end of the war in Europe. This unruly mob stopped at a red light at an intersection. They waited for it to change, then went on their joyful way.

As Canada adjusted to the post-war world, out of which it had emerged richer and more powerful, politicians strove to meet the expectations of better educated Canadians. In 1960, Premier Jean Lesage led the "Quiet Revolution in Quebec." Eliminating patronage and corruption, the Liberals removed power from an ossified, worn-out, exhausted clerical and political hierarchy. Peter Newman subtitled his book on change in Canada between 1985 and 1995, "From Deference to Defiance." Its main title, *The Canadian Revolution*, is misleading. Newman merely describes the acceleration of existing domestic and international trends in that decade. What is disturbing in recent years has been the widening gap between government and the people, rich and poor, those who have access to power and resources and those who do not. The traditional rituals, ceremony and rhetoric that once worked to ensure Canadians that all was well in their world increasingly fail to convince them that this is so.

The pent-up energy, frustration and anger of those who feel excluded from power and control over their own destinies finds expression in riots, blockades, stand-offs, sit-ins, civil disobedience and other forms of direct action. The Innu sat down on runways at Goose Bay, Labrador, to protest the way in which flights over their land disrupted their lives and those of the animals on which they depended.[45] Dissatisfied Indians elsewhere have specialized in blockading roads. These demonstrations followed a predictable pattern: Media coverage of confrontations, followed by boredom on both sides of the barriers. If the "warriors" become too aggressive, the police arrive and either convince them to tone down their actions or arrest them. After the Oka incident in Quebec in 1990, the federal government set up a Royal Commission on Aboriginal Peoples in the pious and unrealistic hope, that this ritual would solve their problems.

During the French and Russian Revolutions, hordes attacked the Bastille and the Winter Palace. Both served as symbols of a decadent and oppressive social order, but had few other uses. In our time, protesters surge towards parliamentary buildings and another familiar scenario unfolds. Police form a barrier between the rioters and the politicians. After a great deal of slogan chanting and waving of banners and placards, the demonstrators return home while their leaders engage in formal negotiations with those they consider their oppressors. In industrial disputes, business people simply wait until the strikers run out of money, and realize they will lose more than they can possibly gain by staying on the picket line. Then both sides decide to negotiate a settlement.

In Canada, the frustration with the ways of government and business, the anger at people's inability to match their expectations of life with daily realities—known as "cognitive dissonance"—push people closer and closer to the breaking point. This internal revolution, this overturning of the personality, has created the victim society. As Robert Nisbet puts it:

> "But there is very different and wholly political meaning today to the words *victim* and thereby *victimology*. The meaning is inseparable from the welfare Leviathans that have been built up in the West during the last century or two. The source of this meaning is the do-gooder and uplifter that became widespread in the nineteenth century. Those who were poor, unemployed, chronically drunk, and even criminal in tendency were, by some sociological legerdemain, decreed to be victims—of society."[46]

In the past, politicians promised to care for people, to be Good Samaritans, binding up the wounds of the hurt, taking the damaged people in society to safety. This image of the Samaritan state has been eroded in recent years. For as Margaret Thatcher tartly observed, the Good Samaritan could not have succoured the wounded man had he not had the money to do so. And now, while the ideal of caring for the less fortunate members of society is still promoted by people in power, they do not have the money to bridge the gap between their rhetoric and the real lives of the casualties of change.

As the Shadow over the lives of Canadians becomes larger, more and more people turn their anguish and energy inwards and begin to rip themselves, their groups and their communities apart in random and unpredictable ways. Hans Selye's pioneer research showed that a certain amount of stress was necessary for a healthy life. But many Canadians feel excessively burdened by stress, together with anxiety, depression and fear of the future. In 1975-76, publicly funded psychotherapy by psychiatrists and other physicians cost Canadian taxpayers $72 million. Ten years later that figure stood at $280 million.

Child abuse, spousal assaults, drug and alcohol problems, random acts of violence have increased over the last decade in Canada and the traditional ways of dealing with them appear to be failing. One of the saddest stories came from British Columbia. A young boy, starved, tortured and emotionally abused, was smothered by his mother in 1992. At least twenty-five social workers provided services to Matthew and his mother, and sixty reports on the five-year old had been submitted. In 1992-93, ten young natives committed suicide on Big Cove reserve in New Brunswick. Here the welfare budget rose from $3.7 million in 1990 to $6.3 million in 1994. An internal Indian Affairs report on the reserve stated: "There appears to still be the fallacy operating that money will 'cure' social ills. The myth that money or funding will solve the problems needs to be addressed."[47]

Industrial society, in turning people into workers, generates identity through occupation. People are what they do. Protests against seal hunting in Newfoundland did not appreciate that for many young men, "going to the ice" formed part of a *rite de passage* that moved them from childhood to adult status in their community.[48] Sealing formed part of the identity of many Newfoundlanders. When it was curbed they lost part of their being as well as of their income. In halting cod fishing in Atlantic Canada, the federal government failed to put in place measures to deal with those who lost not only their livelihoods, but also their sense of worth and identity. These people were seen merely as victims of change, not individuals with potential to run their own lives, make choices, act as responsible human beings. In 1966-67, Ottar Brox, a Norwegian sociologist studied the Newfoundland fisheries. This outsider saw clearly the roots of many of its problems:

"The most striking feature of Newfoundland's economy, as seen from the other side of the Atlantic, is the dualistic nature of its development. On the one hand, there are modern, sophisticated, technologically up-to-date industries. On the other, economic practices and techniques exist that appear to be almost medieval, such as inshore fishing and the processing of salt fish, where no innovation whatsoever seems to have taken place, either in the tools or in the work habits. What is more remarkable is that the gap between modern and traditional sectors seems to be widening."[49]

Brox's words reflect the fundamental dilemma of Canada—the imposition of industrial (and post-industrial) ways and assumptions upon pre-industrial people in many parts of the country. Brox suggested better organization at the local level, more vigorous enterprises, intermediate technology and upgrading of outports to move the fisher folk of Newfoundland into the modern world and make them more productive. He saw "Cognitive Change" as the key to doing this, pointing out that government agencies cannot *determine* the actions of Newfoundlanders in the way that management in a company can control the behaviour of its labour force. They must understand how others live, their values, the choices they face, their realistic options for action and development. Governments and large entities can give you a choice—but not an identity other than the one through which they define you for their own convenience.

The Atlantic Groundfish Strategy (TAGS), designed as a temporary measure while the industry in the region restructured itself is being seen as a form of entitlement by many fisher folk. The programme ran out in 1998, after the expenditure of $1.9 billion. In theory, this money was supposed to be used for retraining people in the fisheries. In practise more and more of it went towards income support—paying people to do nothing. This caused bitter divisions in many Atlantic communities, with some people struggling to make a living while others received government cheques without making any effort to retrain or find alternative work.[50] Some people have left the region to find work, or moved to the cities. In 1997, with the end of TAGS in sight, some Newfoundland fisher folk sat in government offices to pressure politicians to continue it.

Compounding the problem of the over-exploited fisheries on the east coast is the division between those engaged in it. Nova Scotia fisher folk have seventy different associations representing them.[51] In the past, some communities developed ways of collectively managing the resource so that *everyone* received their fair share of the harvest of the sea. In 1919, Calvert in Newfoundland initiated a lottery so that every family had the same chances to fish in the best places.[52] The Fundy Fixed Gear Council in Nova Scotia has developed a system of community management. Its members set their own quotas week by week, discipline each other, secure advice from a wide range of people on their advisory board, and undertake studies of the ecology of the Fundy shore. On Isle Madame, in Cape Breton, after the collapse of the fishery, local people formed their own development organization with the help of government money. Development Isle Madame (DIMA) began a vigorous search for new employment opportunities. A survey of the community by consultants came up with four hundred suggestions for local development. Aquaculture, a bilingual call centre, the export of kiln-dried lumber to Europe, heritage tourism and other possibilities for generating jobs and income are being explored and expanded. The consultant decided that community economic development was the island's only real hope.

In Newfoundland and Labrador, the provincial government has pinned its hopes for future development and employment on Hibernia,

Voisey's Bay, and high tech. But it too has discovered community economic development. In 1995, a task force on community economic development in the province published *Community Matters: The New Regional Economic Development*. It claimed:

"Community economic development emphasizes that the people of a community themselves should be directly involved in pursuing and managing their own economic development...Only if we foster local commitment and accountability for economic development will the innovation, entrepreneurship and productivity necessary for success in the new economic conditions we face be unleashed."[53]

Thus, after the expenditure of billions of dollars in the name of regional development, after experts have studied Atlantic Canada and come up with endless reports on its ills and their special solutions to them, governments have decided that local people should take charge and become involved in directing their own development.

This brings up the third option of the powerful—the encouragement of community development, mutual aid, and self help. Quite suddenly, the word community is on everyone's lips. In the past and the present, its invocation as the answer to all human problems has arisen from crises, from a feeling that the world is out of control. The personal and collective dislocations and disintegrations of the last decades—the inability not only of the centre but of practically every other place of stability to hold—has led to the rise of the therapeutic industry. When individuals faced crises in the past, they went to their priest. Now they head for the psychiatrist, the psychologist, the healer. Along with the increasing prominence of professional therapists has come an upsurge in the numbers of gurus, wizards, miracle workers, messiahs, each offering his or her cure for what ails suffering humans. Some methods, like those in the conventional fields of therapy, work better than others. Halifax has become the centre of Tibetan Buddhism that has attracted a number of New Agers in search of peace and personal tranquility. While some of the leaders of this group have been less than perfect, the Buddhists of Halifax have proved to be an asset to the community, setting up small businesses, starting alternative schools and offering their knowledge (for a price) to anyone interested in acquiring it. Increasingly, more and more Canadians are refusing to see themselves as victims, and are redefining their place in society as survivors of its excesses. A large number of self-help groups, modelled on the twelve-step approach of Alcoholics Anonymous, have sprung up in Canada. Here individuals find acceptance and can come to terms with their demons while understanding the social forces that awaken them. Individuals adrift in society, like governments that have failed to find magic solutions to creating employment and generating development, especially on the margins of Canada and among the "disadvantaged," are increasingly attracted to the concept of community. They see in it an elixir, a way of turning the lead of social change into the gold of progress. The very word community generates feelings of togetherness, a sense of warm fuzziness, a belief that it is possible to return to the good old days when people lived in harmony with each other.

But what is community and its development all about?

The Myths of Community

"If we have no sense of community, the American dream will continue to wither."
President-elect Bill Clinton, quoted in *Time*,
16 November, 1992.

We all live these days in the centre of twin vortices.

One pulls us towards the international scene where decisions are made that will affect us in the months and years to come—trade relationships, currency shifts, weather patterns. The other draws us to the local level where we have our day-to-day beings. Thus we have to understand what is happening in the world community and around us, on our home turf.

The word community, however, has been so misused that it has lost any real meaning. The media and intellectuals constantly demand that something called "the international community" act to curb the excesses of totalitarian regimes and solve problems of starvation, poverty and human misery throughout the world. This community, however, is a figment of the imagination of policy wonks and other abstract thinkers. The Internet has been promoted as a way of creating a "virtual community." This concept may comfort isolated individuals now able, through their computers, to contact other like-minded people. But the belief that people, sitting in front of their screens and exchanging information and gossip constitutes a community is another intellectual fallacy.

Some governments have set up departments to stimulate and encourages community development. The mission of Alberta Community Development is "to support community development, and through leadership, protection and partnership, help all Albertans participate fully in the social, cultural and economic life of the province."[54] The government agency's mandate includes supporting the independence and well being of seniors, helping Albertans appreciate their history, culture and diversity, and dealing with addictions treatment and prevention. Alberta Community Development, created in December, 1992, brought together a number of departments and agencies to provide a wide range of services. Then came streamlining and downsizing: "...the ministry has moved from the direct provision of services in many areas to an emphasis on establishing partnerships and providing consultation and advisory services that assist in building self-reliant communities."[55]

In Canada's richest province the rhetoric of community development, and of self-reliance, has been invoked as its government recognizes its inability to do things for people and seeks to work with them in partnership ventures. Unfortunately, too many projects of this kind have resembled the fabled horse and rabbit pie made up of equal parts—one horse, one rabbit. Since the aim of governments and other powerful institutions is to control people, they tend to dominate all aspects of such joint ventures. Singapore, a tightly regulated country, has a Department of Community Development.

Faced with shrinking budgets and increasing demands, police departments have jumped on the community bandwagon. Community policing involves going back to the future and having officers walk the beat. There is no strong evidence that community policing cuts down on crime. These days, the real money is in white collar crime, not in the petty activities of small-time thieves and scoundrels. The presence of police on the streets, however, helps quiet the nerves of the fearful middle class.

Another mythology about community revolves around the belief that there is a vast number of institutions in society willing and able to take responsibility for others when governments do not have the resources to do so. During the past two decades, mental institutions have sent patients into "the community" which is supposed to take care of them. The result of treating community as an abstract entity can be seen in the number of homeless and lost souls on the streets of our city. A professor at a Halifax university studied what happened to "de-institutionalized" psychiatric patients. In hospital, they claimed: "I'm fine. It's this place that's driving me crazy." After spending time in the community, all the patients in the study returned to the psychiatric ward, saying: "We don't belong out there, we belong here." This place was "community" for these people.[56] In France, a Christian community contacts homeless people, informs them of their eligibility for state pensions, and finds them decent accommodation if they wish to move off the streets.

Community exercises great fascination for politicians bereft of ideas for solving pressing human problems. Addressing the Character Education Conference in May, 1995, President Clinton stated:

> "Religious and community institutions have an important role to play...if every church in America...had not only a vigorous program for its own members and the people it's recruiting, but also an outreach to a fixed number of families and children to fight the problem of out-of-wedlock birth, teen pregnancy, school drop out...it might have more impact than all the government programs we could ever devise."[57]

This same theme echoed through the Speech from the Throne by the new Progressive Conservative government in Ontario in

September 1995:

> "...neighbours helping shut-in seniors, corporations sponsoring nutrition programs for children, service clubs funding community projects, private sector employees and executives volunteering for public service—this is the spirit of Ontario."

With the huge profits made by Canadian corporations coming under public scrutiny, the Conference Board of Canada launched its "Business in the Community" project. In Britain, a similar organization works with community groups to strengthen their ability to become more self-reliant and dynamic. The Canadian venture has all the hall marks of a public relations effort.

In Britain, a leader of Business in the Community (BiC) stated: "...this was not just a charitable venture; it was in the direct interests of businesses, their employees and investors...Community involvement policy is not just a matter of public relations—it should be part of the mainstream thinking of corporate life." BiC's deputy director noted:

> "People realize that dependence on the state is not the answer. Governments either withhold services and resources—or offer them on unacceptable terms. Middle class people used to come into poor areas, do useful things on the main street, then go home in the evening. We see the need for partnership with local people who own the turf. The crucial issue today is how to give people more pride in their environment, involvement in their housing and control over their lives to increase confidence, develop new organizational skills and new enterprises."[58]

The private sector has discovered community as "the invisible key to success." Writing in *Fortune* on 5 August, 1996 Thomas Stewart in his column, "The Leading Edge" stated: "Shadowy groups called communities of practice are where learning and growth take place. You can't control them—but they're easy to kill." Stewart based his piece on the work of Etienne Wenger at the Institute of Research on Learning in Palo Alto, California. His fundamental finding is that learning is social, and that "communities of practice are responsible only to themselves. No one owns them. There's no boss...People join and stay because they have something to learn and to contribute."

Thus communities are groups of people engaged in mutually beneficial undertakings. Not exactly a new discovery! Emphasizing the *concept* of community often blinds people to the reality of the problems around them.

The use of the term community development to rationalize the downloading of government services on to citizens recalls William Blake's claim that "...he who would do good to others must do it in Minute Particulars: General Good is the plea of the Hypocrite and Scoundrel." Interviewed after the throne speech, Premier Mike Harris invited churches to support his community agenda and to help people: "That's what they're for, to help their neighbours, to help their communities." Religious groups are very active in North America at doing what Premier Harris suggests. Habitat for Humanity builds houses for low income people with their participation and that of volunteers. It started in Koinonia, a Christian community in Georgia whose members were persecuted by their neighbours. In Ottawa, the Grey Sisters of the Immaculate Conception offer cheap rental space in a former high school to groups providing hope to people in need of economic, spiritual, emotional and physical support. In January, 1997, the sisters at the Benedictine monastery in Winnipeg offered a free retreat to unemployed people, the fourth time they have done this.

At the upper levels of the religious world, as among politicians and business leaders, there is confusion about what community development involves. Most of the mainstream religious groups, beset by declining congregations, internal divisions, and shrinking budgets, have turned inward, become obsessed with their own problems. Evangelical sects, preaching personal piety and individual salvation rather than collective activity and the redemption of all lost souls, attract increasing numbers of people. The struggles in the church reflect the ongoing religious tension between "pie in the sky" visions and those concerned with recreating Jerusalem on earth.

The Catholic Church in Latin America, its power and congregations dwindling, has sought salvation in the idea of Basic Christian Communities. Their creation owes something to the lack of priestly vocations and the unwillingness of the Vatican to permit the ordination of women. In 1969, Catholic bishops in Medellin, Colombia, issued a statement on this new approach to Christian spiritual development.

"The Christian ought to find the living of the communion to which he is called in his 'basic community,' that is to say, in a community, local or environmental, which corresponds to the reality of a homogenous group and whose size allows for personal fraternal contact among its members. Consequently, the Church's pastoral effort must be oriented towards the transformation of these communities into a 'family of God,' beginning by making itself present among them as leaven by means of a nucleus, although it be small, which creates a community of faith, hope and charity."[59]

Here again, a powerful centralized organization has gone back to its roots to find a new way forward, for it was in basic Christian communities that the early followers of Jesus lived, having all things in common. In those days, however, these small communities did not have bishops and women played leading roles in them.

Twenty five years after the Medellin Document on Basic Christian Communities appeared, the Catholic Church in Quebec espoused this approach to revitalizing itself. Its bishops issued *Risking the Future: Basic Communities in Quebec (Risquer l'avenir)*, identifying the ills of the church:

"...the process of secularization...has marginalized the church...church communities were too impersonal to generate any sense of fraternity. The church became a church of liturgical services, encouraging a religion without commitment and consumerism in faith."

The Welfare Revolution displaced the Catholic Church from its historic role of offering charity to the poor. Now, with aging congregations, sexual scandals, alienated youth, it seeks, at least in Quebec, to take part in the Democratic Revolution. *Risking the Future* sees basic communities as "outwards looking...critical of the modern world and yet reaching out to evangelize it." These communities would offer leadership roles to lay people. But is this move by the Catholic Church an attempt to liberate its followers and offer them a fuller and more abundant spiritual life—or simply another effort by an enfeebled organization to maintain its control over them?

Jesuits in British Columbia operate a Basic Christian Community Project. Its newsletter however, describe activities that strongly resemble prayer groups or encounter sessions.[60] In these basic communities, Catholics, freed from clerical domination, openly express their anger and pain at the ways of the institutionalized church. Will they return to their church after involvement in a basic community— or drift even further away?

Only too often, community becomes a refuge, a safe place, a retreat from responsibility and the demands of individualistic societies. In *Habits of the Heart*, Robert Bellah and his colleagues set out to examine individualism in American society and the erosion of community.[61] They note the difference between a community and a lifestyle:

> "Whereas a community attempts to be an inclusive whole, celebrating the interdependence of public and private life and so of the different callings of all, lifestyle is fundamentally segmented and celebrates the narcissism of similarity."[62]

Cities on the Hill by Frances Fitzgerald, promoted as "a brilliant exploration of visionary communities," looked at four places: The Castro area of San Francisco (a centre for gays), Liberty Baptist Church in Virginia (home of Jerry Falwell's Moral Majority), Sun City, Florida (a seniors' retirement town), and Rajneeshpuram in Oregon (a bizarre venture founded by a free love guru with a penchant for Rolls Royces). All these "communities" celebrated sameness and uniformity, serving as refuges for individuals unable or unwilling to cope with the demands of modern, individualistic America.

As Bellah points out:

"Americans, it would seem, feel most comfortable in thinking about politics in terms of a consensual community of autonomous, but essentially similar, individuals, and it is to such a conception that they turn for the cure of present ills. For all the lip service given to respect for cultural differences, Americans seem to lack the resources to think about the relationship between groups that are culturally, socially, or economically quite different."[63]

Some American ideas about community have filtered into Canada. Scott Peck, a psychiatrist, claimed that "In and through community lies the salvation of the world."[63] In dealing with the distressed, alienated members of the American middle class, Peck came to see the value of togetherness. He outlines three stages of community building. First comes pseudocommunity, based on denials of difference to avoid conflict. This usually leads to the formation of committees and organizations to deal with problems. Spontaneity and dissent are stifled, damped down by routine. If individuals can open up, rid themselves of their prejudices, preconceptions, biases, their need to control others, then barriers to wholeness begin to dissolve and a sense of community emerges. Peck's approach to generating community has its roots in the religious tradition through which the rejected and alienated person loses himself or herself by coming together with others in a cathartic event that casts out the demons. In true religion, the group admits shortcomings before God—or His representative. Now that the therapist has replaced the priest, confession and baring of the soul takes place before a secular saviour.

Peck's approach to community has overtones of what used to be called the Human Potential Movement that used group dynamics, sensitivity training, and encounter groups as ways of achieving human perfectibility. Of the community movement, he writes: "There is no viable alternative—no other way out of survival."[64]

Peck helped to set up the Foundation for Community Encouragement (FCE), a non-profit educational foundation which "teaches the principles and values of community to individuals, groups and organizations."[65] Its literature quotes Peck, who is no longer involved with FCE: "The only obstacle to introducing community into a business is politics...If the top managers of a company are the kind of people who want community, they can have it." The FCE uses a "Community Building Model" to show how "Any group can build and experience genuine community provided they understand the demands and responsibilities involved and are willing to commit themselves to the process." One participant in an FCE workshop asked plaintively: "How on earth can I go back to my board of governors and sell them on love?" The belief that you can separate politics and the exercise of power bothered a Newfoundlander who wondered how the techniques that may work in a closed seminar room could be applied to outport villages.

Community as therapy is becoming increasingly popular as stress levels rise. There is no great harm in bringing people together and having them open up to each other. But can they learn the processes involved in short seminars and workshops, as if the creation of community simply involved a set of techniques? As the presence of the lichen on earth shows, generating lasting symbiotic relationships between people takes great skill, a lot of time and involves an appreciation of the mysterious, the sacred, the unknowable in the world. As the Pilgrim Fathers (and Mothers!) crossed the Atlantic to find new lives and found new communities in a new world, their leader John Winthrop told them: "We must consider that we shall be a City on a Hill, the eyes of all people upon us." The Americans, a dynamic, open and generous people have created many cities on hills. But they have also built rickety dwellings and infernal communities, and we can learn much from them about how *not* to create communities.

Increasingly, despite Coca-Colonization and Disneyfication, Canadians are showing that they are very different from Americans. As Noam Chomsky put it:

"Americans have great and noble principles and they go to hell trying to live up to them. Canadians also have great and noble principles, but they go to heaven figuring out ways to get around them."

In January, 1994, the CBC gave John McKnight, a disciple of Saul Alinsky, an opportunity to promote his vision of community on its *Ideas* programme.[66] McKnight defined community as "the space where citizens prevail." Echoing the views of his mentor, who called social workers "pimps of the poor," McKnight stressed how outsiders weakened many communities by their interventions. Life for residents had been worsened by these efforts to help them—with most of the money going to service providers and not to the poor. McKnight noted that "as communities grow richer in social services, they often grow poorer in competence and solidarity." The outside "helpers" encourage dependency, and often neuter local leadership—especially if it is strong and competent, but lacks professional credentials. McKnight urged Canadians to take back control of their lives from professionals and large corporations. By forming local associations that help them to identify, strengthen and share their gifts, people can revitalize their communities. This "do-it-yourself" approach to community has some validity in Canada. But it can be dangerous, as it rationalizes neo-conservative efforts by governments to offload responsibility for services on to communities.

The Americans have a positive mania for creating associations to meet local and national needs. Alexis de Tocqueville, watching the new American society emerge, recognized this tendency. But he wondered how it would mesh with the strong strain of individualism that already marked the United States in the first decades of the nineteenth-century. He saw egalitarianism as eliminating individual differences and identity by submerging individuals in an anonymous crowd. However, the French visitor observed that:

"...whatever may be the general endeavour of a community to render its members equal and alike, the personal pride of individuals will always be to rise above the line and to form somewhere an inequality to their own advantage."[67]

75

In the United States and Canada, the rich never concern themselves with community. They can choose to meet and mingle with people like themselves—or seclude themselves in gated communities or behind walls and bars. The poor suffer from too much community—too many demands on too few resources. If you're affluent in America, you live in lifestyle enclaves like Sun City. If you're poor, you live in a welfare ghetto which has its own lifestyle.

Faith Popcorn, the American "futurist," coined the word "cocooning" to describe the musk-oxen stance of threatened people who retreat into gated communities to shut out the unsafe, uncertain world. In 1994, the Fraser Institute promoted an American version of community in Gordon Tullock's *The New Federalist*. This book describes life in Sunshine Mountain Ridge, a village in Arizona. A major developer built 250 houses. Each buyer signs a contract pledging to become a member of the homeowners' association, to obey its rules and pay an annual fee. The right-wing think tank saw such intentional communities as a way of countering the omnipresence of government. As Tullock puts it: "...government does not have to be monolithic but can be broken down into parts."[68] Because of the costs of the houses in Sunshine Mountain Ridge, the population is very homogenous, with few children. From this single example, the leap to seeing the future of North America as lying in self-contained, locally ruled lifestyle enclaves is easily made by those who seek to live their own way, sealed off from demands from "others" outside their boundaries.

But no community is an island, complete unto itself.

British Columbia has a number of planned communities for retired people. Such developments seek to recreate the feel of lost village life—with handy access to golf courses, The names of these new developments echo the past—The Village at Gallagher's Canyon, Craig Bay, Ambleside and Longwood, Fairwinds, Arbutus Ridge. Kelowna has ten gated communities.[69] Under the rubric of the "New Urbanism" a group of architects and planners is seeking to recreate the lost sense of community in cities, to encourage people to interact with each other on a daily basis.

The passion for community has found expression in a new political movement, which is gaining ground in the United States and elsewhere. Communitarianism began in 1990 when fifteen ethicists, philosophers and social scientists met in Washington at the invitation of Amitai Etzioni, a leading academic. They discussed the ills of America and created the Communitarian Network in 1992, issuing a twenty-nine-page position paper stressing the role of the two-parent society as the cornerstone of society, and suggesting a ten-year moratorium on the creation of new rights. Communitarians believe that everyone should accept responsibilities as well as enjoying rights.

In *The Spirit of Community: Rights, Responsibilities and the Communitarian Agenda*, Etzioni hammered away at the grievance/victim/resentment/entitlement culture that pervades affluent societies.[70] People keep demanding rights while refusing to honour obligations to others. Communitarians criticize liberals for their permissive, individualistic view of society in which anyone can do anything, as long as it does not harm others. Etzioni believes that the old labels in politics—conservative and liberal, left and right, have no validity these days. He promotes the idea of community for free individuals but does not explain how this can be achieved. Like most intellectuals, Etzioni is happier dealing with neat, theoretical abstractions than with messy reality and complex facts.

Will Kymlicka, a Canadian academic, points out that the communitarians "argue that liberals both misconstrue our capacity for self-determination and neglect the social preconditions under which that capacity can be meaningfully exercised."[71] Etzioni and his followers believe that the state should not be neutral but engage in "a politics of the common good." As Bernard Shaw put it: "Do not do unto others as you would have them do unto you. Their tastes may be different." Communitarianism has many aspects of Puritanism in a new dress, and is infused with ideas of perfectibility. The world is divided between "us" who know what constitutes the common good and "them" who don't.

Managing a gated community where people share a common lifestyle offers some challenges. But it is simple compared to organizing diverse people with very different values and ways of living in one geographical location, whether at the local or the national level.

During the Sixties, many young people in the industrialized world accepted the rural myth and left the cities to find individual freedom and togetherness in communes. Seeking to escape the rigours of mainstream society, these idealists discovered just how difficult country life could be. In creating new lives in new settings, they had to find new ways of making a living—and of relating to each other. The record indicates that most of these intentional communities lasted about two years. Some have survived. Twin Oaks in Louisa, Virginia, founded in 1967, serves as the mother house of the commune movement.

The Federation of Egalitarian Communities in the United States has issued a booklet whose title reflects its continuing idealism. *Sharing the Dream* tells how intentional communities survive and thrive. Their members hold land, labour and income in common; assume responsibility for each other; practice non-violence and democratic decision-making; conserve natural resources and preserve the environment. The booklet notes:

> "It takes a special kind of person to thrive in community, to forgo private income in favor of shared wealth, to accept the challenge of decision-making among equals, to embrace diversity among community people and to revel in the richness of complementary strengths. You need courage to break from a competitive, consumption-oriented culture—and attempt with us the formation of an alternative society. We cannot promise utopia, but if you are seriously interested in our joyful struggle, we invite you to come and see for yourself."[72]

The dream of community, of making better worlds survives in small corners and remote locations in North America and elsewhere in the world. The successful collective ventures all have one thing in common—a strong moral and spiritual basis.

The word "community" still retains its evocative powers. But to understand ways of creating the good community, you must go beyond instrumental concerns and personal fantasies and ask why communities have been and are being created. In *Creating Community Anywhere*, subtitled "Finding support and connection in a fragmented world," a woman writes about how she coped with the death of her marriage.[73] Finding herself unable to raise her two children on her own, she created a "community" of volunteers who took the place of the nanny she could not afford. J. Robert Oppenheimer, father of the atom bomb, described Los Alamos, where it was designed and built as "a remarkable community inspired by a high sense of mission, of duty, and of destiny, coherent, dedicated...and remarkably unselfish, devoted to a common purpose."[73a] The common purpose, of course, was to devise a way of killing large numbers of people. A German who later joined the Bruderhof, an intentional Christian community, recalled how the Nazis created a sense of collective identity. Involvement in the Hitler Youth, with its club nights, excursions, campfires captivated and enthused its members: "community, one for all and all for one." After all, what could be greater than dedication to the Fatherland—"and to die laughing and proud for its sake."[74]

One source on community claims that the term is "one of the most elusive and vague in sociology and is by now largely without specific meaning."[75] It identifies three elements in community—collections of people with a particular social structure, "a sense of belonging or community spirit," and all daily activities taking place within a geographical area in "self-contained entities." A study carried out over forty years ago examined ninety-four definitions of community and concluded that "beyond the concept that people are involved in community, there is no complete agreement as to the nature of community."[76]

Until recently Canadians have not shown the same enthusiasm for creating local associations and founding intentional communities as have the Americans. In the American West, the pioneers went out ahead of the law and had to learn to live together. In the Canadian West, the law, in the form of the Mounties, went into the seemingly empty land before the settlers arrived. The dominance of government in Canada has made officialdom the main point of reference in our lives. And economic policies in the past have tended to favour large corporate entities rather than community interests. Canada does not have the same degree of individualism as is found in the United States, and we tend to be more pragmatic than the idealistic Americans.

We are a different country and tackle the quest for community in different ways.

COMMUNITY IN CANADA

"Perfection is the enemy of the good."

Anon.

The concept of community is tied up with the ideal of perfect harmony in human relationships. The stressed middle class have created a growth industry in therapy in the industrialized nations as they seek to harmonize their inner and outer beings—and heal their relationships with the earth whose exploitation enables them to have the standard of living they enjoy.

In *The Tyranny of the Group*, Andrew Malcolm, a Canadian psychiatrist, cast a critical eye over the various techniques for acquiring inner harmony.[77] He saw little merit in nude encounters, Syanon, gestalt theory, T-groups, sensitivity training and other ways of manipulating people's emotions. Malcolm praised the Israeli *kibbutzim*. At one time they were held up as a model for creating ideal, egalitarian communities. The *kibbutzim* are a realization of the vision of modern Jews bent on recreating their ancient community in the Promised Land. The very harshness of the land and the enmity of local Arabs strengthened the sense of community among the early settlers. The *kibbutz* and the *moshev* (settlement of co-operative smallholders) gave residents freedom from alien oppression, their own communities and a sense of belonging to a new kind of society.

Today, *kibbutzniks* have to balance their communal ideals with the realities of the modern world. A Canadian professor who lived on a *kibbutz* with his family for six months in 1981 and returned in 1992 noted a number of changes. Children once lived in separate houses, but now sleep at home. Thus some houses have to be enlarged at the expense of the community. And decisions about funding these expansions create tension in the *kibbutz*. No longer is it "a tightly knit commune of single youth during a pioneer period." Kibbutz Ein

Hamifratz is now "a multi-generational community of families with very modern values."[78] Another commentator sees the ideology of the *kibbutz* rooted in European revolutionary Marxism: "From its very inception, the kibbutz has constituted an economic unit that confronts the market...the *kibbutz* model is a form of socialism that accepts, and functions within, capitalism."[79] There is increasing focus on the family, the privatization of social life and individualism. Hierarchies have appeared, with high-status positions bringing privileges and technocrats playing leadership roles.

The population of the Israeli *kibbutzim* has remained steady at around 120,000 in recent years. Commenting on the survival of the *kibbutzim*, George Woodcock noted:

> "One of the most depressing and yet the most obvious conclusions I very quickly reached was that except under very unusual circumstances, nonreligious communities had little survival."[80]

Creating community requires practical and social skills. But without a shared spiritual foundation, intentional communities can become places of fear and exploitation. Roch Theriault, leader of the Ant Hill Kids commune in Quebec murdered one of his followers and forced a woman to amputate her own arm.[81]

In British Columbia, the perils of communities that relied on charismatic leaders become apparent in the sagas of Sointula and Brother Twelve. Sointula, "a place of harmony" in Finnish, lasted for three years on Malcolm Island. Founded by Mattii Kurikka (1862-1915), a political refugee from Finland, this utopian community attracted idealists with very little practical understanding of working the land, the forests and the sea. By 1905, the venture had vanished. But it left traces of the co-operative ethic in the small community that took its place. This scenario has been played out again and again in intentional communities. Even if they fail, they leave traces on the landscape and in the memory of members and others.

The story of Brother Twelve has mystical overtones.[82] While on his sick bed in a village of southern France in October, 1924, Edward

Arthur Wilson, a British sea captain, had a vision. Through it, he learned that he had been selected by an occult brotherhood to do great spiritual works. The Great White Lodge named him the twelfth master of the group, so Captain Wilson became Brother Twelve. This taking on of a new persona, a new name, occurs again and again in the history of community creation. Brother Twelve attracted women and disenchanted intellectuals and seekers to his community. At the headquarters of his Aquarium Foundation at Cedar-by-the-Sea, eleven kilometres south of Nanaimo, BC, Wilson proclaimed the "First Trumpet-Blast of the New Age," and gathered around him a band of the faithful. He set them to work building the foundation headquarters and breaking the land for a farm on De Courcey Island.

The venture began in 1927. Brother Twelve worked his flock hard while extracting money from them and his other followers. He acquired a mistress, Madame Zee, and told everyone to prepare for the coming Armageddon. He also began to stash $20 gold coins in Mason jars. In 1933, Brother Twelve's overworked followers on the farm rebelled, demanding an accounting and control of the community. The prophet fled with Madame Zee, settling in Neuchatel, Switzerland. He died there on 7 November, 1934. Or did he? His lawyer claimed to have seen him on a luxury liner in San Francisco a year and a half later.

In the past, Canada welcomed religious groups who lived communally. Leo Tolstoy helped 7,400 persecuted Doukhobors to settle in what became Saskatchewan in 1899. The newcomers registered for homesteads on an individual basis, but were allowed to live communally. Other religious groups such as the Hutterites, Mennonites, Amish live and farm together, following traditional ways of life. These efficient farmers often arouse the ire of their neighbours as they attempt to expand their holdings and demonstrate their self-reliance. The religious communities are not homogenous. Some have flourished while others have vanished. Old Order Mennonites in Elmira and St. Jacobs, Ontario, will not speak to strangers or have their photograph taken in case this smacks of the sin of pride. Other Mennonite communities use advanced technology and welcome visitors. These Christians have an outstanding record throughout the world for their work in local development. During the Tet offensive in Vietnam in 1968, the house occupied by the Mennonites in Hue remained untouched. Both the Americans and their enemies recognized and respected their pacifism and neutrality.[83]

The late George Woodcock wrote of visiting a Doukhobor community in British Columbia in 1949.[84] His encounter with these people shows how difficult it can be to separate a true mystic from a manipulative maniac. Woodcock and his wife, travelling through British Columbia, saw a sign near Hilliers on Vancouver Island proclaiming the presence of "The Union of spiritual communities of Christ." Woodcock, an anarchist with a strong interest in collective ways of living, decided to stop in for a visit. The couple met Michael the Archangel, leader of a breakaway group of Doukhobors, who ruled the community. He had received a vision and set out to create a new Jerusalem, where his followers would wait out time and mortality. In God's earthly kingdom, its leader decreed, women had freedom, sexual relations were unrestrained and family life discouraged. Michael practised what he preached, while claiming that no one had any rights over anyone else. The hard work and dogged devotion of his followers had made the land fruitful. But Michael had become a tyrant, exploiting his followers. Jailed for disturbing the public order, he died in prison. Ten years after their visit, the Woodcocks passed the site of the community. Fallen fences and thickets of thistles marked the site of the new Jerusalem.

Intentional religious communities have flowered in Britain and the United States. But they are few and far between in Canada. A small Christian community in Rochdale College in Toronto survived as the venture was invaded by squatters, vagrants, drug dealers, bikers and freeloaders.[85] The North East Kingdom Church, persecuted in Vermont, moved into Nova Scotia in the Seventies. It drew upon the Old Testament with members taking new names from it when they joined. These godly people met prejudice and harassment in the province and eventually moved to Winnipeg. Fear of sects, uninformed media coverage and the competition that the group's restaurant in Barrington Passage offered to the local greasy spoons played some part in this persecution. Authorities became concerned about the claim that members of the community disciplined their children in the belief that sparing the rod spoiled the child. The members of the church lived in the New Testament way, sharing all things, and were excellent workers. The community offered a place where lost and lonely people could find meaningful roles serving others while finding personal peace. A woman leader in this community told me that making the decision to join it was the hardest one she had ever made in her life, for she had given up everything—house, boyfriend, job.

The Grain of Wheat Community in Winnipeg, another intentional community, operates from a communal house, with other members living on one street. This group has a strong Mennonite component.

One of the most curious and unlikely examples of community in Canada originated in a meeting between a British aristocrat and a wandering American. Ron Graham devoted a chapter in his book *God's Dominion* to the Emissaries at 100 Mile House in British Columbia; no mention is made of this religious community in the National Film Board series based on the book.[86] Graham told of a high school friend who had "fallen into the clutches of a strange cult run by a British Lord," and was living on a commune. This friend had drifted through university "minoring in political radicalism and majoring in psychedelics and spiritual understanding." Attending a lecture by Michael Cecil, a member of the great English family of that name, he joined his community.

Once known as the Emissaries of Divine Light, the venture at 100 Mile House began with a revelation received by an American, Lloyd Arthur Meeker. He left home at sixteen, wandered around the United States and had a vision in 1932 at the age of twenty-five. Founding the Emissaries, Meeker renamed himself Uranda and set out to promote spiritual regeneration. Buying a dryland farm in Colorado, he called it Sunrise Ranch. In 1940, Uranda met Lord Martin Cecil who later became the seventh Marquis of Exeter. He had been sent by his father to manage the family ranch at 100 Mile House. One of the mysteries about the creation of community lies in the way in which diverse people come to share a common vision and turn it into a reality. Cecil made the lodge on the ranch the headquarters of the Emissaries in Canada. When Uranda died in a plane crash in 1954,

Cecil took over his leadership role. His writings combine Old and New Testament theology with overtones of earth magic.[87]

The community now has five centres in the United States, three in Canada, and one each in France, Britain, Australia and South Africa. It's easy to dismiss these ventures as hippie havens and refuges for the alienated middle class. But the Emissaries' community seems to work well for those who join it.

Martin Exeter, who succeeded his father as leader of the Emissaries, has a clear vision of community:

"Being in community implies the presence of individuals whose sense of self is solidly in place, and knowing the golden threads of their very selves, they are free to be together and to create together. Neither the individual nor the community is dependent...This is the experience of being in community, not in competition, conflict or comparison. It is complementation, the conjunction of diverse elements which have their places together without losing their diversity."[88]

This statement has overtones of the Lichen Factor, of symbioses between very different kinds of people. In communities like the Emissaries, a strong, spiritual bond holds members together as they seek to grow both individually and as members of a collective.

Sustaining the original vision of a better life together while adapting to change offers constant challenges in communities. In 1952, several Quaker families "with their heads in the sky and their feet on the ground" and tired of the Cold War environment in the United States moved from California to the old silver mining town of Argenta at the north end of Kootenay Lake in central British Columbia.[89] Greeted initially with suspicion by the locals, they revitalized the old community. In the Nineties, however, the residents had to cope with newcomers moving into the area who did not share their values of openness, honesty and caring and also with threats and divisions over logging on the community watershed. Nancy Argenta, the Canadian soprano, took her name from this remarkable Canadian community.

Even those communities whose members adhere to the same religion have had difficulty weathering the strains of change and new demands. In 1992, a dispute split Hutterites in Manitoba and ended up in the Supreme Court of Canada.[90] Daniel Hofer of Lakeside Hutterite Colony made hog feeders patented by another colony. The elders told Hofer to stop production. He refused. So the elders voted to ostracize him and his followers. Hofer claimed that the leader of the Hutterites had introduced restrictive American ways into Canada: "Their idea was that if a member doesn't obey to the letter exactly like management says, he should be expelled and kicked off the property." The Supreme Court ruled six to one in Hofer's favour, concluding that the colony had failed to follow the laws of natural justice by ordering him and his followers to leave.

The clash between individual values and collective life emerges in the words of a woman who grew up in a Mennonite farming community in southern Manitoba:

"Later, during adolescence, the net of family that held us so completely as children began to feel more like a trap. We were itching to leave home and invent our own lives, and the burden of belonging to this fixed entity, with its fixed story, fixed rules, no longer seemed safe and inviting, but unbearably narrow and confining. We began to feel the weight of guilt, the price of non-conformity, and to remember the pain of being disciplined, severely, religiously, as children into the family code."[91]

Governments in Canada have seldom been sympathetic to collective endeavours. In 1944, nineteen veterans started a co-operative farm at Matador, Saskatchewan.[92] Despite the urgings of the provincial CCF government, Ottawa refused to amend the Veterans' Land Act to allow collective farming. The members of the co-op took individual title to the land, worked it collectively and shared the profits. They also started their own school and store. As the founders aged, they faced the problem of keeping the collective venture alive. As with the Israeli kibbutzim the next generation did not face the problems of starting up and sustaining a new enterprise against difficulties and opposition from outsiders. The NDP government made the transfer of the land easy by allowing the co-op members to sell their holdings to the provincial land bank, which then leased it back to their sons.

Government inflexibility hampered another collective venture in British Columbia. In 1947, several members of a credit union and co-op store in Vancouver decided to found an intentional community.[93] Borrowing $10,000 from the Robert Owen Foundation, they bought 130 acres of land near Nanaimo. Many ex-servicemen wanted to join the community. The federal government refused to give them their demobilization grants if they did so. The community did not last very long. Members sold the land for a small profit, repaid the loan, and went their separate ways with "good memories of an interesting experiment" in the words of one member.

For some people, time spent in an intentional community forms part of a lifetime of learning about themselves and others. For others it becomes an obsession or an escape from the demands of the world. For still others, community living is a sensible, economical and pleasant way to meet their own needs and serve others. Co-housing is very successful in Scandinavia and has received government support.[94] In these ventures, people come together to plan and develop their own community, with individually-owned houses and shared services and facilities. In Barrie, Ontario a group of people seeking to start a co-housing venture encountered suspicion and hostility from the local council whose members thought they were founding a commune.

In a time when political ideologies have been drained of meaning, the notion of community appeals to right wingers like Michael Harris—and to leftwingers who have realized the follies of promoting state control of the economy and the intervention of professionals in the lives of the poor and the disadvantaged as the only ways to create a better society. Pat Lorjé, a Saskatchewan NDP member of the Legislative Assembly, suggested that the party abandon its emphasis on central planning and control in favour of encouraging a community approach to meeting human needs:

"Many of these things [social and economic problems] are big questions. That's the kind of planning dear to the hearts of New Democrats and socialists everywhere. But maybe what we really need is...community-owned and controlled small and practical ideas, rather than big ideas...that are being squashed under the heels of voter resistance. Let's start talking small with plausible community proposals for tackling crime, helping the unemployed, improving education and the quality of life."[95]

James Laxer is described as "one of the leading political thinkers in this country" on the jacket blurb of his book *In Search of a New Left*. Now a university professor, Laxer was one of the founders of the Waffle group in 1969, and almost became the leader of the national NDP. His book looks at "Canadian Politics after the Neoconservative assault" in the words of its subtitle. Laxer damns the wickedness of the rich and exalts the nobility of the poor, defining socialism as being "about the struggle from below for the fullest possible extension of democracy...[which] starts from the premise that social justice is concerned, first and foremost, with the condition of the non-affluent."[96]

After lamenting corporate greed and the excesses of the neoconservatives, Laxer jumps on the community bandwagon, seeing it as the future of politics in Canada:

"Another society exists within the exo-skeleton of the one just described. And that society is not subject to the tunnel vision of utilitarianism. It is all around us, although when we analyze great economic and political questions, it is scarcely visible.

The other society is made up of communities based in every region in the country that have formed around churches, trade unions, schools, cultural bodies, associations of various kinds, and sporting and recreational bodies. The values system within these communities is vastly at odds with the global, market-driven economy of the late twentieth century."[97]

Laxer also sees the various social movements that have sprung up in Canada such as the Action Canada Network and the Council of Canadians as playing a vital role in creating the ''New Left.'' Like many other enthusiasts about community and social movements, Laxer resembles the man who bought a bottle of beer, liked it, then went out and bought the brewery.

Community cannot be forced on unwilling people.

And social movements have a trajectory that is well documented in the literature on them.

Throughout history, concerned men and women have dreamed of making a better world by human effort. Others have tried to turn this vision into realities and founded communities where individuals could live fuller lives. Some of these efforts have worked better than others. These visions of new society almost inevitably arise at times of personal and collective crises. By looking briefly at the world history of the concept of community it's possible to identify forces and factors that encourage and enhance collective ways of tackling human problems.

Like every other magic word, "community" has a history of effective use—and simplistic misuse. But the idea behind it haunts and tantalizes us still, and the concept is not going to go away.

And so we plunge into history...

A SHORT HISTORY OF COMMUNITY

"The world is full of people whose notion
of a satisfactory future is, in fact,
a return to an idealized past."
Robertson Davies, *A Voice in the Attic*, 1960

THE IDEALIZED PAST

"Would that I had not been born in this age,
but either before or after it."
Hesiod, eighth century (BCE) Greek poet.

Hesiod's lament echoes down the corridors of time. The Judeo-Christian heritage enshrines a belief in the Garden of Eden. The faithful who die for Islam live eternally in a beautiful garden, waited upon hand and foot by houris. The hoboes during the Great Depression in the United States sang of the Big Rock Candy Mountains where all the jails were made of tin—"And you could bust right out again/Just as soon as they put you in."

Northrop Frye writes of the pastoral myth and the progress myth: "Many people like to assume that the society of their childhood was a solid and coherent structure which is now falling apart."[98] The progress myth implies that all past history was a kind of bad dream. Thus the invocation of community in our time hovers between dreams of a perfect past and expectations of some wonderful future state free of all tensions.

After Hesiod's time, the aristocracy in Greece tightened its grip on power. Footloose people flocked to the cities in search of work and a better life. The arts began to flourish. The Greeks gave up their barbaric warrior ways as communities become refined and cultured. Natural phenomena that once generated reverence, awe and fear came under the scrutiny of philosophers in Ionia and elsewhere who began to explain them. The arbitrary and capricious ways of the gods made less and less sense and lost their power over men and women as these early scientists identified rational reasons for what happened in the natural world. Reason and scepticism became prevalent as wars, social mobility and migration strained the social fabric of traditional life.

A dictator invented democracy. In the sixth century Cleisthenes seized power from the ruling oligarchy in Athens and presented a new constitution to the people in 508-507 BCE. In place of an exclusive coterie of four tribes and 360 clans, the dictator divided Athenians into ten tribes, depending on where they lived in the city. These districts were known as *demes*, from which the word democracy comes. Foreign freemen became citizens of the *demes* in which they lived and the roll of voters doubled. Religious ceremonies honoured local heroes, strengthening the sense of community through collective rituals.

This early attempt at creating community shows some enduring patterns. Initiated by a powerful, enlightened individual who centralized power and then decentralized it, the changes he initiated gave individuals a new identity and opportunities to participate in new rituals, enhancing their sense of belonging at the local level. The reforms of Cleisthenes ushered in the golden age of Athens, rich in drama, literature, art, sculpture and philosophy. The Athenians, imbued with a sense of pride and identity, defeated the invading Persians. With prosperity came arrogance and hubris; the Peloponnesian War (431-404) between Athens and Sparta ended the golden age. Over the next century, Athens fell into decline. The two founding philosophers of western thought lived in those days of defeat and offered radically different ideas on how to create the good life. Plato was born in 428 BCE. Aristotle died in 322. The former favoured centralized government run by priest-kings. The latter promoted decentralization and local rule. Living in a time of social disintegration and moral decline, Plato looked back to the past for inspiration. When aristocrats ruled, everyone had stability and security. His ideal government would ban money and unrestricted freedom in the arts, immorality and factionalism. Aristotle saw the creation of small, pluralistic states as the way of the future.

In Palestine, the Jews developed their sense of community through the ceremonies that governed their relationships with one god, an unusual practice in the ancient world. Even the power of Rome could not crush this sense of Jewish identity and destiny. The Roman Empire reached its peak around 14 AD when Caesar Augustus died.

Moral rot set in as enormous wealth from captured lands and trading ventures poured into Rome. Gurus, magicians, cultists and wonder workers offered instant solutions to the problems of rich and poor.

Some of the discontented and oppressed joined a new sect founded by the followers of a man crucified by the Romans in a remote part of the empire, who had risen from dead. The name Christian was first applied to these people in Antioch around 40-44 AD, and used as an official designation for them by the Romans. Blending elements of Hellenism and Judaism, the Christians preached *agape*—loving kindness to all. They lived in community, sharing what they had. Aristide, a pagan, wrote to the emperor Hadrian about the members of this strange sect:

> "They love one another. They never fail to help widows. They save orphans from those who would hurt them. If they have something they give freely to the man who has nothing: if they see a stranger, they take him home and are happy, as if he were a real brother. They do not consider themselves brothers in the usual sense, but through the Spirit, through God."

Although the leaders of the early Christian Church disagreed about who should be allowed to join their new community, the sect attracted more and more followers. Persecution by Roman emperors, especially Nero, bound the small band of believers together and weeded out those not prepared to suffer for their faith. In 313 AD the emperor Constantine proclaimed the equality of all religions. Christianity, freed from persecution, soon became an arena where men struggled for power and preference. As Rome fell into decline, the barbarians poured over its borders. In 410, Alaric and his lusty lads sacked the city, inspiring St. Augustine to write *The City of God*. He came up with the doctrine of necessity. No matter how chaotic life might be in the present, God had a plan for humans. We must all struggle along as best we can, putting up with evil and wickedness. In time, we shall reach a new community, the City of God: "How great will be that facility, which shall be tainted with no evil, which shall lack no good."

Some early Christians fled into the desert, living in solitude, rejecting the temptations of the flesh. St. Pachomius (290-346) drew hermits in the Egyptian desert into communities. The former Roman soldier wrote a set of rules to regulate life in these first monasteries. The members lived in separate cells, coming together to work and to eat, enjoying privacy and community.

The directions that Pachomius drew up have been lost.

But they influenced St. Benedict of Nursia (480-547) who set out to create a system of monasteries. St. Benedict's first venture at Subiaco failed. Resenting his high standards, followers tried to poison him. Benedict organized twelve communities of faith, and built a large monastery at Monte Cassino south of Rome. While the Huns ravaged northern Italy and the leaders of the Christian Church squabbled among themselves, his monks established islands of peace, productivity and human harmony.

During the Dark Ages, the monasteries became points of light and sanity, making their lands fruitful, offering shelter and succor to wanderers. St. Benedict's rule directed the daily round of life in his communities. Spiritual and physical work complemented each other—*laborare est orare*. Benedict counselled moderation and patience with those who broke the rule. Asked what he did in a monastery, a monk replied: "We fall and get up, fall and get up, fall and get up again." Unfortunately, as they became wealthy, the Benedictines fell very short of their original ideas:

"They ruled men, collected rents, maintained buildings, provided hospitality for the great, and kept up a ponderous dignity in all the affairs of life and death. No one looked to them for new ideas or new forms of spiritual life: they looked to them for stability, pageantry, involvement in the aristocratic life of the upper classes, and a visible display of continuous religious and family history."[99]

By the end of the thirteenth century, the Benedictines had become part of the establishment, resisting reform. Other monastic orders picked up the ideal of community and set up sacred communities in the wilderness. The Cistercians, an offshoot of the Benedictines, went to the frontiers of Europe to colonize them for religious, military and agricultural purposes. The monastic orders educated a new kind of thinker who sought to link religious and secular ideas. St. Thomas Aquinas (1225-1274), educated at Monte Cassino, saw virtue in decentralized societies and the ideas of Aristotle. He promoted the concept of *communitas communitatum*—a community of communities—as the most effective way to create the good and holy society.

A thousand years after the death of St. Benedict, Sir Thomas More (1478-1535) coined a new word to describe his version of the ideal community. Utopia ("no place") has passed into the English language to describe an idealized society that can never become a practical reality. More wrote his book as traditional ways came under attack in Britain. Henry VIII centralized power in government and curbed the power of the monasteries which he then proceeded to privatize. He oppressed guilds, local community bodies or any group that threatened his hegemony. Villagers lost their right to graze animals on common land which ruthless men then enclosed and used for individual gain. Powerful families enjoyed huge incomes, while the poor starved or were hung for stealing food.

Utopia appeared in Latin in 1516, in English forty years later, and is still in print. It can be read as a moral allegory, a political tract or a traveller's tale. Few idealists who yearn for Utopia would like to live in the world that More envisaged. His vision of the ideal community reflected life on the great country estates of his day. Everyone in Utopia worked and took what they needed from the common pool of goods; slaves did not have this privilege. Two hundred "Stywards" elected the mayors of the towns by secret ballot. District councillors had responsibility for thirty houses, all of which looked alike. Utopians worked for two years on the land, then changed places with those living in the towns for two years. Priests, elected by the community, could be male or female. Utopia had few laws. But those who broke them were executed if they persisted in doing so. Opportunities for repentance and forgiveness remained ever present. Utopians did wonders with barren land, practised good husbandry and ate a well-balanced diet.

This vision of communal bliss began to fade as individualism became rampant in western Europe.

THE RISE OF INDIVIDUALISM

> "Liberty consists of doing what one desires."
> "The liberty of the individual must be thus far
> limited; he must not make a nuisance
> of himself to others."
> "The worth of the state, in the long run is the worth
> of the individuals comprising it."
> John Stuart Mill *On Liberty* (1859)

The Renaissance and the Reformation preceded the Democratic and Industrial Revolutions and gave them their rationale. A new image of man emerged, freed from the constraints of the traditional community and feudal ways, a creative individual able to conquer the physical world with new mechanical and social technologies. Self-created and self-sustaining, this new being had no need of help and succor from God. The secularization of society broke that ancient, holy bond between humans and God upon which the sanctity and security of society and individuals rested. Before the revolutions, you could be poor, a holy mendicant and still find favour in the eyes of other men and women—and God. In Russia, *poustiniks* dedicated themselves to "prayer, penance, mortification, solitude, silence, offered in the spirit of love, atonement, and reparation to God."[100] A *poustinik* could be a peasant or an aristocrat, learned or unlearned, who lived in solitude but helped anyone in need, for example, a farmer trying to bring in hay before it rained. The intentional Christian community at Combermere in Ontario, founded by Catherine de Hueck Doherty, seeks to keep this tradition alive.

As the Industrial Revolution gathered speed, the worth of humans was measured by what they produced and consumed—not by what they contributed to the common good. The rising middle class defined itself through the possessions its members acquired and flaunted.

In the nineteenth century the bourgeoisie in Europe overthrew the old aristocratic order. Now a prophet arose who claimed that they, in their turn, would be displaced by the proletariat. *The Communist Manifesto* (1848) begins: "A spectre is haunting Europe—the spectre of Communism." Karl Marx saw an irreversible trend in world history—the powerful were always being overthrown by the powerless. He scared the bourgeoisie and the governments they dominated with his ideas on the inevitability of class warfare as the poor, the downtrodden, the workers became aware of their plight. Communism, so often presented as the way of the future in our century, in fact represent a return to an ideal past. Through Marxist-Leninism, an intellectual vanguard would take power from the old order. Then, slowly but surely, the state would wither away. Once again men and women would live and work together as they had done in the past, free and unfettered, serving each other rather than the insatiable need of the middle class for profit and power. But while Marx railed against the "money fetish" and the "commodity fetish," he recognized the need to have some sort of a regular income to survive. In 1862, he wrote to Engels, who was supporting him: "If only I knew how to start some sort of business! My dear friend, all theory is dismal and only business flourishes. Unfortunately I have learned this too late."[101]

Throughout the nineteenth century, idealists offered alternative visions of the good society that avoided the excesses of capitalism and communism.

Marx believed in the "bottom-up," grassroots way of creating a new society. Robert Owen espoused the "top down" approach to change. Born in 1771 in Newton, Wales, he saw co-operation, not competition, as the basis of the good society. Owen believed that people could learn to live and work together in "mutual confidence and kindness." At the New Lanark mills in Scotland, he put his ideas into practice in the early part of the nineteenth-century. Establishing a model community, Owen improved housing and working conditions, set up an Institute for the Formation of Character, established a school (including the world's first day-nursery and playground and also evening classes) and opened a village store where workers could buy what they needed at slightly above cost. New Lanark became the cradle of the co-operative movement in Britain.

In 1813, Owen published *A New View of Society*, claiming that human character is formed by circumstances beyond the control of individuals. Change the environment in their early years, and they would learn to live good lives. His *Report on the Poor* (1817) appeared as mass unemployment followed the end of the Napoleonic wars. Owen proposed settling idle people on vacant lands in co-operative groups of five hundred to 1,500. Here, through farming and small-scale manufacturing, they could become self-sufficient. He tried to put these ideas into practice by founding the community of New Harmony in Indiana in 1825. Under his direction, the co-operative venture flourished with representative government and a constitution embodying collective ownership. The community attracted idealists with few practical skills for living from the land, and its members became divided over religious differences. The venture absorbed most of Owen's money and dissolved in 1828. He then devoted his life to trade unionism and spiritualism, dying in 1858. An inspired improver, Owen spent his last days in his birthplace, drawing up plans to reorganize the town's education system. Grateful residents of Newton erected a statue to him. In a nearby graveyard the tomb of an ironmaster carries the simple epitaph: "God forgive me."

A few people followed Owen's path, and in the United States a wide range of intentional communities came into being. Oneida in upper New York state—"the merriest of our nineteenth century Utopias" in the words of Alfred Kazin—began in 1848.[102] Its founder, John Humphreys Noyes, saw the community as a bridgehead over which "the armies of Christ would soon advance to establish God's kingdom on earth." After several futile attempts to generate businesses, the community began to make money by selling animal traps, then moved into job-printing and silk-spinning. Oneida attracted all the unwarranted attention that cults and communes have suffered in our time. It has survived in a very modified form. In the early Nineties Oneida Ltd. produced china tableware and industrial wire products as well as sterling silver and silverplate. It was also the world's largest manufacturer of stainless steel cutlery.

The communal reaction to aggressive individualism in Europe found its voice through men like Pierre-Joseph Proudhon, Michael Bakunin, Alexander Herzen and especially Peter Kropotkin and followers of the anarchist tradition. Prince Kropotkin gave up power and his privileges in Russia, was imprisoned there and in France and found refuge in England. He sought to counter the concept of Social Darwinism and the belief in the survival of the fittest, a phrase coined by Herbert Spencer in 1852. Kropotkin travelled widely in Eastern Siberia and Manchuria in his youth. In the harsh edges of Russia, he saw a "paucity of life" as species struggled against "inclement Nature." In areas of rich and abundant life, Kropotkin failed to find:

"...that bitter struggle for the means of existence, *among animals belonging to the same species*, which was considered by most Darwinians (though not by Darwin himself) as the dominant characteristic of struggle for life, and the main factor in evolution."[103]

The belief in competition, in nature red in tooth and claw, nicely served the needs of aggressive business people and nationalist politicians in the nineteenth century as they expanded their power. Kropotkin found many examples of mutual aid and support in nature, concluding that "no progressive evolution of the species can be based...upon keen competition."[104] In *Mutual Aid*, he wrote about cooperation among humans and animals, pleading for the decentralization of power and for governments to encourage people to work together for the common good. For Kropotkin, the greatest pleasures in life came from benevolence. He deplored egotistical individualism as leading to destructive and selfish forms of hedonism. Returning to Russia after the revolution, Kropotkin soon clashed with Lenin over his ruthless pursuit of the perfect state.

This short survey of the philosophical basis of community and the origins of the clash between it and individualism shows how thinkers have attempted to deal with the tensions implicit in creating perfect societies. The concept of community becomes increasingly attractive as the existing systems of handling these tensions appear increasingly difficult for their leaders. Prime Minister Trudeau cast himself in the mould of the priest-king while Joe Clarke has promoted the idea of Canada as a "community of communities." The ghosts of Plato and Aristotle still wander the corridors of power. Robert van de Weyer, a former hippie who found enlightenment—and Christ—in an ashram in India, used the Pachomian model when he founded the Community of Christ the Sower in England. A Dane, frustrated with the pressures of life in Copenhagen, drew upon More's *Utopia* for inspiration when he started a co-housing venture in a rural area.

But is it possible to move people away from excessive individualism, materialism and greed and have them work together for the benefit of their communities?

There is ample evidence today that this is possible—and not a Utopian ideal. History can inspire people. But blending idealism and practicality, vision and reality and creating a sense of unity in diversity is very tough and demanding in our time. It has been done. It can be done.

THE INVENTION OF COMMUNITY DEVELOPMENT

"To make a reputation
When other ways are barred.
Take something very simple.
And make it very hard."

Anon.

COMMUNITAS

"One's-self I sing, a simple separate person,
Yet utter the word Democratic, the word En-Masse".
Walt Whitman

Individuals like Robert Owen and John Noyes—and many other thinkers and actors in the field of community—burned with a passionate fire. Such visionaries emerge in times of personal and social crisis.

Our age offers a fertile field for the proponents of community. We seem to be hovering between bureaucracy and anarchy, with the world balanced between over-organization and underdevelopment. The old rituals no longer appease the public, the ancient ceremonies of state and the private sector have lost their magic and their appeal. In Canada, the reliance on royal commissions, enquiries and academic studies no longer offer solutions to pressing problems. The Human Potential Movement has shattered into a hundred different methods for soothing the soul. Worried people run from place to place, sampling each one in the hope of finding the answer to their problems.

The work of Victor Turner (1920-1983), a Scottish born social anthropologist, and his concept of *communitas* offers a way of understanding how to deal with the confusion and chaos of our time.[105] He studied how the Ndembu of Zambia dealt with those whose behaviour threatened the integrity of their community. A complex system of rituals, ceremonies, symbols and practices governed relationships between the Ndembu, and between these people and the land that sustained them. Ancestral shades watch over the living: "Are they not the ones who have begotten and born you?" Only recently have people in the West recognized the wisdom of this question: our ancestors live in our genes. The Ndembu word for ritual means "a special relationship" or "obligation." When groups or individuals fail to meet their obligations, they are not blamed for doing so. They have been caught by a shade or afflicted with a misfortune. Their behaviour unbalances the delicate networks that bind the Ndembu together as a community and must be addressed. Afflicted people enter a liminal or threshold state and can threaten others. The word "liminality" comes from the Latin *limen*, the root word of the English "limit" and "limbo." The Romans surrounded their newly-built cities with walls to keep out the physical enemies. They also dug ditches around them to protect residents from spiritual ones. Thus they established *limen* beyond which lay unknown, unsafe territory.

Turner writes:

> "The attributes of liminality or of liminal *personae* ('threshold people') are necessarily ambiguous, since this condition and these persons elude or slip through the network of classifications that normally locate states and positions in cultural space. Liminal entities are neither here or there; they are betwixt and between positions assigned and arrayed by law, custom, convention and ceremonial."[106]

Increasingly, in our time, more and more people fall through the gaps in the systems set up to take care of them. More and more Canadians become threshold people who have lost their place in an old order and can find none in the new one. Bureaucracies set up their classifications and categories on the basis of the way the world worked in the past. These symbolic arrays become increasingly irrelevant to the needs of the present as it merges into the future. The gaps between expectations of the good life and the ability of individuals and groups to achieve it—the persistent shadow—become liminal space where the existing rituals, ceremonies, and symbols lose their power to control people's behaviour.

The Ndembu developed ways for dealing with people who threatened their community by refusing to honour their obligations. A quarrelsome woman was not blamed for what she did and how she behaved; a shade had tied up her reproductive powers. To reintegrate the woman into the community, she takes part in the *Isoma* ritual. Leaving the community, she goes into seclusion, separates herself from others. Native doctors prepare a healing potion of roots and leaves. A tunnel is dug. The woman and her husband crawl through it, marking the passage from death and witchcraft to life and health. Through this process, the couple are healed, and the afflicted woman welcomed back into the community with a festive dance. Thus she moves from separation to integration through a spiritual journey. As Turner points out, these kinds of rituals parallel those involved in *rites de passage*. At critical stages in life, individuals leave their community, travel to hazardous places—in the world or in their own minds—and return to be welcomed on their return home or into a new life. Among the Masai of Kenya, young men had to kill a lion to become adults. In our time, numerous therapies offer opportunities for lost and lonely individuals to "get it together."

Turner studied a wide range of liminal people—bikers, hippies, Franciscan monks. Whole societies have lost their autonomy because they did not develop rituals and practices to handle new demands upon them when confronting liminality. The Icelandic commonwealth in the Middle Ages lost its independence in 1262, accepting the overlordship of Norway, because the rulers on the island failed to develop the appropriate judicial machinery to cope with internal tensions. The Norse colony in Greenland began to disappear in the fourteenth and fifteenth centuries when the climate changed. The settlers continued to farm with increasingly meagre returns, rather than harvesting the sea as the Inuit had done for centuries. Other societies invented new ways of doing things to retain their identity and integrity. The Isle of Man has its own legislature, independent of the British Parliament. In the Tynwald Court, the Council (upper house) and House of Keys (lower house) sit and vote separately. But they transact business and approve bills together. Each year the laws passed are read on Tynwald hill at St. Johns in the centre of the island, on 5 July, old midsummer day. Both languages are used at the reading, and all residents are bidden to attend the ceremony on this holiday. When the tourist industry declined on the island as the affluent British travelled to Europe for their holidays, the leaders on the

Isle of Man passed legislation making it an attractive site for off-shore banking institutions.

The New Testament contains many stories of men and women who renounced an old life to partake of a new one rooted in *agape*. A ruler asked Jesus what he had to do to inherit eternal life. The "good teacher" repeated some of the Ten Commandments. The man replied that he had observed them from his youth. Then Jesus told him to sell all he had and give it to the poor. When this wealthy man heard this, "he became sad, for he was very rich."[116] St. Francis of Assisi followed Christ's advice. Born into a wealthy family, he stripped himself of his rich garments in public, accepting poverty as a holy state, rejecting his old self. The saint drew inspiration from dreams, that liminal land where conscious and unconscious thoughts meet and mingle. St. Francis dreamed of a hen unable to cover its brood. Recognizing that the community he had created needed a new leader with wider wings than his, the saint resigned as its head in 1220.

Einstein defined insanity as continuing to do the same things while expecting different results. One of the fallacies of our time is the belief that innovation and creative approaches to change will emerge from the centres of power. Here the knots of society are tightly tied, each strand overlapping and confining the other. Politics, the quest for power and the urge for control, inhibit any tendency for the strands to unravel and form new combinations. In the corners of society, in remote places, out of the media glare, a great deal of innovation is taking place in Canada and elsewhere in the world. Individuals and group are creating new forms of community, developing rituals, ceremonies and symbols to meet the needs of those who have dropped into liminal space.

Turner points out that as gaps widen in ordered worlds and the powerful begin to panic, "anything may happen." In Canada, the Parti Québécois has united all French-speaking people in the province who believe that the Anglos have pushed them into limbo, denied their separate identity and damaged the integrity of their way of life. In an effort to invent a new ritual, thousands of ordinary Canadians came to Montreal in October, 1995, to show their affection for the people of Quebec before a referendum on sovereignty was held.

Turner uses a new term for community to describe a process that can or might occur as societies and individuals seek new ways of tackling old problems:

> "Communitas breaks in through the interstices of structure, in liminality; at the edges of structures, in inferiority. It is almost everywhere held to be sacred or "holy"."[107]

Turner sees community as a form of "anti-structure"—a counter force to the secularized, rational, ordered society in which we live and move and have most of our being. Thus community cannot be imposed on people or programmed by government. It offers mystery, liminal spaces and sacred places, new avenues for personal and collective development to those willing to confront their own beings at the deepest level, rather than relying on the many quick fixes offered to assuage the ills and fears of materialism and individualism.

Thus there are no "experts" in community development offering objective advice or one methodology, ideology or formula for everyone seeking a better life for themselves and their community. There are only those who have travelled further along the road and can point out some of the promises and the pitfalls of the way. At a conference at the University of Missouri-Columbia in September, 1973, T.R. Batten, the godfather of community development in Britain who had spent twenty years in colonial government and twenty in university life, summed up what he had learned. He noted that people were going to do what they thought was important. They were not going to listen to the professionals, experts and organizers who knew little about their lives. And the best service that anyone intervening in communities could offer was to point out the possible costs and benefits of what those in them proposed to do.

Victor Turner links communitas to the ideas of Martin Buber, the Jewish theologian, and quotes him:

> "Community is the being no longer side by side (and, one might add, above and below) but *with* one another of a multitude of persons. In this multitude, though it moves towards

one goal, yet experiences everywhere a turning to, a dynamic facing of, the others, a flowing from *I* to *Thou*. Community is where community happens."[109]

Turner comments:

"Buber lays his finger on the spontaneous, immediate, concrete nature of communitas, as opposed to the norm-governed, institutionalized, abstract nature of social structure."[110]

Communitas and structure exist side by side in every society. In the latter, others define who you are and what you can do. In communitas, you can explore new identities, new possibilities for thought and action. The existing order need not be taken for granted. Instead it can be analyzed and alternatives to it developed. Thus community development is a form of research and development in human relationships and organizational systems. While many ventures hover between bureaucracy and anarchy, community development offers spaces and places for exploring new ways of tackling problems. New roles in society can be identified and tested in a supportive atmosphere. Through trial and error, new opportunities for revitalizing society emerge, providing maps for others to follow as they move into uncharted terrain in human development.

THE ORIGINS OF
COMMUNITY DEVELOPMENT

"Music is your own experience—your thoughts,
your wisdom. If you don't live it,
it won't come out of your horn."
—Charlie Parker

One of the difficulties of defining communitas and effective ways of creating it is that, like music and electricity, you can see what it does, and describe its effects. But it's hard to say what it is.

Community Development in America, published in 1980, lists nineteen definitions of the term.[111] They include concepts such as "an educational approach" "community improvement," "local decision-making," "supportive human relationships," "self-sufficiency," "voluntary involvement," "co-ordination and integration," "communication," "problem solving process." These vague terms could be applied to almost any field of human endeavour. This source adds that community development can be viewed as a process (a way of moving from one stage to another), a method (a way of doing things), a programme (a set of procedures) or a movement (a crusade or cause to which people become committed).[112] Thus community development—a liminal pursuit—is fitted neatly into existing categories, losing that sense of mystery and unpredictability that marks so many fruitful collective ventures.

Community development became popular in the United States as new opportunities emerged in the burgeoning cities and industries at the beginning of the nineteenth century. The best and the brightest left for pastures new. President Teddy Roosevelt set up the Country Life Commission in 1908 to address rural decline. Its recommendations encouraged the US Department of Agriculture and the land grant colleges to intensify their efforts to improve life in rural America. They sought extension workers who knew how to develop programs *with* people rather than *for* them. The Country Life Commission also identified lack of organization as a major problem of country folk. Several states initiated community organization work: Rural sociologists, many of them ordained ministers, led the way in these efforts.

The Smith-Lever Act of 1914, which sought to put into practice the recommendations of the commission, stated:

> "The theory...is to extend [the Cooperative Extension Service at the land grant colleges] to the entire country by providing at least one trained demonstrator or itinerant teacher for each agriculture county, who in the very nature of things must give leadership and direction along all lines of rural activity—social, economic and financial...He is to assume leadership in every movement, whatever it may be, the aim of which is better farming, better living, more happiness, more education and better citizenship."[110]

This belief that a single individual can save a community has strong appeal in the United States. In 1915, Frank Farrington proposed a different approach to revitalizing declining communities in a book that used the term *Community Development* as its main title. Subtitled "Making the Small Town a Better Place to Live and a Better Place in Which to Do Business," it offered guidelines for those living in places with populations of fewer than ten thousand people. Rather than relying on one person, Farrington advised readers to work through service clubs to encourage local initiative.

Some outstanding—and forgotten—Canadian priests played an important role in fostering what would now be called community development in the Maritimes. In the American west, free men and women settled on free land. On Prince Edward Island, the colonial government handed land over to absentee owners who leased it to residents. Farmers in the Rustico area lacked money to buy land, even if the owners would sell. Nor could these Acadians borrow money from commercial banks. In 1864, with the help of Father Belcourt, the parish priest, they started their own bank. The Farmers' Bank of Rustico never had more than $4,000 in assets and its loans seldom exceeded $40. Farmer members each bought a share for £1 and elected those who ran the venture. In 1883, the farmers sought to renew the bank's charter. The federal government, bent on eliminating small banks, made life difficult for the enterprise. The bank issued its own notes, but commercial banks on the Island refused to honour them. The locally-controlled bank faded away, closing in 1894. But the idea that people could pool their savings to benefit themselves and their community did not die. Alphonse Desjardins studied the operations of the Rustico bank before founding the first *caisse populaire* in Lévis, Quebec, in 1900. This people's bank helped the poor to save and to obtain low interest loans.

After the Acadians were driven from their lands in 1755, the Robin company from the island of Jersey set up a post at Chéticamp on the west coast of Cape Breton Island to exploit the fisheries. Some Acadians trickled back to live there. The *Jersiais* treated them like sharecroppers of the sea, buying their fish at low prices and selling them the goods they needed at high ones. The redoubtable Father Pierre Fiset arrived in the community as parish priest in 1875, serving there until 1909.[113] He organized his parishioners to build the huge church whose spire dominates the community and the coastline, and invited his brother Napoléon to become Chéticamp's first doctor. In 1883, the priest bought a store to provide competition for the Robins, and to break their grip on the fisher folk.

Father Belcourt and Father Fiset had power, presence and status in their communities—as well as being innovators. The Catholic Church sent its priests to communities for extended stays, unlike most Protestant denominations whose clergy were (and are) at the mercy of their congregations or their bishops and had to move on if they became too creative.

The small community initiatives in Rustico and Chéticamp never became part of larger social, economic or political movements. They gave small communities more control over their economic destinies by strengthening their capacity to deal with change. Some ventures vanished with the death of a key person, while others continued the tradition of self-help and self-reliance. No one called their initiatives community development. That term, and the movement associated with it, arose in the British colonial empire during the 1930s. But there had been earlier efforts at encouraging community initiative. In India, in the first decade of the twentieth century, the poet and Nobel Prize winner Rabindranath Tagore (1861-1941) urged young people to work together for village welfare. In 1901, this son of a wealthy Hindu religious reformer founded a school to bring together western and eastern philosophical traditions. In 1914 with the help of Leonard Elmhurst, an English expatriate, Tagore started a rural development institute.

During the Great Depression, the British government ran out of money to run its empire. It had already recognized the shortcomimgs of the colonial education system after a study by an American foundation in 1922. It reported that "the educational policies of governments and missions alike seemed inadequate and largely unreal in so far as the vital needs of Africans are concerned." The educational system in the colonies created an intellectual elite. Albert Schweitzer tells of moving some trees, and asking for help from a passing African. He refused: "I am an intellectual and don't drag wood around." Schweitzer, a physician with three other doctorates, replied: "You're lucky. I wanted to be an intellectual, but I didn't succeed."

A British White Paper, *Education Policy in British Tropical Africa*, issued in 1925, came up with themes familiar in our own time. Education had to be holistic, serving health, agriculture, small business development and the management of resources as well as inculcating ideas of citizenship and service. Emphasis on material prosperity "without corresponding growth in the moral capacity to turn it to good use constituted a danger." The paper pondered the problems of educating tribal peoples in ways that did not disturb and disintegrate their traditional way of life. A Colonial Office brochure, which appeared in 1935, stressed that "a means must be found, and found quickly, whereby the people of a community can understand and appreciate forces which have changed and are changing their lives."[114]

During the thirties, colonial officials found they had to do more with less as budgets and staff shrank. Kenneth Bradley, a District Commissioner in Northern Rhodesia (now Zambia), saw himself as an innovator. The local people, the Angoni, complained that four different mission schools, while teaching their children to write and read, were also dividing the community by putting down each other's religious views. Why did not the Angoni build their own school? asked Bradley. "No money," came the reply. The Angoni had land and also workers. Why did they not build their own school? Bradley asked. If they decided to do so, he'd help them. The Angoni set to work. Bradley scrounged pencils, pens and ink bottles from his own office, persuaded the education officer to give the Angoni a grant to hire teachers, and asked the agricultural officer to lay out a garden for the school. The Chief's Council instituted a levy to pay for textbooks.

And so these people built their own school.

Bradley, convinced that "spoon-feeding was a bad thing" suggested that the Chief's Council set up "ministries" and appoint capable young men to build latrines, better housing and meet other expressed needs among their people. This idea upset the colony's governor, an amateur anthropologist, who claimed that the Angoni did not have such roles in the old days. The chiefs told him that they were more interested in solving their present problems and moving into the future.

Bradley tried to spread his ideas to other tribes in his district, telling them how the Angoni had become more self-reliant. Some chiefs saw the wisdom of this way. Others simply wanted more benefits for themselves and their families. After talking for an hour and a half in one village, Bradley fumed when the chief asked him for a pair of boots. As he wrote: "...the people expected the Government to do everything. Did it not have power, and wisdom beyond imagining?"[115] The agricultural officer planted maize in two plots. One he cultivated in the traditional way, the other he manured and weeded with excellent results. Then he invited the local people to compare the two plots. They shrugged: "It is wonderful what the government can do with all its money." Then they went back to cultivating the land in the traditional manner.

Both Bradley and the people for whom he was responsible were thrown into liminal space by budget cuts and the activities of outsiders bringing new ideas to their communities. So they invented new roles, rituals, symbols and ceremonies to meet new needs. In liminal space, some people will embrace change and challenge. Others will jump back to the old ways, no matter how inadequate they are to meet changing circumstances and will rationalize this response in their own peculiar manner to explain their refusal to change.

Bradley did not call what he did community development.

He just used common sense and initiative to help the Angoni to solve their problems and gain more control over their lives.

The Second World War cut off the colonies from the mother country, and thousands of their people served in foreign fields. In the east, the Japanese defeated and humiliated the British, Dutch, French and American colonial rulers. Colonized people began to think about taking control of their own affairs, of rejecting the yoke of imperialism. During the Forties, demands for independence from colonial elites increased. The British began to describe the unofficial policy of community development started by men like Bradley as an official prelude to giving colonial peoples control over their own destinies. The move to independence for the British colonies was helped by the fear that their rulers might have to spend more money on them than they extracted in revenue.[116] Community development became defined as a form of mass education, a way of preparing traditional peoples for self-government and self-reliance. In 1948 a group of field officers from the colonies met in Cambridge to pin down the butterfly of community development. They defined "mass education/community development" as:

> "A movement designed to promote better living for the whole community with the active participation and, if possible, on the initiative of the community, but if this initiative is not forthcoming spontaneously, by the use of techniques for arousing and stimulating its active and enthusiastic response to the movement...[it] must make use of the co-operative movement and must be put into effect in the closest association with local government bodies."[117]

In 1954 another conference in Cambridge defined community development as: "A movement designed to promote better living for the whole community with the active participation and on the initiative of the whole community." This definition, slightly modified, became the official United Nations' one in 1955. By that date, the agency had published twenty-four major papers on community development in four languages. Although governments agreed on the goals of the movement, they took different paths to achieve them. India set up a ministry to handle community development in 1956 and hired *gram sevaks*, village workers equipped with an official manual to guide them. By 1967, forty thousand *gram sevaks* worked hard to meet the needs of villagers, with limited success.

T.R. Batten became a proponent of the non-directive approach to community development. He noted:

"In the late 1940s, when this community development way of working was first introduced by some government officers in the rural areas of Asia and Africa, its immediate results were impressive: and many politicians and high ranking government officers regarded it as a breakthrough."[118]

In *Once A District Officer* (1966), Bradley wrote:

"...hundreds of small, independently conceived experiments in self-help eventually came to be translated into a policy, and presently there was a whole new philosophy of administration for all underdeveloped countries, with its own title, its own jargon, and its own academic school of theorists. Community development under different names has spread from Latin America to Thailand."[119]

Community development in its early days demonstrated the Mayo or Hawthorne effect, as well as the presence of the Lichen Factor. Elton Mayo (1880-1949), a Harvard Business School professor, studied a spinning mill in Philadelphia where one department had a turnover of 250 per cent. Mayo suggested introducing rest pauses and giving workers more control over their duration and frequency. Morale soared and the turnover went down to six per cent, the average for the rest of the mill. Mayo ascribed the results to the rest pauses that broke the monotony of the work, improving the mental and physical condition of the men tending the machines.

Then Mayo undertook another experiment at Western Electric's Hawthorne plant in Chicago. Two groups of workers were isolated and their performance studied. The lighting conditions in the place where one group worked were varied, those of the other group kept constant. No significant differences in productivity in either group were seen. In fact, whatever was done to the lighting, productivity rose in both settings. The research team segregated six women in one part of the factory, and kept changing their working conditions. No matter what they did, output kept increasing. The women became a team, developing informal values and practices to help each other and produce more. Physical conditions had little impact on them. Mayo concluded that "the breakdown of traditional values in society could be countered by creating a situation in industry conducive to spontaneous co-operation."[120] Mayo and his colleagues, hired by the company, acted as mediators, enablers, facilitators, and showed great respect for the women whose work habits they studied.

Elton Mayo, an Australian, did not adhere to the American management values propagated by another business guru, Frederick Winslow Taylor (1856-1915), the father of scientific management. He introduced time and motion studies into industry, and saw workers merely as extensions of their machines:

"In our scheme, we do not ask the initiative of our men. We do not want any initiative. All we want of them is to obey the orders we give them, do what we say and do it quick."[121]

Mayo did not treat the workers he studied as objects of his research or mere cogs in the industrial machine. He pointed out that: "Management succeeds or fails in proportion as it is accepted without reservation by the group as authority and leader."[122]

The credibility of early efforts in community development in the British colonial empire derived from individuals who knew how to work with local people and also had a firm grasp of what management involved. Short of money, the officials used imagination and common sense to solve problems. While it began as a genuine, *ad hoc* bottom-up, grassroots ways of meeting local needs, community development soon became respectable in government circles in newly independent nations and turned into a top-down policy to strengthen political and bureaucratic control. The British held their colonies together through the rule of imposed law, the presence of the military and a benevolent paternalism that assured the colonized that they were lucky to be living under the control of such nice people. When colonies gained their independence, they had to set about creating a new sense of nationhood among very diverse people. Nigeria has 250 tribal groups. Community development was used as a way of generating consensus at the local level, harnessing people there to national goals and easing the passage from colonialism to independence and self-reliance.

Most of the leaders of the newly independent nations had been educated in Britain and the other centres of colonial power. Others, like Idi Amin of Uganda, had been trained by the military. Only too often, external colonization was replaced by internal colonization through which certain families, tribes or opportunistic groupings took power over their people. They built up large bureaucracies to strengthen their grip on every aspect of the lives of "liberated" peoples. As Basil Davidson, the historian of Africa, put it: "Bureaucracy ruled together with clientism, and gradually became the same thing...the ideal became not so much to occupy a job as to occupy a wage."[123] He quotes Claude Ake, an African:

"Development strategies in Africa, with minor exceptions, have tended to be strategies by which a few use the many for their purposes. They are uncompromisingly top-down. There is not, and never has been, popular participation in political and economic decision-making."[124]

During the Cold War, leaders of new nations played up the myths of democracy and public participation in decision-making to extract money from western nations. President Nyerere of Tanzania had spectacular success with this ploy, extracting millions of dollars in Canadian aid.[125] Other capitalist nations, enchanted with Nyerere's policy of *ujamaa* (working together), also sent experts and money for state-run schemes masquerading as community development. Centralized control and bureaucratic imperatives stifled efforts at self-help. Ideology, not pragmatism, ruled. Farmers refused to sell their crops to state agencies, and agricultural production declined. Under private ownership, workers on sisal estates cut the crop from two in the morning until ten, avoiding the heat of the day. Cutters, paid on the basis of their productivity, had an incentive to work hard. On nationalized farms, cutting began at seven in the morning and everyone received the same wage.

Some former colonies have become kleptocracies, looted by a ruling individual or one of the new dominant classes. Robert Klitgaard spent two years in Equatorial Guinea, working for the government on a $13 million project to rehabilitate the country's infrastructure. He notes that, "The harsh conditions of underdevelopment encourage tropical gangsters of every variety—government, business, and international aid giver."[126] The depredations of the late dictator of Zaire, Mobutu Sese Seko, typified the excesses of the new ruling classes in many former colonial nations.

Anyone who has spent any time in Africa appreciates the fundamental decency of the people there, even as they struggle for survival with so few resources. In the face of oppression and insult, they recognize the truth of the Yoruba proverb: "Not even God is wise enough."

In the late Sixties, the United Nations surveyed the community development scene and presented its findings in a report in 1971.[127] It revealed that almost any activity could be described as community development, from the activities of fire brigades in new towns in Poland which served as cultural animators, to the creation of fortified villages in Vietnam to protect residents from the Viet Cong. A Romanian bureaucrat claimed that in his country "all power belongs to the people." The country's dictator, Nicola Ceausescu, had turned it into a personal fief and ruined its economy with mad schemes. In the former French colonies, governments used social animation as a technique for generating community initiative and creative participation in the affairs of newly independent nations. Cadres of animators sought to involve local people in decision-making. In single party states, they were government appointees. Serving as the sole link between the centres of power and the villages, the animators blocked any local initiative that threatened the rulers.

The United Nations report demythologized community development:

"That village uplift could not be independently realized was all too apparent, given the lack of resources and the resistance of traditional-minded local leaders to modernization. Aid from the central government became a necessary condition for rural development. In a country where a tributary relationship existed between the village and the central authorities, the implementation of CD programmes placed strains on this traditional relationship which effectively hampered rural development."[128]

T.R. Batten noted the reasons why community development had not lived up to its early promise: "...people cannot want possibilities that they do not know exist...many of the things that people do want, often do not fit in at all well with the requirements of national and regional development programs."[129]

Governments used community development funds to make villagers conform to official top-down schemes. The rich and powerful saw community development as a way of strengthening their grip on poor people. In Bangladesh, a rich landlord gathered bogus signatures to claim that he managed a co-operative. He also bribed local officials to install a $12,000 tube well, funded by the World Bank, on his land, planning to charge farmers for using "his" water.[130]

The true light of community development was kept burning by individuals and small groups in isolated parts of the world. Kishan Baburao Hazare retired from the Indian Army in 1975, and returned to his native village. The sole survivor of an attack on his company during the war with Pakistan, Hazare lived simply in a temple, dedicating himself to improving the lives of the people there. By 1993, incomes had risen eight-fold in the village. Farmers who had once only grown enough rice for their families produced surpluses for export. Sixty-five other villages began to learn from the way in which Hazare had transformed life in one community.[131]

About the time that many nations had determined that community development was not a quick-fix for all their problems, the Canadian government discovered it. Initially it was seen as a way of bringing the poor, the marginalized, the outsiders into the mainstream of Canadian society, a form of nation building. The proponents of community development in the federal and provincial governments treated it simply as a new technique. Although small, isolated and short-term in many places, the history of efforts by Canadians to gain more control over their lives has shown what works—and what does not. Some of the small beginnings in generating local autonomy and economic self-reliance have been very successful, perhaps too successful, and become bureaucratized and inflexible. In the west, co-operatives have flourished, and in Quebec the *caisse populaire* movement is big business. In Atlantic Canada, co-operatives and credit unions serve many communities, and Ontario has a strong co-operative movement.[132]

Three early community development ventures—although they were not called that—in Alberta, Nova Scotia and Prince Edward Island reveal familiar patterns that illustrate the potential and the limitations of do-it-yourself social, political and economic democracy.[133] These early efforts, led by a remarkable band of men and women, belong to the history of adult education as well as to that of community development. Adult education has a number of techniques that are extremely useful in encouraging people to confront the problems and powers that oppress them, and to move into action to deal with them. But community development is more than a technique. All the early efforts in Canada were led by individuals with compassion for others who demonstrated, in their thoughts and actions, a certain, intangible spirit that's hard to describe in words. They did not seek to rub raw the sores of discontent among the poor and isolated people with whom they worked. Nor did they impose their ideologies or programmes on people. They tried to meet people at their point of need and help them to achieve goals they set for themselves. And they worked outside the mainstream of society, away from the corridors of power, although some early leaders in adult education/community development had strong supporters there. They were an odd blend of idealist and realist, seeking better ways of meeting human needs than their societies offered the ordinary people of their time.

Beginnings in Canada

"Our movement has grown in large part out of
the dissatisfactions of great numbers of people
with the formal education we have."
Moses Michael Coady, *Masters of Their Own Destiny* (1939)

Canadians have always done things in a gradualistic way. Throughout this century, the federal government slowly gained more and more dominion over the affairs of Canadians. In a parallel process, the provinces began to shake off the hand of Ottawa as their legislatures acquired more powers.

Alberta became a province in 1887. Three years later the University of Alberta came into being. In the American West, the land grant colleges had to serve their communities. Most Canadian universities followed the British model of "town and gown", with very little interaction between the two. Rather than serving the community, the universities concentrated on training scholars and future leaders.

The first president of the University of Alberta, Henry Marshall Tory, recognized the need for the new venture to gain credibility and visibility in the eyes of the ordinary people of the province. If the university did not serve them, the legislators could certainly find other uses for the money they gave it. Tory took education to the people. The faculty went to churches, schools and other places in communities and gave lectures on everything from sewers to Shakespeare. In 1912, Edward Ottewell became secretary of the university extension department, launching a travelling library, and a publishing programme covering women's suffrage, consolidated schools, immigration and other issues. During the winter of 1914-15, Ottewell distributed thirty plays suitable for amateur theatrical production to help people to pass the long nights and increase the sense of community. Starved of culture and entertainment, residents of small places formed theatrical groups to put on the plays. In 1921, Ottewell hired E.A. ("Ned") Corbett as his assistant. Soon the extension department had its own radio station, travelling libraries and a large collection of films and slides. Local theatrical groups flourished, especially during the Depression when movie theatres closed. In some communities, everyone took part in the theatrical performances. Corbett recalled one production of *Macbeth* where the witches learned and recited their lines as they cooked the family meal on their stoves. Many of the pioneer immigrants came from cultivated backgrounds to seek a new life in Canada. The hard life of breaking the land wearied most of them—and killed quite a few. Drama offered opportunities for role playing, demanded organization, collaboration, and gave these pioneers an outlet for their talents and abilities. In the plays, individuals could live out fantasies while entertaining the members of their communities.

No one called the work of the University of Alberta community development. But its staff certainly encouraged it in every way. By 1933, Alberta had three hundred small drama groups. Word of the university's achievements reached the Carnegie Corporation in New York which provided a grant of $10,000. The extension department hired Elizabeth Haynes to work with theatrical groups to improve their skills. While president of the Alberta Drama League, Ned Corbett came up with the idea of a summer school. The other members turned down the idea. Corbett took $1,000 from the Carnegie grant, drove to Banff, met with community leaders and secured their support for hosting a summer school. To everyone's surprise, 190 people enrolled. In 1935, the summer venture became the Banff School of Fine Arts, now one of the main economic bases of the town.

While Ottewell, Corbett and Haynes focused their efforts on theatre and culture as ways of encouraging creativity and community, three men in Nova Scotia set out to make rural people in that province "masters of their own destiny." Father Moses Michael Coady took these words as the title of his book, published in New York in 1939, which told "The Story of the Antigonish Movement of Adult Education Through Economic Co-operation." Coady dedicated his book to "all those unnamed noble souls who without remuneration are working overtime in the cause of humanity."

The Antigonish Movement did not begin in that university town in eastern Nova Scotia. It originated with the vision of a fiery priest, Father Jimmy Tompkins, who sought to make Saint Francis Xavier University respond to the needs of ordinary people.[134] He wrote in later life:

"There was more real adult education at the pit heads, down in the mines, out among the fisherman's shacks, along the wharfs and in the kitchens and wherever you can get the farmers and their wives to gather and sit and talk in the evenings, than you can get from one hundred thousand dollars' worth of fossilized formal education. It springs from the hearts and pain of people."

The words bespeak the man—blunt, respectful of ordinary working people, scornful of formal education that trained the best and the brightest of the local sons to leave the region and work for the oppressing classes. Father Jimmy, as he was known, joined the faculty of Saint Francis Xavier University in 1902, after studying in Rome. At that time, the Catholic Church, recognizing the appeal of socialism, communism and nationalism, sought ways to retain its hold on the hearts and minds of workers. On 15 May, 1891, Pope Leo XIII issued his encyclical *Rerum Novarum*. Stressing the rights of the family against the incursions of the state, it proclaimed: "Labour is not a commodity." Workers should receive their just rewards, and be helped to form trade unions and co-operatives to counter the growing power of the state and give them more control over their lives.

During Father Jimmy's time at the university, the economy of the region slowly changed. The old self-reliant ways and the small communities began to decay. Men left small farms to work in new industries and farmers and fishermen were drawn into the world market economy. A few activist priests helped farmers to form co-operatives and buying clubs. The first co-operative in Canada, established at Stellarton in 1861, simply served its members. Other co-operatives, founded by British miners, tended to close in on themselves. The Webbs, the guiding lights of British socialism and the co-operative movement, had proclaimed that workers could not form productive ventures but they could become storekeepers through consumer co-ops. The genius of the Antigonish Movement lay in the way in which its members linked the formation of credit unions and co-operatives with adult education. Its slogan—"Listen! Study! Discuss! Act!"—pointed learners towards the goal of creating a better life for themselves, their families and their communities.

In 1921, Father Jimmy published a pamphlet, *Knowledge for the People*. It drew inspiration from the Workers Educational Association in Britain, the Gaelic League in Ireland, the University of Wisconsin, and adult education programmes in Quebec and Saskatchewan. The priest used to say: "Ideas have hands and feet. Get them out and they will work and travel for you." His booklet noted: "It is a law that popular governments and popular institutions, whether religious or secular, are subject to decay if they lose touch with the people." It called for "a handful of devoted men" to go into the highways and byways, bring knowledge to the people and put them in touch with the best minds of the world to help them solve the daily problems of existence.

Promoting adult education with visionary zeal, Father Jimmy espoused another cause with equal energy and fervour. And this caused his downfall and exile. Most of the universities in the Maritimes originated with religious bodies. The Carnegie Corporation of New York offered to fund their amalgamation, and Father Jimmy became its champion. His superiors in the university and the church did not share his views, fearing loss of power and control over the minds of Catholic youth. And so they sent Father Jimmy into the wilderness.

At the age of fifty-two, in 1922, after being vice-president of the university for a number of years, the priest went to Canso to serve the people there. At that time, the town had a lot of modern equipment and facilities (including a movie theatre), but the population was divided between poor fishermen and a band of fish barons who lived up the hill and controlled their lives. Canso looked like an unlikely place to foster change. In this windswept, foggy community, Father Jimmy put his ideas about adult education into action. A voracious reader, he handed out books, pamphlets, articles to everyone, using the pulpit to spread his messages. With his help, local fishermen built their own lobster plant and set up a co-operative to secure better prices for their catches. A nun who worked with Father Jimmy called him "God's great nuisance."

Every social movement has a defining moment, a trigger that inspires wider action. The seas around Nova Scotia yielded bountifully in 1926-27, flooding the markets with fish and depressing prices. While inshore fishermen, with their small boats, scrambled to make a living, large offshore trawlers scooped up more and more fish. On 1 July, 1927, fishermen at Canso assembled on the dock, complaining that they had little to celebrate on the sixtieth anniversary of Confederation. Father Jimmy urged them to organize a mass meeting and petition Ottawa.

The media covered the protest, and Ottawa set up a royal commission to study the fisheries. The MacLean Commission took only seven months to complete its report, submitting it on 4 May, 1928. The document presented a grim picture of empty harbours and idle men as the steam trawlers of large companies overfished the offshore waters. The report recommended the formation of fishermen's co-operatives. Ottawa acted promptly, hiring Father Moses Coady, Father Jimmy's cousin, to start the process. In 1928, St. Francis Xavier University had set up an extension department with Coady as head. He recruited A.B. MacDonald, a school superintendent, and a team of gifted local men and women, and the Antigonish Movement began.[135]

Father Jimmy's ideas on social change differed from those of his cousin. He wanted people to know what caused their present miseries. Coady, a large, charismatic figure, gave out simple instructions for solving immediate problems of poverty. His co-workers held meetings in small communities and encouraged the people to pool their nickels and dimes to form credit unions. Then they helped them to start co-operatives, in a process that took up to two years—and did not work in many communities. Only about eight per cent of the full and part-time labour force in Nova Scotia in the 1920s worked in the fisheries. The typical Nova Scotian adult was more likely to be a coal miner or an urban wage earner than one of the fisherfolk. In 1935, Father Jimmy moved to Reserve Mines and helped a group of miners form a co-operative to build their own houses. Offering his own books to anyone interested in reading them, he sowed the seeds of the regional library system. By the end of 1931, 173 study clubs had been set up, most of them in rural Catholic Scottish Catholic parishes. Eight years later, 342 credit unions and other forms of co-operative endeavour had come into existence. Just before the Second World War broke out, 19,600 people were studying in 2,265 self-help groups in the Maritimes.

The war stripped away the leadership of the movement, as the pioneers aged. Support for the Antigonish Movement came from the Carnegie Corporation, and the federal and provincial governments were supportive, if not very generous, in assisting Coady. In the Fifties, St. Francis Xavier University tried to obtain grants from Carnegie by claiming to be fighting communism. A magazine story even claimed that the Antigonish Movement had turned back the red tide in eastern Nova Scotia.[136]

The social and economic changes in the post-war world led to the demise of the Antigonish Movement, which a sociologist has referred to as a "Celtic ghost."[137] Co-operatives became more concerned with ideology than new technology and failed to adapt to change. Large, privately-owned fishing companies expanded their facilities and extended their reach, luring co-operative fishermen away from their organizations by offering a few cents more a pound for their catch. As life became better in the boom years after 1945, Nova Scotians and other Atlantic Canadians went down the road to find jobs elsewhere in Canada. Many did remarkably well in making new lives in new communities. At home, Unemployment Insurance removed the need for fishermen to hazard their lives in dangerous seas all year round. "Fishing for stamps"—spending only enough time working to qualify for UI—became a way of life in the small coastal communities. The old industrial base, founded on coal mining and steel making, began to vanish as the economy changed and the mines and mills became less and less productive and competitive.

The legacy of the Antigonish Movement can be seen in the Maritime landscape where co-op and credit unions signs dot the countryside. When you talk with those who worked with Tompkins, Coady and the other co-operative pioneers, their voices and eyes light up as they tell of their experiences. These were great days, as personal development went along with organizational development. The credit unions and co-operatives offered employment and careers for young people who wanted to stay in their communities and work towards their development as well as their own. But the Antigonish Movement never confronted the old political ways in Nova Scotia, based on patronage and special privilege.

On Prince Edward Island, a remarkable academic blazed a path for local democracy. John Tougas Croteau came from Acadian stock, and held a Carnegie-endowed chair in Economics and Sociology at Prince of Wales and Saint Dunstan's Colleges in Charlottetown from 1933 to 1946. His account of his effort to improve the life of people on the Island lacks the polemics of Coady's book.[138] Croteau describes, with insight and humour, just how hard it is to organize self-help among rural people. His work weakened dependency and the pervasive patronage upon which Islanders relied for jobs and benefits, upsetting many local politicians. Croteau tied co-operative action to a network of regional libraries that he helped to develop, rather than relying on a team of extension workers. He had no illusions about local people. They poached fish and lobsters, broke regulations and showed no interest in new sources of income. Croteau pointed out that Irish Moss could be harvested and sold, but his ideas were ignored. Nor did fishermen show much enthusiasm for collecting and processing cods' livers during the war when the oil was in demand. Croteau found a design for rendering oil from the livers. The provincial government offered them to fishermen's organizations at nominal cost. Some communities fell in love with the co-operative ideal. One village built a cannery—then found it had nothing to can.

Croteau recognized that local merchants had no more control over the forces that affected them than did fishermen and farmers.

Writing about a visit to Labrador in 1939, Croteau described the efforts of the Grenfell Mission as "well intentioned." But what could they do "in face of a highly monopolistic business structure, with a handful of St. John's merchants controlling credit, production and marketing." These barons manipulated the government, supporting a "regressive tax system—low income taxes and high customs duties on essentials."[139] Newfoundland offered few services to its people and a pittance in welfare, barely enough to keep them alive. Charities like the Grenfell Mission were no substitute for enlightened, compassionate government policies that complemented bottom up efforts in self-help with those coming from the top down.

In the Thirties, governments ran out of money, and their operations became lean and mean. Individual civil servants worked with Coady and Croteau. The Department of Fisheries gave grants to St. Francis Xavier's Extension Department. When the federal and provincial governments rediscovered community development in the affluent Sixties, their efforts at bringing about change from the top down involved many dedicated and concerned people. But everyone was in too much of a hurry to solve the problems of poverty, isolation and disadvantage to learn from the efforts of the pioneers of community development in the depressed Thirties.

THE REDISCOVERY OF COMMUNITY DEVELOPMENT IN CANADA

"It is not the brains that matter most, but
that which guides them—the character, the heart,
the generous qualities, progressive ideas."
Dostoyevski, *The Insulted and the Injured*

The social and economic movements of the Thirties had been grassroots ones, relying in the *caisse populaires* on locally generated capital, and in the Antigonish Movement and Croteau's work on support from an American foundation. In the Sixties governments took the initiative in community development to improve life for the rejected in society. These people had been pushed to the edges of Canadian society—the Indians on to reserves, the poor into inner cities, the Blacks on to barren land in Nova Scotia.

In July, 1966, Prime Minister Lester Pearson wrote in glowing terms about the approach in *The Journal of the International Society for Community Development*:

"As a philosophy and a method, community development offers a way of involving people more fully in the life of their communities. It generates scope and initiative which enables people to participate creatively in the economic, social and cultural life of the nation. It provides, above all, a basis for a more profound understanding and a more effective use of democratic processes. These are essential elements in Canada's social policy. These principles underlie our current and social programmes which, in essence, are designed to make it possible for people to overcome low income, poor education, geographic isolation, bad housing, and other limitations on their environment."

Before this piece appeared, a Saskatchewan research centre and a Manitoba government agency had already tried to turn these ideals into realities—with limited success.

Alarmed at the signs of rural decline, the Saskatchewan government set up a royal commission on agriculture and rural life in 1952. Its director became head of the Centre for Community Studies at the University of Saskatchewan in 1956, and sought to implement its recommendations. Funded by the province, the centre studied communities, supported organizations involved in community development, and offered training to those in the field. The government saw community development as a cheap, safe way of tackling rural development through encouraging self-help and mutual aid. The academics at the university, who viewed their institution as non-political, became uncomfortable with community development, which sought to combine theory and practice in creating a better life for rural people. The process did not fit into academic disciplines as it used holistic approaches to local development.

The Centre did useful work. But the staff soon became aware that many community problems originated in government plans and policies drawn up without local involvement. Market and other forces beyond their boundaries and the ken of community residents also influenced life on the land. Large scale investment from outside sources and policies and plans that respected local conditions would be needed for communities to develop their potential. Seeking academic credibility, the director dropped the Centre's community action programme and concentrated on research. This effort to make the institute part of the university life failed. In 1964, the provincial government changed, the Centre lost it funding and the staff moved off the campus. Struggling to survive on government grants and contracts, it slowly faded into history. One commentator described the Centre as a "prairie dust devil" which spring up in high winds and vanish when the air becomes calm.[140]

Around the time that this initiative disappeared, another innovative prairie venture in community development was being phased out in Manitoba. Its origins lay in a study of native peoples which revealed poverty, despair and discrimination in Indian and Métis communities. Published in 1959, the commission report also noted that many white communities in Manitoba had similar problems, and identified community development as the best way of helping people of Indian ancestry to solve their own problems. This approach might seem to be idealistic, the report noted, but community development programmes were operating successfully in many parts of the world. Community workers could win the trust of local people and then help them to identify their needs, prepare them for action, assist them in using local resources, co-ordinate the work of other government services, and serve as bridges between native and white residents in communities.

Setting up a Community Development Branch in the Department of Welfare, the Manitoba government hired Jean Lagassé, a Métis who headed the study of the native peoples, as director. As he put it: "Community development is not a livelihood. It is life itself." He also outlined the fundamental beliefs behind this approach to social change:

"1) That all people, no matter how unambitious they may appear, have a desire to better themselves.
2) The difficulties preventing the fulfilment of peoples' needs are too great for the resources which they have.
3) All groups can do something to help themselves when given an opportunity to do so on their own terms.
4) In order to achieve lasting change it is necessary to influence simultaneously various aspects of human behaviour."[141]

Lagassé sent his community development staff into the field as facilitators, enablers, organizers, animators, first-aid technicians and mediators. When one worker arrived on a reserve, some residents asked: "What are you going to do for us?" He replied: "Nothing! I'm here to find out what you can do for yourselves."[142] In many communities, white outsiders who stayed in them for short periods of time held all the power.

In its first four years, with a highly able director and a corps of dedicated workers, Manitoba's community development programme

137

worked well. It began to falter when Lagassé joined the federal government and moved to Ottawa in 1963. During the Sixties, the provincial government sought to "develop" its north through pulp and paper mills and hydroelectric schemes. The small-scale efforts in community development appeared insignificant in this new scheme of things. And the programme slowly fell prey to bureaucratization, losing its autonomy and flexibility, and support in the upper echelons of government. The programme ended in 1968.[143]

Community development efforts by Indian Affairs suffered the same fate. The British off-loaded responsibility for Canada's Indians on to Canada in 1867, under the BNA Act. Ottawa knew little of the complex and diverse ways of these people. An Athapaskan Gwich'in from the Mackenzie Delta has as much in common with a Mi'kmaq as an Englishman has with a Polynesian. The very name "Indians" stems from Columbus' mistaken belief about the land he reached. A joke among Canadian Indians is that it's just as well he did not think he had reached Turkey. Sir John A. MacDonald announced that "the great aim of our legislation has been to do away with the tribal system and assimilate the Indian people in all respects with the other inhabitants of the Dominion, as speedily as they are fit to change." From being "Them," Canada's Indians would become part of "Us." The process of assimilation became increasingly difficult as Indians were herded into reserves, pushed on to barren land, or banished to the fringes of white communities. Their old way gone, and the avenues to a new one barred, Indian communities lived on the very edge of existence.

An act "protected" their rights, and a quasi-military bureaucracy administered it. Over the years the legislation and the government structures became an iron cage, trapping Indians. Dependency on government offered some measure of security to people adrift in Canada. Some of the old self-reliant, land-based way of life persisted among Indians, especially in northern regions. A photograph taken on the Ermineskin reserve in Hobbema, Alberta, in 1900 shows seven young women. They are neatly dressed and hold violins and mandolins, reassuring evidence that they are becoming "just like us." To some Canadians, the Indians became "noble savages," representing a primitive way of life in harmony with the land. But to most Canadians, the Indians were simply invisible. With federal government efforts to create a sense of nationhood in the Sixties, Indians became more visible. As the abysmal conditions under which many of them lived appeared in the media, Indian Affairs launched a community development programme to encourage self-help on the reserves in 1964. Recruiting a corps of dedicated, idealistic young men—and even a few women—the agency sent them into the field to bring about change. A community development worker found that an Indian superintendent had been robbing the Indians for years, telling the chief and council to sign blank resolutions, and then filling them in to meet his own needs. The community development worker also asked the chief and council to sign blank resolutions.[144] Then he typed in their resignations—and showed them what he had done. "They never signed a blank resolution again," he reported. One chief expressed his appreciation for being taught about the "two ccs" by community development workers—collect calls and carbon copies. The newcomers on the reserves showed the Indians how to tap into resources to which they were entitled as Canadians and other ways of bypassing the colonial bureaucracy that dominated their lives.

As in Manitoba, the bureaucracy eventually overwhelmed the community development process in Indian Affairs. One study noted:

> "Superintendents resented the threat to, and loss of, their authority, and the dissatisfaction rebounded up the bureaucratic hierarchy to senior officials who were quickly becoming disenchanted with the program."[145]

The main promoter of community development left Indian Affairs which handed responsibility for it to Indian organizations and bands. Stephen Brooks, an English writer, travelled across Canada in the Eighties and visited two Alberta reserves with about the same population and resource base. One appeared to be well run. Band councillors took responsibility for various tasks, supported by the community development officer. On the other reserve, councillors were "an unhealthy bunch, overweight, potbellied and heavy in voice."

In a "pugnacious and overemphatic" manner they complained bitterly of injustice to Brooks. He wrote that "it seemed easier to reject possibilities than to propose solutions." The councillors wanted "self-determination"—and more social assistance: "All their problems were blamed on others, and for all their talk of self-determination, the council kept concealed any signs of being capable of it."[146]

The reactions of the two bands to change recalls Kenneth Bradley's experiences in Northern Rhodesia in the Thirties. One group of indigenous people showed willingness to work towards solving their problems while the leader of another was interested only in securing gifts from the government. Canada's Indians often find themselves betwixt and between old ways and new demands, caught in liminal space.

The official rhetoric of both the federal government and the leaders of the First Nations focuses on the need for self-government and self-reliance among Canada's aboriginal peoples. But most of the resources devoted to "the Indian problem" go towards maintaining existing systems, on and off the reserves. Canada's aboriginal peoples are passing through the painful processes of decolonization *and* debureaucratization as they struggle to blend traditional ways with the demands of the modern world. Some Indians have asked Indian Affairs to take control of their communities or to investigate the band council's handling of government funds. But the official bureaucracy that controls so much of the lives of aboriginal peoples shrugs off such demands, claiming that it does not want to interfere in the day-to-day administration of first nations. Only when a situation on a reserve hits the media does Indian Affairs respond. In September, 1997, after revelations of poverty and despair on the Stoney Indian reserve west of Calgary, where payments from the federal government and from natural gas royalties totalled $3.3 million in 1996—about $10,000 for every resident—Indian Affairs stripped the band council of its spending powers.[147]

In the same month, the department moved to place the Fort Albany First Nation in Ontario in trusteeship.[148] Here, the per capita payment for nine hundred residents in 1996 came to almost $20,000 for a total expenditure of $17.5 million. A volunteer forensic accountant working under a co-management agreement with the band through Canadian Executive Services Organization (CESO), objected to the improper use of band funds. The council passed a resolution banning him from the reserve. He wrote to the Minister of Indian Affairs, detailing the widespread misuse of band funds.

In the past, many of those who sought to help aboriginal peoples, especially missionaries, made them feel guilty about their traditional ways of life. Some Indians have become very skillful at reversing the process, and making white outsiders feel guilty and responsible for their current ills. When a reporter suggested to an Indian woman in Nova Scotia that welfare was widely used on reserves there, she replied: "Welfare is blood money for what our people went through."[149]

To protect the integrity of their way of life, many aboriginal peoples have drawn circles around their communities to deter outsiders from intervening in them. The situation in many places strongly resembles what has happened in post-colonial nations. Some Indian bands and communities have become the domain of certain families or clans who distribute benefits among themselves. Many aboriginal peoples find themselves caught in an iron cage where they live, inside the iron cage of official government policies that limit and constrain their activities.

In Teslin, in the Yukon, an Indian woman confronted David Crombie then Minister of Indian Affairs, and told him she wanted to talk to him about self-government. A writer described the encounter:

> "Self-government! Fantastic idea! If there's anything [Crombie] learned already, it's that Indian people deserve and have the right to run their own affairs. Absolutely. She let him finish, paused a long moment, then said: 'That's all very well. But self-government here just means my family will never get another house.'"[150]

The Sawridge band in Alberta has been called "a family compact." To limit the number of people receiving royalties from oil and gas development on their land, the Sawridge bought out band members with golden handshakes worth $200 - $400,000. The band took the federal government to court over Bill C-31, passed in 1985, which changed the Indian Act to allow women who had married non-Indians and their children to reclaim aboriginal status. Any Sawridge seeking to rejoin the band has to fill in a forty-three-page questionnaire and write essays on how they would adapt to life on the reserve. The band made a large contribution to the Progressive Conservative campaign funds, and Prime Minister Mulroney showed his appreciation by appointing its chief to the Senate.[151]

The way in which certain families and clans have gained control over reserves and their resources is not unique to Canada's Indians. Edward Banfield, an American social scientist, lived in a village in southern Italy in the Fifties. Isolated and poor, the residents practised "amoral familism," showing an "inability to concert activity beyond the immediate family."[152] The dominant ethos of the community was: "Maximize the material short-run advantage of the nuclear family; assume that all others will do likewise."[153]

The constant media coverage of tensions on Indian reserves obscures the efforts of Canada's indigenous people to blend old and new ways of living. The Lichen Factor can be seen in many Indian ventures where insiders and outsiders have worked together effectively. To mark the fiftieth anniversary of the United Nations, a panel of international advisers chose fifty model communities showing outstanding collective approaches to environmental issues and social development. Three aboriginal communities, Walpole Island First Nation, near Windsor, Ontario, Sanikiluaq Inuit community in Hudson Bay (the Belcher Islands), and the Oujé-Bougoumou Cree of Quebec made the list. In the Cree community, a committed individual, Abel Bosum, who had operated a hardware store, came home to lead his people out of the wilderness. The Quebec government told the Cree it would not help the band until it was recognized by Ottawa. But Ottawa said that it wouldn't recognize the band until it had land in the province. Quebec then replied that it did not want to see any more reserves under federal jurisdiction in the province.

This impasse and other blocks did not daunt the spirit of the Cree, and they finally developed their own community. Another triumph took place at Alkali Lake in British Columbia. Here the people descended into alcoholism and violence as they lost their old way of life and became increasingly dependent on welfare. Seeing what her drinking was doing to her relations with her children, one woman abruptly quit. Her husband joined her. With the help of an outsider, they started an Alcoholics Anonymous group. The man became band chief, and set about eliminating bootlegging on what was theoretically a "dry" reserve. A priest with a drinking problem opposed this move—and was told to leave. Indian Affairs and the band council supported a scheme to issue vouchers instead of cash for food and supplies to cut down the money spent on liquor: two local stores agreed to accept them. Elders from other communities came to talk about their lives and experiences. The people of Alkali Lake built a sweat lodge as they began to recover lost traditions and rituals. And they told the story of their struggle from 1940 to 1985 in a video documentary, *The Honour of All*. Residents travel to other aboriginal communities to assist them to deal with problems of alcoholism and despair.[154]

Why have some aboriginal communities spun downwards in spirals of despair and powerlessness while others have been able to work with outsiders to make a better life for all? The Royal Commission on Aboriginal Peoples recognized that many indigenous communities lacked the skills and resources—and the organizational structures—to lift themselves out of deprivation and despair and to become self-reliant and independent of welfare. It called for a new relationship between aboriginal and non-aboriginal peoples and the expenditure of large sums of money to rectify the problems of Canada's native peoples. Non-government groups like CESO, Frontiers Foundation, and Habitat for Humanity have worked with aboriginal peoples and communities, helping them to solve the problems they identify.[155] In doing so, their members have learned to respect the strengths of the traditional ways of life—and their shortcomings. And, in turn, some aboriginal peoples have come to recognize the demands of the outside world and learned how to deal with them.

Traditional peoples live in circular worlds, within limits, facing inwards. Westerners, believers in progress, favour linear thrusts into the world, into what they believe to be empty space. When the two peoples met, the linear thrust of the west has turned the circular world of traditional peoples into spirals. Some of these, based on mutually beneficial interactions, have moved upwards, giving traditional peoples more control over their lives. Other thrusts from outside have started a downward spiral, as indigenous peoples have been exploited, lost control of their lives, and descended into despair and darkness.

Simplistic assumptions about the power of community development as a technique to assuage all the ills of humanity and its mindless application without regard to local values, attitudes and realities led to a decline of interest in this approach to change in the Seventies.

THE NATIONAL CONTEXT
OF COMMUNITY DEVELOPMENT

"There is no greater evil
than forcing others to change."
—Lao Tzu

In 1967 the Canadian Research Centre for Anthropology published Antony Lloyd's *Community Development in Canada*, an overview of the field.[156] It identified a wide range of initiatives across the country, including Manitoba's programme, the Agricultural Rehabilitation and Development Administration (ARDA), the *Bureau de l'Aménagement de l'Est du Québec* (BAEQ), community development efforts among Black Nova Scotians and many other attempts to stimulate self-help. The publication did not mention the Company of Young Canadians, a federal initiative set up in 1966 to fight poverty. It attracted people who thought they could run the revolution on government money—and a lot of naive idealists. Sent to marginal communities to work with the poor, they soon confronted the reality of poverty and powerlessness. In Montreal, CYC members were accused of being communists. In 1969 a Parliamentary committee investigated the organization and the federal government appointed someone to make sure that money was being spent properly. Unable to handle its internal tensions or to meet the demands made upon its resources by those it set out to serve, the Company faded away, being abolished in 1976.[157] The National Film Board launched its *"Challenge for Change"* series to help communities understand the processes of change. Some of these ventures, such as the one on Fogo Island, Newfoundland, played a useful role in helping communities to strengthen their ability to co-operate and to improve their economy.

By the early Seventies, the fire had gone out of the community development movement in Canada.

Government became suspicious of community development as its proponents disturbed the tranquility, stability and routines of bureaucratic agencies. Some government agencies used the process as a means to extend their control over communities. The social work and adult education professions tried to claim community development as their turf. The former became increasingly involved with case work, as first the extended family, and then the nuclear family, as sources of support for individuals began to disintegrate. To adult educators "the prospect of encouraging real thinking seems too radical and not applicable to their professional role."[158] The few academic programmes to train people in community development in Canada, including an M.A. course at the University of Alberta and a diploma at Algonquin College in Ottawa, did not last very long. Community development, an egalitarian, holistic approach to change did not fit into the hierarchical, segmented academic world. Community development became a nursery for new leaders, who strove to keep alive the idealistic spirit that first motivated their involvement in it. Barbara Hall, a member of the Company of Young Canadians, became mayor of Toronto. George Erasmus, co-chair of the Royal Commission on Aboriginal Peoples, and Ovide Mercredi, former Chief of the Assembly of First Nations, started their careers in community development.

Every decade has its own mood, feel, spirit.

Community development suited the ambiance of the Sixties. Pierre Elliott Trudeau, Canada's philosopher king and dedicated centralist, came to power in April, 1968. This charismatic individual presided over two contrasting movements in Canada. The state exercised more control over the lives of Canadians as bureaucracies expanded to take care of their every real or imagined need. And the increasing sense of individualism that came with economic affluence fueled ideas about personal freedom and liberation. The governments appeared to have money for any personal fantasy, and debts at the federal and provincial levels began to rise alarmingly.

Over the past thirty years, in Canada and elsewhere in the world, community development has been seen by revolutionaries as a way of overthrowing the *status quo* and by government as a way of placating the restless peasantry and proletariat. Community development has only too often served as a safety valve for agencies that have lost touch with their constituencies. Or it has been used as a way for certain individuals to "self-actualize themselves" and find meaning and a role in life. Action at the local level, from the bottom up, *must* be paralleled by policy changes at the top levels of government. During the Sixties, the federal government discovered that many seniors lived in poverty after lives of hard work and struggle. In 1969, 41.4 per cent of families headed by people aged sixty-five or over lived below the poverty line. Ottawa raised old age pensions (renamed old age security) so that in 1992, only 8.5 per cent of families fell below the poverty line. No community development or self-help effort could have brought about that change.

In British Columbia, NDP governments tended to favour community development, while Social Credit ones cut them and looked to the private sector for salvation.[159] In Quebec, social animation became popular as a way of creating awareness among marginalized peoples about their problems and ways to solve them.[160] The provincial government blew hot and cold about public participation in decision making, and community development became a battleground between militants and maintainers. The leaders of some community ventures welcomed programmes like EXTRA, which gave welfare recipients an extra $25 a week to gain work experience. Others saw it simply as a way of dumping poor people on their doorsteps instead of tackling the problems of poverty at the policy level, and restructuring society to eliminate unemployment. Tensions also developed between professionals in the field of social service and local people with little training, but lots of street smarts, who staffed local health and social agencies founded by their own community members. The Partie Québécois government favoured community development, but increasingly saw it simply as a cheap way to deliver services to the poor and the disadvantaged.

A study of 150 local organizations throughout the world concluded:

"The style of public administration prevailing in most developing nations is threatened and complicated by assertive publics. So civil servants, preferring to deliver prepackaged services to a waiting and receptive community, may see little benefit and much trouble in organized groups, especially among the poor."[161]

Seeing community development merely as just another form of social engineering or as a way of giving power to the powerless tends to overlook the political, social and economic context in which it operates. Community development revolves around changing relationships between humans, and this involves politics—who gets what and how. One of the paradoxes in the process is the way that those involved have to practice politics in a non-political manner or at least a non-partisan manner. Every political ideology strives to come to terms with the gap between theory and practice. Every ideology must take into account national and local realities and mythologies and try to separate one from the other.

Community development operates in the shadowland where dreams and desires encounter limits and restrictions. Sometimes these visions of a better future can be made flesh. But sometimes the myths nurtured over the centuries have to be shown for what they are— unreliable and comforting stories that have no current relevance. One of the enduring myths about Canada claims that it is a resource-rich country. The warehouses in the German concentration camps in which the loot stolen from those sent there to be killed was stored were called "Kanada." Canada's development has been a story of booms and busts. The belief that riches lie just over the next horizon dies hard in this country.

Martin Nordegg came to Canada from Germany in 1904 and saw how the rich coal deposits of the eastern Rocky Mountains could fuel the expanding railway network and the new industries of the west. Backed by German financiers and with the help of political connections, Nordegg started a coal mining company, built a railway and founded a town in Alberta that still carries his name. He prospered, then lost control of the enterprise, retiring to Rockcliffe where he helped many refugees before moving to New York during the Second World War. Nordegg claimed "The Possibilities of Canada are Truly Great!" An editor used this phrase as the title of his memoirs from the years 1906 to 1924.[162] By the early Seventies, only neglected houses, abandoned mine shafts and rusting rails remained of the once bustling community that Martin Nordegg built. Its decline came as diesel-electric engines replaced steam-driven ones on Canada's railways.

Community development can very easily raise the expectations of residents in places that have no resources or whose resource base has been exploited or rendered obsolete by change. The scenario that unfolded at Nordegg has been played out again and again in Canada. When Napoleon blockaded the Baltic States, the Royal Navy cut down the tall trees of New Brunswick to make masts. Philemon Wright led a group from Massachusetts in 1800 to settle on the site of Hull, seeking to start a farming community. Lack of success in working the land turned his eyes to the stands of white pine in the Ottawa Valley and Wright became a lumber baron. In the early days of the Klondike Gold Rush miners shook nuggets from the roots of plants in creek beds. They called the ephemeral communities they created Ophir, Paris, Grand Forks. As hand-mining gave way to dredging, fewer and fewer men were needed to reclaim more and more gold. The towns around the creeks dwindled, then vanished, leaving only Dawson as the service centre of the region. Here the great days of the Gold Rush serve the needs of the tourist trade. Evaporated milk is know in the Yukon as "high grade"—the best part of the product. The ethic of "cleaning up and clearing out," part of the heritage of resource-based economy, persists in Canada. An old-timer in Dawson articulated the creed of the optimistic pioneer: "There's more gold in the hills than was ever taken out of the creeks."

The early gold miners externalized many of their costs, paying no attention to the damage they were doing to the land (or to themselves) and ignoring any claims the indigenous people might have to it.

The belief in Canada as a land of inexhaustible resources lies behind the huge deficits piled up by the federal and provincial governments. Why bother to conserve funds when the big strike and instant wealth from the land will soon be ours? For over two decades, Nova Scotia governments hoped that offshore oil would make them a "have" province. They poured millions of dollars into ill-advised schemes to generate an offshore bonanza. Only in 1997 did it appear as if the Atlantic would yield its riches in the form of gas. This development took place just as the results of over-exploiting the east coast fisheries became increasingly obvious. In 1977, Canada declared dominion over the two hundred mile (340 kilometre) zone around our coasts. Fish plants sprang up in every cove while communities buzzed with activity, building boats and making gear. Fish are a common resource—anyone can catch them. Aided by government subsidies, large companies and small operators expanded their activities, and the fishery became crowded. When large corporations like National Sea ran into difficulty as the consequence of their over-exploitation of the resources of the sea and their inefficiency, governments stepped in and bailed them out.

The possibilities of instant wealth from natural resources still tantalize Canadians. Robert Friedland made several billion dollars from the mineral deposits of Labrador without dirtying his hands. The belief that quick money could be made suffered a dent with the Bre-X fiasco. Its promoters, however, made millions out of it. Only in recent years has the concept that intellectual resources—what men and women carry in their heads, hearts and hands—found ready acceptance in Canada. The string of economic disasters by those who lured governments into mad schemes that looked like instant answers to problems of unemployment is long and tragic in Canada: Dome Petroleum, the Sprung greenhouse in Newfoundland, the Westray mine in Nova Scotia. A western bumper sticker sums up the end of the illusion about resource development: "Oh, Lord, give us just one more boom and we promise not to piss it away this time."

Another inhibitor of community development has been the belief that luck, rather than hard work, hard thinking and dedication will turn dreams into realities. In 1969, the federal government amended the Criminal Code to permit lotteries. If you are going to hit the 6-49 jackpot—the chance of winning is one in fourteen million—why bother to work with others to solve your community's problems?

At the national level, community development efforts have had to take into account the fact that Canada is a land of large corporate entities. Concern about corporatism has risen among intellectuals in

Canada in recent years and was articulated by John Ralston Saul in *The Unconscious Civilization*. Oddly enough, this attack on large organizations originated as a series of talks on the Canadian Broadcasting Corporation, a large corporate entity. In its early days, like any frontier, the CBC attracted idealists and opportunists. Harry Boyle worked for the corporation, and noted:

"In the beginning [it] attracted two types...people who were creative and people who wanted to work for a new organization and dig themselves in. These second people dug in and assumed control. In the old days people sacrificed titles and offices for the sake of programs. But titles are what a bureaucracy lives for. See, the only thing they will sacrifice is the talent...Some of these people would be much happier if there were no programs."[163]

A large country like Canada requires large corporations and other bodies for its efficient operation. In the affluent Sixties, these national bodies expanded their scope and operations. Life in them became secure and comfortable, and the maintainers routinized their activities. Now downsizing and outsourcing have thrown thousands of Canadians out of work. And with the loss of a job comes a loss of identity. And for those who remain, life is hectic, uncertain, unpredictable. How much time can anyone devote to community concerns as individuals struggle to survive in these lean and mean times?

Slowly but surely the belief among Canadians that someone else is going to save them from the consequences of their own mistakes is giving way to a greater willingness to take personal responsibility for one's own actions. The famous and perhaps mythological characteristic of Canadians—deference to authority—arises from the domination of our lives by large corporations and government. The other side of deference is defiance. The megastructures of society operate on the command and control model. Governments talk about development, but essentially their role is to control people, to keep them in line, ensure that they adhere to the norms of society. Government is about maintaining. Development—personal, institutional, community—is about change, creativity, initiative, enterprise, all the qualities that politicians and business leaders praise in public but hate in private because they erode their power over others.

Canadians have shown exceptional abilities in subverting, undermining, bypassing and otherwise neutralizing many of the systems set up by the megastructures to control their lives. A fish plant on Cape Breton employed three hundred people but had a staff of nine hundred. Each year, one set of workers would spend four months in the plant. At the end of that time they would hand over their jobs to others in the community and go on pogey. In turn, these three hundred workers handed over the jobs after four months and drew unemployment insurance. And then the circle was repeated, with each worker having four months work and eight months paid leisure.

Beating the system if it limits your choices, as much as conforming to the demands of the powerful, has been as marked a feature of Canadian life as has deference to authority. It's the reason for the Underground Economy, which has deep roots in Canada. In 1784, the British forbade the mining of coal in Cape Breton to protect their export trade. This did not stop illegal mining. In 1819, two thousand tons of coal were stolen from the island. In 1960, the federal government passed the Technical and Vocational Training Assistance Act. Premier Joey Smallwood paid the chef in the cabinet dining room kitchen from this fund, claiming that he was an instructor at the vocational school in St. John's. In 1995, General Motors of Canada, with a profit of $1.03 billion in the previous year, colluded with the Canadian Auto Workers' union so that laid-off workers could receive UI payments as well as money from the company to maintain their standard of living. *Jobs with a Future*,[164] published in March, 1995, recorded a wide variety of ways in which groups and individuals, with the help of government officials, sought to beat systems that did not meet their needs. A lighthouse required only seven people to operate it—but provided employment for twenty-eight workers. In Quebec, a novel occupation developed—that of "winter barman/summer barman"—combining extended holidays with access to UI.

This kind of creativity and sharing of scarce jobs represented a rational adaptation to life in communities with few resources. But it bothers the policy makers and bureaucrats seeking to direct the lives of Canadians into areas where individual initiative and entrepreneurship are considered essential to revitalizing the economy.

The unwillingness or inability of Canadians to behave the way they should—or how rational analysis of the economy suggests they should—brings up another powerful thrust in recent years. At one time, old people were respected in communities for their ability to survive. Experience, knowledge learned in the school of life, street smarts counted for more than theories about how the world worked.

Art not only reflects reality. It anticipates it.

During the Forties and Fifties, a new art movement emerged in the United States. Abstract expressionism sought to catch the essence of an idea, rather than to portray reality. After the Second World War, universities in Canada and throughout the world expanded and new ones came into being. Here abstract intellectualism flourished and it has become one of the dominant forces of our time. At one time, people simply solved problems with what they had at hand. But now, no problem can be tackled until it has been studied. Just as art ceased to represent nature, so the intellectuals moved further and further away from looking at the real world, and began to generate theories on why things happened as they did—and how things could work better. The sense of wonder at the mystery of the world vanished, replaced by a sterile, objective examination of its ills and sorrows. It proved hard to fit human beings into the theoretical abstractions, and the impact that individuals could have on events was ignored or neglected. As Henry Kissinger put it: "As a professor, I tended to think of history as run by impersonal forces. But when you see it in practice, you see the difference personalities make."

Our universities teach young people to analyze, criticize, dissect the world as if it were a frog in a biology class. Seldom do they learn how to synthesize theory and practice, to recognize their own biases and how they structure their view of the world, and to determine the line between the rational and the mystical, the knife edge along which many people struggle as they seek to make better lives for themselves and their children. In recent years, participatory research—academics working with people in communities on the problems the residents identify—has begun to gain ground in Canada. This is yet another example of "bottom up" approaches that are giving local people a better understanding of their world and how they can change it for the better.

Atlantic Canadians have long been the victims of ideas that their proponents have presented to governments as the final solution to their economic development problems. The move towards emphasizing community development in the region stems, in part, from the failure of many of these theories and strategies to improve the economy. In *A Day at the Races*, Groucho Marx approaches a window at a race track to bet on a horse. Chico intercepts him, ostensibly selling ice cream from a cart. He persuades Groucho that he knows which horse will win the next race: No one cons more easily than a con man. Soon Groucho has to juggle with a number of books that will lead him to the name of the winner. By the time he finds it, the window has closed—and the horse on which he originally planned to bet has won the race. This "Marxist" scenario has been played out again and again in Canada as those able to manipulate symbols have taken over from a generation accustomed to a hands-on approach in dealing with problems. You can always tell an "underdeveloped" area or country by the number of studies carried out on it.

During the Sixties, most of the emphasis in community development focused on social concerns and on bringing the outsiders in Canadian society into its mainstream. A great deal of experimentation took place in social change. Much was learned about ways of strengthening local identities and abilities in problem solving with small amounts of resources and lots of local commitment. But when communities became too competent and individuals in them too assertive, governments began to worry that things were getting out of control.

During the Seventies, the political climate in Canada began to change. Governments promoted public participation as a way of encouraging Canadians to become involved in the decisions that affected them. Only too often, attempts at co-operation by government turned into the co-optation of local people to meet agendas and plans that the bureaucrats had already decided were in the best interests of everyone.

Their actions brought reactions.

And new communities—and new forms of community development—emerged. During the Seventies, Canadians began to organize "communities of interest," to oppose change and to press the government and other large corporate bodies to meet the needs of the people they claimed to represent.

COMMUNITIES OF INTEREST

"National life has become a struggle for advantage
among large and powerful organizations—not
simply trade unions and corporations.
Organized pressure groups abound."
Robert Stanfield, 1977. [165]

The beginning of the Canadian public participation movement can be dated to 1971.[166] Bill Davis, the newly elected premier of Ontario, cancelled the proposal to build the Spadina Expressway in that year. It would have cut through the heart of downtown Toronto, and affected the lives and property values of people living there. They organized, protested vigorously and Davis listened to them. Hailed as a triumph for local democracy, the cancellation of the expressway merely shifted the problems of gaining access to central Toronto to other parts of the city. After the euphoria of the Sixties and the summers of their youth, the members of the middle class settled down, bought houses, and started up the career ladder. They wanted stability in their lives—not constant turmoil and change. Their motto became: "What we have, we hold." Adopting the musk-oxen stance, they opposed any move that threatened their lifestyle and property values. In Toronto, and elsewhere, the word "developer" became equated with "enemy" in the early Seventies. In his book, *Marlborough Marathon*, Jack Granatstein, an historian at the University of Toronto, told the story of his fight to protect his street, his community, from developers. It was threatened by a scheme by Marathon Realty, a subsidiary of Canadian Pacific Railway, to develop land the company owned in downtown Toronto. Granatstein's street contained old time residents and members of the new professional classes who had gentrified working class houses. Granatstein fought "to protect the money I had invested in my house (really the interests

157

of the mortgage holders), to ensure the safety of my children as they went to school, and to improve the general quality of life in my immediate neighbourhood."[168] As a member of a ratepayers' association, Granatstein was invited to view Marathon's plans. A lawyer who belonged to the nearby York Racquets Club cautioned: "Ratepayers' associations can do a great deal of good if they are reasonable and responsible, just as they have been known to do a great deal of harm when they become irrational and irresponsible."

Granatstein saw himself as a street fighter. He upset his middle class neighbours by suggesting throwing garbage on the steps of the Racquets Club as "a symbolic act of urban guerilla warfare." Setting out a memorandum of complaints, the historian spent $3.25 for 100 copies: "Once the money had been spent, I was irrevocably committed." Granatstein managed to beat back the threat to his street. Such isolated actions aimed at preserving the *status quo* took place all over Canada in the Seventies. Some succeeded, some failed.

The kind of *ad hoc* opposition to the activities of government and large corporations in Canada represented no real threat to them. They could take their money and spend it elsewhere. And the opposing groups disintegrated when they won their victories—or faded out of existence when large well-endowed corporate entities wore them down with legal wrangling, bureaucratic obfuscation or stalling tactics.

Watching the rise of fascism and nationalism in Europe, the Italian jurist Gaetano Mosca (1858-1941) concluded: "The dominion of an organized minority, obeying a single impulse, over the unorganized majority, is inevitable."

As governments appeared increasingly unable to organize the economy and society to the satisfaction of Canadians, interest groups began to proliferate. They brought together like-minded people in communities that transcended geographical boundaries. The history of communities of interest in Canada parallels that of geographical communities as they sought to adapt to rapid change. Many interest groups took the musk-oxen stance. Others butted heads internally and externally, perpetually locking horns in struggles over territory, power and money. A few developed symbiotic relationships with those beyond their boundaries, mirroring the lichen.

During the Seventies, the media carried more and more stories about insult and injury to humans and the environment. Interest groups became more strident in seeking to correct the damage being done by large corporate entities.

Communities of interest are not new in Canada. They emerged in the past when the existing methods for dealing with problems proved inadequate, or when a personal experience, especially a tragedy, confronted an individual or a group with a failure in the system.

Women have been pioneers in Canada in forming groups to protect the common good. The Young Women's Christian Association began in Saint John, New Brunswick, in 1870 to save innocents from sin: By 1885 it had become a national body. The National Council of Women, launched in 1893, drew attention to the plight of women and children in poor circumstances. Two years later, Mabel Bell, wife of the inventor Alexander Graham Bell, and a small group of women in Baddeck, Nova Scotia, voted to buy books and globes for the local academy. Their local initiative blossomed into the Canadian Home and School Association. The Women's Institute started in Stoney Creek, Ontario, in 1897. By 1912, one in every eight women in Canada belonged to it or to a similar organization. These communities of interest operated in a genteel manner, with hosts of volunteers devoting their time and resources to tackling issues ranging from the safety of milk to women's suffrage.

Interest groups founded by men usually focus on economic issues. The Canadian Manufacturers' Association began lobbying around 1900. By the end of the First World War, it "seems to have become an accepted part of the policy process" in the words of Paul Pross, a leading authority on interest groups.[169] The Canada Grains Act, passed in 1912, became law after the federal government listened to the concerns of interested parties.

Pross divides communities of interest into two categories.

He calls the kind that Jack Granatstein started "Issue Oriented." They form around a specific threat or issue and vanish when it is resolved or when forces beyond the control of participants make it impossible for people to act effectively. Granatstein won his battle with the developers. In the Nineties a group in Halifax tried to preserve a movie theatre built in 1916 and turn it into a community arts centre. The volunteers put together a business plan for the venture and one of them, an architect, designed the proposed new centre. The movie theatre, which had been closed for several years, belonged to a large, locally-owned grocery chain. Although Halifax city council and its bureaucracy proved sympathetic to the idea of creating a community centre, the owners allowed the building to deteriorate and knocked it down in 1997.

The other category identified by Pross is the "Institutional" group which has continuity, cohesion, stable leadership and wide membership. Those involved in these groups know how government works and seek good relationships with politicians and bureaucrats.

During the Sixties, as Canadian learned more about their country and what was happening in the world, new kinds of communities of interest began to form and expand. Wickedness and evil appeared to be rampant, and Canada entered the era of "isms"—environmentalism, feminism, consumerism, multiculturism. Unlike the early interest groups, those in the new institutional ones looked to the government for support for their activities. Confronted with their demands, politicians and bureaucrats adopted the Russian sleigh technique. A story claims that when Russians in a sleigh saw wolves following them and coming closer, they threw out one of their number to appease them. While the wolves dined on this unfortunate, the sleigh raced ahead, striving to outpace the animals. As interest groups snapped at their heels, governments threw out bags of money to keep them at bay. The rationale for funding interest groups was that they were tackling problems that the government should be handling, and hence deserved public funding.

Like geographic communities, interest groups have to learn how to handle the impact of external forces on their operations and the internal tensions that come with any form of collective activity. In the Sixties, there was never any doubt that Canada's environment had been damaged by the reckless greed of individuals and businesses whose only concern was for taking the best and leaving the rest. Nor was there any doubt that women in this country did not have access to the same opportunities for advancement as did men.

And small and large businesses continued to foist inferior products and services upon consumers. Poverty, oppression, abuse of human rights, inequality—evidence of this in Canada and elsewhere in the world appeared on our TV screens every day.

Discontent with existing systems always generates social movements.[170] These pass through several stages as those involved in them try to make a better world. At first, participants in social movements are restless and uneasy, acting in random fashion. Prophets and reformers arise who focus the concerns of the discontented and speak out against the evils of society and the existing system. Agitation becomes widespread, loosening the hold of individuals on previous attachments and former ways of thinking and acting. As social movements enter the liminal phase, arousing new feelings and impulses, generating excitement, they attract the rootless in search of new identities. The old ways, the old ceremonies, the old rituals lose their magic and their hold over people. Shedding former allegiances and relationships, the adherents of the movement begin to see themselves as special people, brothers, sisters, comrades in arms. Convinced of the rightness of their cause, they seek to occupy the high moral ground as they divide everyone into "Us" and "Them." Critics—or anyone daring to question the received wisdom of the groups—soon leave or are ejected. Greenpeace has copied the Jehovah's Witnesses in their campaign for a pristine environment. Recruits go out and knock on doors to solicit funds. Every rejection is an affirmation of the rightness of their cause. Building a sense of community and identity in social movements is as important as raising money. Ceremonies and rituals strengthen group solidarity, and a well articulated philosophy and psychology binds believers together as goals, doctrines, ideologies and myths develop to rationalize action—any action—to defeat the evils of the world.

Over the years, some interest groups have become bureaucratized. Others have simply fallen apart. As money became tighter in the Eighties, governments cut back on their support for communities of interest, creating tensions as those running them struggled to do more—or even to sustain their activities—with fewer and fewer resources. Governments in Canada suddenly discovered the volunteer ethic as

161

they had less and less money to meet more and more demands upon them. During the affluent Sixties, and by funding interest groups, governments at all levels paid people to do what once they did for free as volunteers.

In the past, to be a radical, to go against settled ways and the oppressors of others, meant persecution, harassment, exile. In Canada, however, governments have funded social movements aimed at confronting and abusing them. Jean Charest, when Minister of the Environment, stated that funding interest groups was not popular in cabinet. His colleagues complained that most of them "wouldn't exist without our funding, then they turn around and criticize government."[171] Greenpeace began in Vancouver in 1970 when three Canadians decided to stop a proposed atomic blast in the Aleutians. Through its well-publicized activism it raised millions of dollars and never had to rely on government funding. Some other interest groups have played the numbers game to secure funds from government. The National Action Committee on the Status of Women added up the number of members in its affiliated organizations and claimed to speak for three million women. Generously funded by the federal government after it came into being in 1972, it has seen this support dwindle in recent years. If NAC really represented three million Canadian women then a dollar from each of them would be enough to sustain its operations and render it independent of government.

The communities of interest that arose in the Seventies reflected the fears of the new middle class and their desire to control what affected their lives. Environmental pollution, over exploitation of resources, damage to the land and those who lived on it had been described by two books published in 1948. Fairfield Osborn's *Our Plundered Planet,* dedicated to "all who care about tomorrow," and William Vogt's *The Road to Survival* told vividly of the degradation and destruction of the earth's resources. But it was not until the publication of Rachel Carson's *Silent Spring* in 1962 that the members of the middle class became alarmed about environmental pollution and demanded that the government do something about it. The book pointed out how pesticides were entering the food chain, and suddenly environmental issues became very personal. In Canada, Robert

Bryce, secretary of the cabinet, read Carson's book and took the appropriate bureaucratic measure of setting up what became the Department of the Environment, now Environment Canada.[172] The provinces followed suit. Governments believed that pollution was merely a technical problem, and hired lots of engineers to tackle it. Others recognized environmental issues as being rooted in human, social and political concerns. The battle lines between the two camps hardened over the years as governments became more bureaucratic and ineffective in dealing with environmental problems and citizens groups more militant and aggressive in the cause of saving the world.

Only too often, interest groups that set themselves up as watchdogs of government turned into lap dogs. To protect consumers from the consequences of their own silly buying habits, the federal and provincial governments established departments of consumer affairs. Ottawa also funded the Consumers' Association of Canada. It began in 1941 when the federal government enlisted fifty-six women's organizations to monitor prices to aid in wartime rationing, becoming formally established in 1947. Over the years, the business community began to pay more attention to the needs of consumers, improving products and services, installing 800-lines for feedback from the public and generally becoming more attentive to what buyers really wanted.

In 1988, the Consumers' Association of Canada, deeply in debt, had to be bailed out by the federal government and the Consumers' Union in the United States. Then the group split apart because it could not handle its internal tensions. By 1992 it had lost two-thirds of its membership and been forced to cancel its magazine. In July, 1994, the newly-elected president of the association stated: "We are not a special interest group. We are a public interest group. It is an important distinction."[173] In that year, the federal government gave the Consumers' Association of Canada $500,000 in grants.

The women's movement in Canada has polarized around the radical feminists of the National Action Committee on the Status of Women (NAC) and REAL Women, founded in 1983. When the latter organization applied for government funding, its request was rejected: "The objectives of your organization are not in harmony with those of the women's movement. Your organization appears to be supporting a way of life, a concern for the family unit rather than actually promoting the status of women."[174]

A woman manager found herself called "part of the problem for women in the workplace," by a NAC leader. She wrote: "Instead of seeking to include all women, NAC's policies and policy makers have increasingly excluded and alienated the majority of Canadian women."[175] Government funding of the NAC generated jealousies within the community of Canadian women. The Toronto chapter of the Infertility Awareness Association of Canada complained it was being "marginalized and ignored" by NAC. Its director sought a "modest $130,000 grant" for her office and a 1-800 line. She lamented:

> "NAC has a sizable federal grant and a national profile...Many of us in the Infertility Awareness Association are feminists who have fought for feminist causes, including the right to choose abortion...Women we should be able to count on, who have access to politicians, the media and money, have turned on us as we experienced the greatest crisis of our lives."[176]

Communities of interest have played a significant role in enhancing and bettering Canadian society over the past thirty years. Politicians, while willing to fund them, have seldom recognized their role and promise in a democratic society. Government money has only too often been taken by interest groups as official sanction and recognition for whatever they do. The environmentalists seek to create a pristine world, free of all blight and insult. Like true believers, they refuse to compromise, to make deals with "Them," to find middle ground between conservation and development.[177]

In November, 1994, John Bryden, a back bench Liberal MP stripped away the security blanket in which many interest groups had wrapped themselves. He published a reasoned analysis of forty non-governmental organizations, highlighting misuse of government money, inflated administrative costs and salaries, small bases of public support and volunteer involvement, lack of accountability and other shortcomings.[178] Bryden estimated that special interest groups, charities, and non-profit organizations make up a sector worth about $100 billion in the Canadian economy. He identified several organizations doing good work in the public interest, including the Canadian Council on Multicultural Health and Pollution Probe. They served as reliable sources of information and ideas for anyone concerned about acting on the problems in their areas of concern. They had strong volunteer involvement, and modest salaries and administrative costs. In the past, the level of rhetoric emerging from an interest group has usually been in inverse proportion to its ability to act effectively. In the future, the only option for such bodies to attract public or private money is for them to be well run, transparent, accountable and responsive to the needs of those they claim to serve. It will no longer be enough for any body of people to claim that they are against sin in society and in favour of truth, justice and beauty. They have to show their effectiveness in pursuing the goals they set and manage their affairs in an efficient manner.

Victor Turner's concept of liminal space helps to explain how the successful voluntary organizations operate. Structured society— government and large corporations—operate on *a priori* grounds, always defining in advance what a problem is and how it is to be tackled. In their policies, plans and programmes, human beings, reduced to symbols, are expected to conform to certain preordained norms of behaviour. While human beings can be made to behave in certain ways through offers of reward and threats of punishment, it becomes increasingly difficult to control them in a time of enhanced individualism and pluralism. The so-called management revolution in recent years was sparked by a need to see human beings as innovative, creative, unique individuals with the potential to be more productive if they are informed and involved in the decisions that affect them.

Robert Putnam's work on civil society in Italy, recorded in his book *Making Democracy Work*, indicates how the informal structures of society—chess clubs, choral groups—strengthen and reinforce the formal one through generating spaces where mutual respect, trust, and co-operation can be fostered.[179]

In his story *The Crack Up*, F. Scott Fitzgerald wrote:

"The test of a first rate intelligence is the ability to hold two opposed ideas in mind at the same time, and still retain the ability to function. One should, for example, be able to see that things are hopeless yet be determined to make them otherwise."

In their seminal business book, *In Search of Excellence*, Thomas J. Peters and Robert Waterman put the first sentence from Fitzgerald's statement at the head of the chapter on "Managing Ambiguity and Paradox."[180] In recent years, Tom Peters has been advising business leaders to "go crazy" and break down their existing systems and structures. He is advising them to discover liminal spaces as they realize that the old ways of doing things don't work. But business has a bottom line, whereas voluntary and non-government agencies do not. They are dedicated to personal, organizational and community development, and it is hard to measure how successful they are because the outcomes from their activities are intangible. The recent emphasis on the bottom line in all aspects of Canadian life—the importation of a business concept into non-business areas—has done much damage to the fabric of society. Of course, many interest groups have been badly run and poorly managed. Altruism, an essential underpinning of voluntary groups, often becomes an excuse for inefficiency. *Bridges of Hope?*, a survey of Canadian voluntary agencies involved in the Third World, noted that they had to "resist a simple response to human suffering" and "base their programming on careful consultation with beneficiaries."[181] These agencies had to "avoid the assumption that good motives necessarily lead to right actions: altruism is not an end in itself." *Bridges of Hope?* notes that many voluntary agencies have not been particularly well managed in the past. But it also points out the "ill-concealed irritation of senior CIDA (Canadian International Development Agency) staff" at the way in which a Parliamentary Committee held up small NGOs (Non-Governmental Organizations) projects as examples for their agency to emulate. In a time of tight budgets, and the need for large organizations, especially governments, to retain and extend their control over human behaviour, liminal spaces in society are needed more than ever. While governments praise volunteerism, they always want to channel it into the areas they believe need attention or where official efforts have been ineffective. But as June Callwood puts it: "Volunteers are free-lancers. No one owns their swords."[182]

The British have long referred to community development as a way of making democracy work. But for community development to flourish, it requires spaces and places where people with common concerns can develop their own programmes and approaches to problem solving, rather than having them imposed upon them in the way that governments do with their pre-packaged ways for resolving tensions in society. For many people, communities of interest offer a point of reference in their lives, a haven, a place to explore new opportunities for personal and community development and make new connections.

In 1971, a group of enthusiastic idealists founded the Ecology Action Centre in Halifax. It has always had the look and feel of happy chaos about it, and never received provincial government funding on a sustained basis. Run by volunteers, with a few paid staff from time to time, the centre lived on the edge for years, raising money through memberships, auctions, contracts. Through its doors passed large numbers of young people who learned a lot about themselves and the world as they struggled to protect the environment. Among other things, the centre developed the best information system on the environment in the province. Meanwhile, the provincial government stumbled and fumbled around trying to solve the mega-problems of the environment through mechanical and social engineering. An attempt to clean up Halifax Harbour ended unsuccessfully after the expenditure of more than $50 million. A scheme to deal with the Sydney Tar Ponds—the most polluted site in North America—fell apart when the equipment designed to process the sludge failed to perform properly. This fiasco also cost over $50 million.

On the other hand, culture has flourished in recent years in Nova Scotia with government support for "anti-structures." In the Seventies, adult educators in the provincial cultural agency met with representatives of writers, theatre groups, artists and other creative people. The agency then provided core funding for voluntary cultural agencies to encourage writing, dance, theatre, crafts, visual arts, heritage, choral work and multiculturalism. Each developed its activities and programmes in line with the needs of its membership, with the goal of enhancing professionalism and fostering excellence in the arts. They continue to do this in a variety of different ways by holding educational camps, organizing juried shows for crafts, sponsoring competitions for writers. Anyone can join these cultural organizations which must also serve non-members; the provincial government provides grants for a co-ordinator/director and a secretary. The cultural ventures offer advice to government and provide feedback on the needs of their members to larger corporate entities in the public and private sector. Culture in Nova Scotia has been fostered by a unique combination of bottom up and top down initiatives, rather than being controlled and commanded by a central bureaucracy.[183]

The Working Centre operates in Kitchener's city core.[184] Its founders, Joe and Stephanie Mancini, went as volunteers to Tanzania with a missionary effort organized by the Precious Blood Fathers, an Italian-Canadian religious order in Toronto. The Mancinis, not married at the time, took part as students, ostensibly to help to install windmills. Their summer in Tanzania helped to shape their views about the good society. Joe Mancini wrote his M.A. thesis in history on Julius Nyerere's efforts at socialist development there after his summer in Tanzania. Like many ardent and idealistic young people, the Mancinis wanted to help others. Their concerns found a focus during the 1982 recession as the Catholic Church preached anti-capitalism and the need to create more humane structures in common life. The couple opened the Working Centre in the spring of 1982 with a small grant from PLURA, an interdenominational church agency promoting grassroots projects aimed at redistributing power, knowledge and resources. The Mancinis and their colleagues have created a space where unemployed people can come, explore opportunities for work, discuss and share their experiences, determine solutions to their problems while analyzing the social framework of Canadian society and how it defines success and failure. In January, 1983, the centre received a one-year grant of $50,000 from the Canadian Community Development Project and opened a storefront office to carry out research and offer resources to the unemployed. The centre spawned two other ventures—a drop-in centre and soup kitchen operated by St. John's Anglican Church and a worker-controlled recycling business. The former still serves meals five days a week, but the latter collapsed when the market for paper changed in 1991. It is extremely rare to find accounts by the beneficiaries of those voluntary ventures. A publication on The Working Centre contains a piece by an alcoholic telling how St. John's Kitchen helped him to turn his life around after he had run the gamut of treatment centres, rehabs, hostels, doctors and food lines:

> "...I noticed right away something very central to the philosophy of so many of these other services was missing at St. John's—that overriding you-guys-are-losers, condescending attitude was not there!"

The writer recalls lining up with others at a hostel, waiting for a meal. They were handing their tickets to the staff "when someone at the back went 'Moo! Moo!'." Everyone in the line burst out laughing: "We all knew what the guy meant, all of us that is except 'the staff' at the front with the puzzled look on his sainted brow."[185]

Many interest groups, especially in the environmental field, take a "holier-than-thou, wiser-than-thou" attitude to everyone who does not share their assumptions or support their activities. Some issue report cards, giving grades to government indicating their shortcomings while avoiding any criticism of their own activities.

The work of Mary Douglas helps to make sense of interest group activity, especially in the environmental field. In *Purity and Danger*, she analyzes concepts of pollution and taboo. It is very difficult for the mainly middle class members of so many Canadian communities of interest to accept that their culture, their values, their way of life, their assumptions are not absolutes, but represent only one way of being and acting in the world. In western society, Douglas notes "sacred things and places are to be protected from defilement. Holiness and impurity are at opposite poles."[186] The wilderness, the feminine, the consumer therefore must be protected from damage and insult by what comes from outside. To some interest groups, society is ritually unclean and must be cleansed of all ills and evils. As Douglas puts it: "...dirt is essentially disorder."[187] This belief in western society has its roots in notions like progress and the fear of chaos. Douglas points out that:

> "In chasing dirt, in papering, decorating, tidying, we are not governed by anxiety to escape disease, but are positively re-ordering our environment, making it conform to an idea."[188]

Interest groups, concerned about disorder in society, usually fail to recognize the liminal space between chaos and order. In the same way, communities with rigid, inflexible boundaries cannot concep-tualize of places around or within them that might offer residents a chance to explore new opportunities for creating a better world in-side their walls. If only evil lurks there, who will have the courage to venture into these unknown, unfamiliar places? Douglas writes:

> "Purity is the enemy of change, of ambiguity, of compromise...When a strict pattern of purity is imposed on our lives it is either highly uncomfortable or it leads into con-tradictions if closely followed, or it leads to hypocrisy."[189]

To affirm life, to deal with its ambiguities and paradoxes and mysteries, you must accept evil as an essential part of the world, and recognize that we all are sinners. Every human has the potential for doing vile and impure things to themselves and others. In taking re-sponsibility for the evil within, by recognizing the errors to which all humans are prone, you begin to blur the line between purity and im-purity while accepting your shared humanity with others. Thus you cease to judge yourself and to berate sinners and can work towards creating a more open, democratic and responsive society than the one that exists today.

Many of those who staff communities of interest bent on eliminating all the evils of the world belong to the "Me/Now" generation. They have been accustomed to getting their own way, to making themselves the centre of the universe, and to having their needs instantly gratified. So they become angry and frustrated at those who will not do their bidding as they strive to protect and enhance what they believe to be the common good.

In the same way, governments make sharp distinctions between those whom they consider to be good citizens and individuals failing to live proper Canadian lives. The unemployed and the poor in particular are seen as lacking something essential in their personal makeups that prevents them from getting off pogey and welfare and making their own way in the world. As the economy worsened in the Eighties, and government programmes failed to generate employment, the virtues of small business and self-employment were touted as the way of the future. Those ejected from the large corporate entities in Canadian society were supposed to find their own solutions to earning a living.

But somehow small businesses and entrepreneurship were not creating employment in many parts of Canada, particularly in the hinterland areas that had been subjected to numerous regional development schemes that failed to stimulate their economies.

In the Eighties, governments began to promote community *economic* development as the solution to the problems of slow growth, high unemployment areas in Canada.

THE COMING OF COMMUNITY ECONOMIC DEVELOPMENT

> "It all comes out like a Jello-definition. Maybe it
> looks good, maybe it tastes good, but if you try to
> squeeze it, it all goes through your fingers.
> I mean, what is it?"
> —Economist Lars Osberg on community economic
> development, *Mail Star* (Halifax) 28 June, 1994.

In 1844, a group of weavers opened a store in Toad Lane, in Rochdale, in northern England, marking the beginning of the modern co-operative movement. These pioneers set down rules and regulations—one member, one vote—to ensure social harmony and business profitability. Many traditional societies had ways of sharing wealth and resources through tontines, thrift clubs and other devices that spread accumulated wealth, limited risk and strengthened the social fabric by ensuring that no-one became too rich or too poor.

What has been called the social economy or the third sector has become big business in Canada and elsewhere in the world. Co-operators make pilgrimages to Mondragon in the Basque region of Spain. Started by a priest and a small band of engineers in 1956, the Mondragon Co-operative Corporation had annual sales of $6 billion (US) in the mid-Nineties. It owns Spain's tenth largest bank and the country's third largest chain of supermarkets, hyper-markets and shopping malls. Consumers in Britain and other western European countries spend about $50 billion (US) on groceries, household needs and services in 14,000 co-operative stores. The community of Earlscourt in Toronto, Ontario, came into being through the efforts of British immigrants who built their own affordable housing through collective effort on the fringes of the city. They practised the precepts of the co-operative movement—thrift, mutual aid, self-reliance, fair shares for all. About half of Canada's population has affiliations with some form of co-operative enterprise. In Quebec, one-third of provincial savings in the early Nineties, about $35 billion, was in co-operatives of some form. About fifty-seven per cent of Saskatchewan's population belongs to credit unions. In theory, co-operatives and credit unions are devoted to serving their members. In practice, most have become big and bureaucratized with their managers keeping a firm eye on the bottom line and the profitability of their ventures. In many developing countries, the rulers decided that co-operatives would free their people from dependency on foreign capitalists and imposed them from the top down. A survey of local organizations in rural development concluded:

"Some of the most unsuccessful [local organization] training efforts have been found among the co-operatives, where there has often been a great deal of emphasis on the philosophy and goals of co-operation, but not enough on the mechanics of making co-operatives operate effectively. This emphasis may derive from the fact that it is easier to impart abstract ideas than to explain organizational dynamics, financial management, or legal issues."[190]

In the co-operatives and credit unions, ideology and practicality often conflict with social and business goals, making their operations difficult to run compared to the private sector's simple obsession with profit.

The modern community economic development movement arose outside the co-operative and credit union sphere and in isolation from it. As the white middle class fled to the suburbs in the United States, inner city areas became depleted and "red-lined"—banks would not lend money to enterprises there. During the War on Poverty, the American government spent billions of dollars on programmes to help the poor: Most of it went to pay outsiders and experts. Residents found themselves cut out of the decision-making process as outsiders and professionals extended their reach into their lives. In 1967, leaders in the Bedford-Stuyvesant area of New York invited Senator Bobby Kennedy to visit their community. It had a population of 400,000—and no local government. Kennedy saw the good and the bad in Bed-Stuy, and concluded that official anti-poverty programmes were not working.[191] With Senator Javitz, the other New York representative, Kennedy sponsored the Special Impact Program to tap federal funds, and brought together black leaders from Bed-Stuy with white businessmen from elsewhere. They created the Bed-Stuy Restoration Corporation as a vehicle for the regeneration of the community. By the late Sixties, the community economic development movement in the United States had become well established, with block associations, churches, unions and ethnic groups backing local self-help efforts. In 1982, the Reagan administration cut back support to community economic development ventures. The Bed-Stuy Restoration Corporation laid off half its staff and sold some of its land. When riots exploded in Los Angeles after the Rodney King decision in April, 1992, the Watts supermarket, owned by a community economic development corporation, went up in flames.

Over the years, some of the corporations collapsed from mismanagement and corruption. But their numbers kept growing, rising from ten in 1967 to 2,500 in 1992 and becoming the leading builder of low-income housing and a major creator of jobs and small business ventures.

Community economic development came to Canada through the efforts of Father Greg MacLeod, a charismatic priest and professor of philosophy at the University College of Cape Breton in Sydney, Nova Scotia. New Dawn, incorporated in 1976 as the first venture of its kind in Canada, had its origin in the frustration of local people with efforts by federal and provincial governments to create jobs in Cape Breton. Again and again, "entrepreneurs" from away took government grants, opened factories, closed them and vanished. Millions of dollars went into ventures such as heavy water plants that had no economic rationale but which created employment and were used for social and political ends.

New Dawn raised some money locally, tapped federal sources and went into the real estate business, building much needed community facilities and housing. By 1985, the venture had $10 million in assets and a staff of thirty, with a volunteer board of directors. MacLeod points out a reason for the lack of interest by governments in genuine self-help ventures: "...when a group has built up equity, it's independent and government officials don't like dealing with local groups that have any kind of independence."[192] New Dawn and similar ventures seek to use business methods for social purposes— "the tools of capitalism for socialist ends." The Sydney venture turned houses on a former military base into homes for seniors who are cared for by neighbours. By 1993 the corporation had built over 230 apartments, and assisted in the development of two co-operatives and eight business or non-profit ventures.

New Dawn has not been immune to the problems of business and reliance on government programmes for assistance. In 1982, the federal government involved the venture in Telidon "to test the viability of establishing a software industry in Cape Breton." Ottawa spent $300 million on the videotext system before recognizing that it was a technology without a market. In 1990, New Dawn misread the market. It launched a cloth diaper service that failed after a year with a loss of $150,000.

This corporation has served as a model for others in Cape Breton and elsewhere. As MacLeod put it: "We adapted, we became 'sea lawyers' clever at finding loopholes...like other community groups...and that's how we kept going. Several times we almost went bankrupt."[193]

Quite obviously, top down efforts at generating wealth and jobs in such places as Cape Breton and other marginal areas have failed, despite a plethora of grants and programmes to aid business and encourage development. During the Eighties community economic development slowly came to be seen as a way of stimulating economies from the bottom up. By 1990, federal and provincial governments were spending $230 million on community economic development through programmes like Community Futures. And they were not too sure what they were getting for their money. In 1990, the Economic Council of Canada published *From the Bottom Up: The Community-Economic Development Approach*. The "statement" noted that, despite decades of government intervention, the "gaps in opportunity" in "have-not provinces" had widened, and "disparities and stagnation remain." It concluded that "top down bureaucracy-driven plans for regional development have fallen into disrepute and policy makers know they need to consider new approaches."[194]

The case studies commissioned by the council showed a wide diversity of approaches to stimulating local economies through collective action. In West Prince County on Prince Edward Island, a dynamic individual with business experience helped to revitalize the local economic development commission and generate a new sense of pride and confidence.[195] When the Bank of Montreal closed its branch in L'Anse-au-Loup on the south coast of Labrador, local people started a credit union.[196] The bank manager stayed on to run it, and the venture received help from a *caisse-populaire* across the provincial border in Quebec. At La Ronge, Saskatchewan, the Indian band created the Kitsaki Development Corporation with the help of a Vietnam veteran who had experience in community economic development and had come north in search of peace and quiet.[197] He helped the native peoples to set up joint ventures with outside businesses.

Some of these initiatives relied on local participation and involvement. Others depended upon government grants and gifted individuals who took on the role of community entrepreneur. Economists in the liberal tradition see only monetary profit as motivating individuals. Thus they have difficulty fitting the concepts of mutual aid, self help and collective initiative—one for all and all for one—into their economic models. When the Conservative government abolished the Economic Council in 1992 the community economic development movement lost a knowledgeable presence that could have explained the concept to the power people in Ottawa. In the Sixties, community development had been viewed as a leading edge technique for bringing about social change. Now, community economic development seems to be looked upon as a rearguard approach, a last resort for creating jobs and wealth when all other methods fail.

In 1980, Employment and Immigration Canada launched Canada Community Development Projects "to create jobs which will enable unemployed people to use their skills in work that has a continuing and genuine value to the individual and the community." As the community development experience shows, this is not easily done. In the Eighties, attention has concentrated on "capacity building" through revitalizing existing organizations to make them more efficient and creating new ones to encourage personal *and* community development.

The Department of National Health and Welfare also discovered community economic development and in 1991 commissioned a series of studies on it. The goal was to determine how social goals could be integrated with business goals through community economic development. Since its bureaucratic mandate dealt with looking after the needs of the poor, the marginalized, the disadvantaged, the department saw CED as a tool to help powerless people and underdeveloped communities. Instead of concentrating on individual problems, the hope was that CED would change the structure of communities and their relationships with the outside world, and encourage residents to become more active in using the available resources. Most approaches and public funding in Canada devoted to eradicating poverty focus on individuals, and past policies have promoted dependency rather than independence and self-reliance. Health and Welfare Canada appeared to see CED as an answer to breaking the cycles of poverty and dependency, very much as community development had been seen in the post-colonial world.

The enquiry showed that practice in CED had outstripped policy and theory. Among the ventures identified as being involved in community economic development were Entre Nous Femmes Housing Society in Vancouver, creating child-oriented, low cost housing for single parents; The Learning Enrichment Foundation in North York, Ontario, which encourages multicultural arts, job training and child services; the Women's Enterprise Bureau in St. John's, Newfoundland, that stimulates business development and entrepreneurship; Carrot Common Corporation which began as a health food store and now runs a shopping centre in Toronto; Mennonite assistance to immigrants in starting "micro-businesses" in Edmonton; the use of community bonds in Saskatchewan to help small towns to develop locally-owned ventures; and the North Portage Development Corporation in Winnipeg trying to renew its deteriorated downtown.

THE DIVERSITY OF
COMMUNITY DEVELOPMENT

"What does it matter if the cat is black or white, so
long as it catches mice?"
—Chinese saying

The constant invocation of community as a solution to the ills of our time has taken on aspects of a magic incantation to drive out evil from our midst. Slapping the word community on a project or adding the word to any and every collective venture has devalued it. The quest for community lies deep in every human psyche, and surfaces in difficult times when the existing systems of society appear to be unable to cope with the problems of ordinary people. Authentic community has deep spiritual, moral and ethical roots, and, as the record shows, creating it involves a blend of theory and practise and leadership by individuals strong enough to transcend their egos. Community development is not a knowledge-free field, as the young enthusiasts in the commune movement of the Sixties soon discovered. But even if a community venture fails, it can leave memories behind that are useful to others seeking a better life, as Sointula, the "place of harmony," showed. Balancing individual and collective needs requires self-knowledge as well as an understanding of what community living involves. Idealism and realism have to come together every day—and in long term planning. Hope must be sustained and creativity encouraged for the common good. As Northrop Frye put it: "All hope is based on fiction. It has no facts to go on. It is where the creative impulse takes over."

There is no "right" or "wrong" way to do community development, and there are risks in it being classified, categorized and neutralized by experts. Its amorphous and ambiguous nature makes members of the media and academe uncomfortable because they cannot pin their usual labels on it. Community development is about solving problems together that cannot be tackled by one individual.

And the record of achievement in this field is very mixed. Only too often government "help" has proved to be the kiss of death. West End Community Ventures operated in a part of Ottawa with a large transient and immigrant population, struggling to combine social and economic objectives while helping people to gain some measure of self-reliance. To provide income and training opportunities, WECV started a clothing store and a restaurant. The agency struggled along until 1990. Then the new Ontario NDP government, bitten by the community economic development bug, chose WECV as a demonstration project and gave it a large grant. The staff increased from two to eighteen, the budget from $100,000 to $700,000. Instead of responding to local realities, WECV had to conform to government policies and demands. The government wanted people on social assistance to become self-reliant through starting small businesses. In the area in which the agency worked, it takes a great deal of time to contact people, talk with them, gain their trust, and encourage them to train and to take risks at starting their own ventures and breaking the cycle of poverty and dependency. In two years, WECV trained six hundred people and founded two businesses that employed local residents. An evaluation by the province claimed that the agency had not achieved the goals set for it by the government and WECV lost its funding.

Carrot Commons, which began as a worker co-op food store created by middle class young people in Toronto seeking a better way to do business, had the help of a philanthropic developer when it wanted to expand. The man and his wife sought to encourage the revitalization of a deteriorating neighbourhood in Toronto. The joint venture between the store owners and the couple created a unique "alternative" shopping centre housing seventeen ventures. The Bread and Roses credit union in that city gives people a choice of investing their money at traditional rates of interest or receiving lower returns for putting their money into socially valuable ventures.

Community development can take any number of forms as people organize around collective needs and concerns. In 1993, when politicians failed to deliver on their promise to build a new health centre in New Germany in Nova Scotia, community members came together, pooled their resources, and built it themselves. In 1964-65, municipal officials in Halifax wiped out the Black community of Africville on the shores of the Bedford Basin. Ostensibly the aim was to give its residents a better life, but many ended up on welfare, grieving over their loss of community. Africville wasn't much—but it was home to many Black people and part of their identity. When it looked as if several Black communities on the Dartmouth watershed might suffer the fate of Africville, organizers invoked what happened there to alert residents to the threats to their existence. Local governments contracted with a consultant who hired three community residents to serve as sources of reliable information and link the grassroots people with the planners, the bureaucrats and the politicians. In time, and after some tension, the Black residents worked with outsiders and developed their own community plan.[198]

Community development, to be effective, requires skilled people inside government who understand its potential and limitations and don't treat those involved in it as threats or as possessors of magic potions. Creating community involves generating or enhancing your own space and your own place, making them better through collective action. As Paul Tillich put it: "Every utopia is a hovering, a suspension between possibility and impossibility."

The utopias of ordinary people tend to be small—and often realizable. In the mid-Eighties, it looked as if the small community of Pilot Mound in Manitoba would lose its resident agricultural representative whose working quarters had become inadequate. In 1985, a woman invited seventeen friends to her house to discuss what could be done to solve this problem. The people of Pilot Mound formed a corporation to erect a building to house the ag. rep. and other services. The money was raised from bank loans, personal pledges, service clubs and other sources, and the new structure opened in March, 1988. It contained offices for a doctor whose wife was a psychologist. As the chairman of the venture put it: "And we didn't ask for a nickel of grant money."

British Columbia attracts highly individualistic people seeking a new life in Lotus Land. Some of them have visions of starting new communities and revitalizing existing ones. When the recession hit

British Columbia in 1980, the deputy premier of the Social Credit government asked the editor of a business magazine for ideas on how to encourage people to think positively and pull together for the common good. The editor suggested "economic participation" and helped to create Team B.C. It promoted the gospel of self-reliance, encouraging self-help and stressing that people should no longer rely on the government to meet all their needs. Although it operated at arm's length from the government, Team B.C. soon came to be seen as an extension of it, selling its agenda under the cloak of public participation. Speeches, newsletters, workshops, upbeat messages on TV and radio—all the tools of business propaganda were used to make British Columbians feel good and optimistic about the future.

Team B.C. faded into history. Meanwhile the tensions between developers and conservationists escalated. In 1987, the provincial government set up a task force to determine how to handle these competing demands. How do you conserve what is of value while finding ways of stimulating the economy that do not destroy it? Conservation looks backward to a real or imagined past. Development looks forward to a better future. How can the interests and demands of the proponents of both be harmonized?

To implement the recommendations of the task force report, *Stewardship and Opportunity*,[199] the provincial government created Community Pride in 1988. Set up as an "arm's length" venture, it was headed by a woman with professional qualifications and a strong background in volunteer work. Unlike Team B.C., this agency, which operated through Heritage Trust, quickly established its role as a politically neutral enabling body. Community Pride served as a "virtual corporation" for four years. A small core staff in Victoria hired specialists and facilitators as and when needed, thus avoiding bureaucratization. Communities seeking to understand how to cope with change could ask for their services, which cost $3-4,000. Community Pride offered two workshops. The first—"Let's Get Organized"—brought together leaders from the three "pillars" of the community (municipal government, the volunteer sector and the business community) to brainstorm about heritage. What did the community want to keep? What did it wish to discard? A consensus and vision emerged. The next workshop dealt with the "how" of local development. "Let's Get Technical" looked at opportunities and limitations in communities. The first question that the facilitators asked was: "How do you eat an elephant?" The answer: "One bite at a time." As the co-ordinator put it: "We're friendly but not flippant, and we seek to convey warmth. The facilitators are not afraid to make fools of themselves."[200] Politicians and bureaucrats did not feel threatened by this approach to community development because they trusted the co-ordinator.

Government did not compel communities to participate in Community Pride, and those that did had to put their own money into it and so had a vested interest in making sure it worked and met their needs in balancing demands for conservation and development.

Some towns in British Columbia followed their own stars to cope with change, developing unique ways of doing community development. In 1980, Chemainus on Vancouver Island had forty businesses. Fifteen years later, they numbered 112. Tourists flock to the town to see its murals. Chemainus has become an "anti-Disneyland," a place of quality and uniqueness, not mass-produced culture. The dramatic change in the community came through the vision of one man with a good idea who came from away. Karl Schutz, born in Heidelberg, Germany arrived in Canada in 1951 and became a successful businessman.[201] Retiring in 1971, he travelled in Europe with his wife. In Moldavia, eastern Rumania, they saw frescoes of Biblical scenes and saints on the walls of ancient monasteries. Back home in Chemainus, Schutz suggested that paintings on the wooden walls of its buildings would attract tourists. The Chamber of Commerce rejected the idea. Then the mainstay of the community's economy began to falter. Between 1979 and 1981, the local mill lost $17.5 million, and it looked as if it would close and Chemainus become a ghost town. While local leaders looked for ways to diversify the economy, the provincial government provided funds to fix up the downtown. A new mayor picked up Schutz's idea of painting murals on the walls of buildings. Most residents were sceptical about this initiative. When the municipality allocated $10,000 for the first murals in 1982, townsfolk buttonholed the mayor on the street, asking him if he was crazy "spending all that taxpayer money on murals when it wouldn't make a pinch of difference."[202]

The town set up Heritage Square, opposite the train station, creating a park with sculptures and a fountain and a large mural depicting the faces of the Salish people whose language gave the town its name. A petition, signed by 120 residents, protested this waste of parking space. The council ignored it. An Indian artist who moved to the town felt uncomfortable every time he passed the mural. It showed the face of his great-grandmother. Other members of the family felt as he did, believing that their ancestors were watching them from *outside* the community. The artist asked the council to sponsor a ceremony to welcome them back to their land. About eight hundred Salish and whites attended the gathering. Dancing and speech-making, a special ritual and prayers, gift-giving by the Indians brought together the living and the dead, traditional peoples and newcomers. By 1995, Chemainus had thirty-two murals brightening up the community, attracting visitors from all over the world. And Karl Schutz had another vision—the Pacific Rim Artisan Village, a centre for learning.

Bad times can foster community cohesion and offer opportunities for inventiveness and initiative when doing more with less becomes a practical necessity rather than a theoretical concept.

But Chemainus would not have survived on the murals alone. Macmillan-Bloedel, which owned the town's mill, also had to re-invent itself. Closing the mill in 1983, the company re-opened it two years later with modern laser equipment that cuts wood to sizes used in the Japanese construction industry. With a smaller, more highly skilled labour force, the mill made a profit of $25 million in 1993. A combination of local creativity, political will and leadership and advanced technology has brought new life and new people to Chemainus.

Each community must find its own way towards revitalization through collective effort. There are plenty of ideas and examples of effective community development in Canada and throughout the world. But they cannot be copied without thought being given to how they fit a particular community at a particular time in its history.

Rossland, British Columbia, took an unusual route to revitalize itself and bring democracy to the people. Here again, an outsider,

André Carrel, born in Switzerland, played a leading role in stimulating public participation.[203] The council of "Canada's Alpine City," which has a population of 3,500, became increasingly concerned about local apathy. Its members set out some guidelines for local governance: In a democracy, people are never wrong; democratic decision making must be a pro-active process; limiting democratic powers leads to retribution from the electorate and retribution is a reactive process leading to negative results.

In August, 1990, Carrel, the community's administrator, drafted a position paper, "A Constitution for Local Government," and circulated it to council and residents. He also sought the advice of a political science professor about effective ways of enhancing local government. The paper suggested introducing a bylaw through which electors could call a referendum on any proposed local legislation. Such an action was permitted under the Municipal Act, but Victoria's response to Rossland's initiative was couched in ambiguous terms. While it "genuinely admires the spirit demonstrated through the enactment of this measure" the bureaucracy added:

> "The Ministry has serious long-term concerns over the capability of Council, under this regime, to adequately address fiscal, health, safety and other concerns that while limited in popularity, do from time to time require action in the public interest."[204]

Carrel had a vision that conflicted with this bureaucratic arrogance and paternalism: "A change in attitude and perception would have to come from where democracy resides—the people themselves." He stressed that the new bylaw, to be effective, would require patience, trust and goodwill as everyone gained confidence on how it operated.

> "When the legislative direction of a community is under the control of its own citizens, that community will truly reflect the character and quality of its citizens. A feeling of ownership and confidence takes hold, and City Hall is not the

bureaucratic enemy which cannot be beaten, City Hall becomes the tool which citizens use to develop their own goals."[205]

The new Constitution Bylaw, put to a vote, passed with an eighty per cent majority. Electors used it to turn down raises for councillors three times. But they approved a proposal to tax every property $100 to build a water filtration plant. Conservers and developers worked together to incorporate a nearby ski area into the boundaries of Rossland. The former saw this move as a way for the town to control land use in a watershed area. Business people saw opportunities for servicing the ski resort. A well organized citizen's group opposed the boundary extension. But the referendum approved it, and the voter roll expanded by fifteen per cent as many people who had never before bothered to vote became involved in the issue. Direct democracy halted protests about a proposal to log a city-owned parcel of land selectively. Opponents blocked access to the forest. An injunction stopped this. The town council appointed a citizens' committee to look at the costs and benefits of the logging project. It approved it. The conservationists launched a petition under the Constitution by-law to halt the logging and turn the forest into a park. They failed to secure the support of twenty per cent of the registered voters to hold a referendum, and so the protest died. Whatever the outcome of the logging venture, the community of Rossland will have to live with the consequences of the action its residents approved.

Rossland had a number of characteristics that fostered innovation. The first local labour union in the province was formed here in 1895 in response to miserable working conditions imposed by mine owners. An enterprising Rosslander built a steam-powered helicopter, the Flying Steamshovel. But the town also had considerable liabilities—a poor property tax base (ninety-five per cent residential), aging infrastructure, and high operating costs because of its alpine setting. It also had an enlightened and visionary administrator, a provincial act permitting referenda, and a local newspaper editor who covered the issue of direct democracy in an articulate and responsible manner.

The Rossland administrator notes how changes in language have reflected the success of this community initiative: "There is a modest but perceptible change in the way in which Rossland voters describe their municipal politicians. The expletives are being deleted!"

International megaprojects and large-scale development ventures have damaged the environment, displaced local people, buttressed the control of the powerful, created huge bureaucracies and promoted the concept of "doing well by doing good." The rhetoric about foreign aid is now rich in talk of decentralization, local decision making, enhancing grassroots democracy, helping people to help themselves. As in Canada, it is as if the international decision makers are saying: We've made a mess of things. Now you, the local people, should set about solving your own problems with your own resources. Unfortunately, we don't have any money to help you to do this. Throughout the world people at the grassroots level are tackling their own problems effectively, with the help of outsiders.

One of the most successful ventures in community development began in Bangladesh, described by Henry Kissinger as a "basket case," and has been imported into Canada. Muhammad Yunnus, an economics professor, theorized that if the poor had money in small amounts they could generate income for themselves. Putting some of his own capital where his ideas were, Yunnus lent $30 to forty-two impoverished artisans who made good use of it to improve their work and their lives. In 1983, Yunnus founded the Grameen ("rural," "countryside," "village") Bank.[206] He recognized that although village people might be poor in cash, some were rich in "social" capital— their reputation for keeping their commitments and repaying loans.

Grameen Bank helps people to form peer group lending circles. One member receives a loan, and until it is repaid no one else is eligible. The bank lends to the poorest of the poor, and the default rate is extremely small. One account compares Grameen Bank to a flock of doel birds sitting on a telephone wire in Rangpur District in India. With their beautiful curved tails, the birds form a sheet of music in the sky. When you photograph it, the snap of the shutter sends them into the air. Then they settle back again, making a different configuration on the wires.[207]

The peer group lending system pioneered by Grameen Bank has been brought to Canada by the Calmeadow Foundation, and is in operation on Indian Reserves and other parts of Canada.

It is possible to analyze community development ventures in rational ways, to identify the forces and factors that make them successful—or fail. But essentially, community development harbours a mystery rooted in the capacity of human beings to be generous or mean, democratic or autocratic, compassionate or cruel, depending on the external dynamics of their world and their internalized ideals, needs, imperatives. Difficult times can make individuals and communities fight like caribou and kill each other, or circle their beings and see anyone coming from outside as a threat or an enemy. But they also offer opportunities for individuals and groups to seek out the Lichen Factor and develop mutually beneficial relationships between what is inside their boundaries and what lies beyond it. To paraphrase Tolstoy, every happy community has the capacity to identify and make use of the Lichen Factor in the same way, while every unhappy community is unhappy in its own way because of the inability of its residents to do so.

In their book, *Is Sex Necessary?* James Thurber and E.B. White complained that the experts had sex on the ground and were breaking its arm. The same thing is happening to community development which has spawned an enormous literature and a band of experts. In truth, much of the writing in this field is dull and repetitive, not so much describing efforts to reinvent the wheel as telling of efforts to reinvent the *broken* wheel.

The arts offer more clues to how community development really works than most of the academic literature. The Sherlock Holmes stories of Conan Doyle tell people to look for clues to what is really happening in the world in unlikely places. *Silver Blaze* revolves around the question of the dog that did not bark. And why did it not do so? Because it knew the man stealing the racehorse.

At the door of the law, a story by Franz Kafka, catches the feeling that pervades communities as they confront change and uncertainty.[208] A countryman arrives at the door of the law, seeking admission. A fierce looking doorman bars the way. The villager peers through the open door, believing that a new life and a new world for him lies beyond it. The gatekeeper challenges him to pass through the door, warning him: "I am powerful. And I am only the lowest-ranking doorkeeper." The ones beyond him are much more fearsome. The man feels peeved. He believes that the door of the law should be open and accessible to everyone. But he decides that sitting outside the door is safer and more secure than trying to tackle the dangers and difficulties inside the law. Years go by as he awaits permission to enter. He bribes the gatekeepers, even pleads with the fleas on his collar for entry. Finally, old, stiff, deaf and nearly blind, he has a sudden insight: "Everybody seeks the law, so how is it that in all these years no one but me has demanded admittance?" The gate-keeper replies: "No one else could gain admittance because this entrance was meant for you alone. Now I'm going to close it."

There is no mystery about where the doors of change lie.

They lie in the liminal territory between these two states: [209]

Responding to crises	Anticipating crises
Reacting to change	Being proactive
Taking specific measures	Taking comprehensive measures
Requiring consent	Requiring participation
Damping conflict	Confronting conflict
Detailed central control	Generalized central control
Small local government units	Enlarged local government units
Standardized administration	Innovative administration
Separate services	Co-ordinated services
Short planning horizons	Long planning horizons.

While Yeats' words about things falling apart have become a common lament these days, little attention has been paid to his extraordinary and hopeful book *A Vision*, published in 1925. Written with the help of automatic writing by his wife, it contains a diagram of two horizontal cones intersecting each other, rather like an hourglass on its side. One cone, labelled "Concord" forms part of another one, "Discord" and *vice versa*. As one increases its spiral gyre—a word favoured by Yeats to describe circular, upward motion—the other decreases. These movements reflect life, with both occurring at the same time as individuals and communities spiral down into despair and hopelessness while others move upwards with feelings of hope and confidence. Yeats quotes Heraclitus: "Dying each other's life, living each other's death."

The main task in community development involves balancing Concord and Discord and encouraging the upward spiral that helps people to do more with fewer resources while building confidence and capability in gaining control over their own individual and collective lives.

Two Canadian examples, one powered by technology, the other by spirituality, demonstrate the pitfalls and potential of efforts to create community. One became an expensive disaster, the other has spread all over the world.

TALE
OF TWO ARKS

"Intervention that is defensible on ethical grounds
must always be paradoxical. One acts for others
only to the point of initiating a symbolic gesture of
genuine respect and concern. This is the first
overture. There is further action if, and only if, the
other responds positively. The response is much
more than consent as we usually think of consent.
After this accepting response, a spiral of action,
reaction and interaction can result between the two.
In the final act of love, who is to say
who is the helper and who the helped?
Then the notion of help is finally irrelevant."
—Alex Sim, pioneer Canadian adult educator.[210]

SALVATION BY TECHNOLOGY

"Whether these [houses] become arks of the
covenant with nature or arks of survival will depend
on us, for [they] express the political ambiguities of
our transitional age. On the one hand, they are
strategies for decentralization,
enabling families to live with high culture in
wilderness circumstances; on the other hand they
are the miniaturization ecosystems
NASA needs for the design of space colonies."
—J. Todd and W.J. Todd,
Tomorrow is Our Permanent Address (1980)

The symbol of the ark as a refuge in troubled times has a strong hold on the imaginations of those seeking safety in a sea of trouble and turmoil.

In 1969, Dr. John Todd, a colourful, articulate, self-promoting Canadian set up the New Alchemy Institute at Woods Hole, Massachusetts to "explore scientific strategies and provide a rational model for bringing necessary change in an acceptable manner." In 1973, the price of oil quadrupled. The federal government sought frantically for ways of decreasing reliance on imported fuel and encouraging self-reliance. Todd sold the idea of building a self-contained community as an answer to the energy crisis. He claimed that his ark,

"...will be a complete integrated life sustaining system for a family unit, in that it will provide food, shelter, and energy systems without external sources, and can be described as a family-sized food, energy and housing complex, including integrated solar, windmill, greenhouse, fish culture and living components."[211]

Ottawa bought the idea and looked for a place to launch it. This wonderful idea of Todd's would conserve energy as oil prices accelerated—and also preserve Canada's endangered environment.

In 1975, the government of Prince Edward Island proposed buying electricity from the Point Lepreau nuclear power plant in New Brunswick. Public protest killed the idea; electricity from this source was obviously dangerous and unclean. Todd's ark would generate power from a windmill and pump any surplus into the Island grid; energy would be derived from a clean, natural source if the project was located on Canada's smallest province with its rural, Edenic lifestyle and landscape. Many people on the Island have lived frugal, self-sustaining lives for years. But their ideas and involvement in the new technology were not sought.

The federal government put up $808,000 to design and build the ark, and the province donated fifty-seven hectares of land worth $128,000 for the site. The federal Department of the Environment issued a glossy, promotional publication which defined the venture as "a structure that provides protection and safety, such as Noah's boat" symbolising "a search for alternative ways of living on earth." It invoked apocalyptic visions of the future: "...without immediate, profound and remedial change on the global scale, our present civilization is unsustainable and the future of mankind is bleak." [212]

Todd assembled a team of experts in agriculture, engineering, fisheries, architecture, computers, philosophy and pest control. While it looked like a diverse group, the individuals shared some common values—belief in technology as salvation, middle-class concern with purity and perfection, and the tradition of transcendentalism and rationalism of Ralph Waldo Emerson and his followers.

Prime Minister Trudeau opened the Ark, together with Premier Campbell, on 21 September, 1976. It began operation in the following February. When Trudeau learned what the Ark had cost, he snorted that he too could be self-reliant, given this amount of money.

The people of the Island watched the ark arise and wondered. The building became a closed community. The residents did everything possible to deter visitors—but they welcomed the media. Its members hyped the project with articles titled "Space Age

Ark—Brave New World" and "This family is ready for the End of the World."

Then, slowly but surely, the Ark began to sink. Some of the technology, including the windmill, the solar heating system, and the chemical toilet, did not work. In 1978, the New Alchemy Institute abandoned ship, handing the Ark over to the provincial Institute of Man and Resources. Treasury Board in Ottawa refused further funding until the venture was evaluated. Islanders had already dismissed the Ark as a make-work scheme for Americans. A group of evaluators determined that the project had lacked effective management in its early stages. And it had produced nothing of scientific value or anything that could be useful to local people.[213] Environment Canada's Public Affairs Adviser stated:

"Taken literally from the public's point of view, the Ark demonstrated that a very large family could be partially self-sufficient if they could, first, afford a very large capital cost, and second, were of independent means such that they didn't have to hold down outside jobs."[214]

One evaluator pointed out that no family could hope to possess all the skills required to run the place. This concern emerges again and again in stories about intentional communities or attempts to revitalize existing ones. Appropriate technology and skills in human relations have to be blended to ensure sustainability and harmony.

A United Nations specialist asked about the needs the Ark was planned to meet:

"...for whom is the ark intended? For a homesteading nuclear family? For a co-operative of like-minded families? For a young people's commune? As a commercial greenhouse-cum-aquaculture operation? As a vision of the future?"[215]

He pointed out that the symbiosis between aquaculture and agriculture touted by the New Alchemy Institute as an innovation, was "borrowed from Asian countries where it has been practised for centuries."

195

The evaluation shook loose more federal funding. But none of the staff wanted to live in the Ark. Guides showed visitors around the structure, and the idea of self-sufficiency vanished. In 1979, a Conservative government took power on the Island, closing the Ark on 1 June, 1981. Soon the "brave new world" stood rusting and stained, its windmill bent and broken, the greenhouse roof gone, weeds running rampant in the experimental garden plot. In March, 1982, the provincial government advertised publicly for proposals for the ruin. A local non-profit co-operative turned it into an inn, restaurant and tourist attraction, at a cost of $525,000.[216]

In the Nineties, a wealthy American tried to replicate this folly on a larger scale. In 1991, Edward Bass gave a group $150 million to build a "biosphere" near Tucson, Arizona. In April, 1994, he ejected the project's top management over allegations of financial and scientific malfeasance. In November, 1996, a news item reported that Biosphere 2, an attempt to create a self-sustaining Garden of Eden in a greenhouse had been placed on hold. As oxygen became locked up its concrete walls, many plants and animals fared poorly or died. Cockroaches and a species of ant flourished, but the scientists could not understand the reason for this.[217]

The New Alchemists bounced back from the Ark disaster, doubtless referring to it as a "learning experience," and continued to promote their magic as a way to salvation. In the spring of 1995, the small community of Bear River in Nova Scotia opened Canada's first Solar Aquatics Wastewater Treatment Facility embodying some of New Alchemy's designs. Bear River, known as the Switzerland of the province, is home to a curious collection of old-timers, in-comers and New Agers, many of them from the United States. Tensions arose between the newcomers who quickly learned how to apply for government grants for community projects, and the original residents who believed that self-help should be encouraged. The community, badly hit by the closing of the nearby Canadian Forces Base at Cornwallis, came together to search for new ideas to meet its needs. A community member came up with the idea of the treatment plant and gained the support of other residents. It uses sewage to feed the biological community in greenhouse. Only a few houses have been connected to the plant, which can handle 150 to 200 homes, but the venture has become a tourist attraction.

Bear River people are not relying on it as the sole solution to their problems. When the Royal Bank closed its branch, the local doctor retired, and the drugstore and other businesses closed, a life long resident lamented: "Bear River was getting to be a lost soul." At a community meeting, residents decided to acquire the bank building and turn it into a health clinic. The bank donated the building, the community raised $30,000 and visiting doctors treat hundreds of patients. And no government money was involved. A United Church minister revived the dormant historical society which opened a museum in 1994, and efforts are being made to recreate an old-fashioned hunting camp. The old elementary school has been converted into a centre for music, arts and crafts, with a craft co-operative based there.[218]

The creation and growth of Jean Vanier's Ark followed a very different path from that of technological wonder that John Todd conjured up to meet the energy and the environmental crises.

AN ARK FOR THE POOR

> "People can only put down roots in a community
> when that meets their deep and secret desire and
> their choice is free—because putting down roots,
> like any commitment implies a certain death.
> We can only welcome this death if there is a call of
> a new life which yearns to grow."
> Jean Vanier, *Community and Growth* (1979)

Community and personal identity are intertwined. Since the exuberant Sixties, the rising middle class, adrift in a troubled world, have sought redemption and salvation inwards and outwards. Personal empowerment, New Age philosophies and theologies, vision questing, running with wolves and other techniques focus on making people whole through individual spiritual renewal. Make the self whole and the world can then be seen as benign and no longer threatening. Others strive to correct the evils of the world—racism, poverty, pollution. In doing so, they make contact with like-minded folk and develop a sense of community—and self righteousness. At a certain stage on these inward and outward quests a moment of truth occurs as the immensity of the problems becomes apparent. After all, what does finding the inner child really mean when some errant gene, over which you have no control, triggers a serious illness? And how feeble individual and collective efforts by activist groups appear when confronted with the situations in the former Yugoslavia, Rwanda and Burma-Myanmar.

As Jean Vanier points out, creating community involves a form of religious conversion, from old sinful ways to new ones. The literature on the Prince Edward Island Ark was rich in rhetoric about six paths to wholeness—"harmonization, symbolization, agriculturalization, civilization, and planetization." In contrast, Vanier writes simply and mystically, embracing brokenness in humans as the point of departure for his concept of community.

In 1963, he went to Trosly-Breuil, ninety kilometres north of Paris, to help to paint a chapel in an institution for mentally handicapped men. When he visited the psychiatric wards, Vanier realized that the place had become a warehouse for the rejected. Inspired by the work and ideas of Father Thomas Philippe, a chaplain at Val Fleuri, an institution in Trosly, Vanier returned there in 1964. He had no great visions about changing the world—"that's not my way." In an asylum to the south of Paris, Vanier was struck by the "screams and atmosphere of sadness, but also by the mysterious presence of God." He met Raphaël Simi and Phillipe Seux who had been placed in the institution by their parents. Buying a run down house in Trosly, Vanier invited the two men to live with him. Aided by an architect and with money from family and friends, he founded the first L'Arche. An existing charitable organization took care of this new venture's administrative matters, with Vanier as its chair.

Jean Vanier had a clear and simple goal for his ark—"to found a family, a community with and for those who are weak and poor because of a mental handicap and also feel alone and abandoned." He saw his venture as a way of saving lost and shipwrecked people drowning in the deluges of civilization. The name came naturally.

At first, its founder saw himself as a generous benefactor sharing his home with two outcasts. Then his view of himself began to change. He slowly recognized that he needed the two men as much as they needed him. That sense of symbiosis and mutuality apparent in the lichen began to flourish, as Vanier saw himself as poor, weak and flawed. Rather than externalizing sin as so many communities do as they seek to make their places and people perfect, Vanier accepted the evil in the world and learned to deal with it. Gabriel, a tramp, came to live in the house at Trosly. When he began to harass Raphaël, Vanier sent him on his way.

As other L'Arche communities came into being, Vanier's philosophy provided a firm foundation for their operations:

"Being in L'Arche does not mean following an ideal or practising a certain philosophy. Being in L'Arche means being a part of a history that already exists; it means belonging to a people."[220]

Jean Vanier's books, grounded in the realities of community life, offer an excellent guide to anyone seeking to create a collective endeavour. He recognizes the value of despised and rejected people wandering in liminal space, unable to find a place in society. Vanier's work embodies the Lichen Factor. He sees qualities of spontaneity, wonder and openness in those we label "mentally handicapped." To Vanier they embody the values of the heart, without which action, power and all the other aspects of daily life lose their meaning.

Vanier has learned how to deal with people who see community as a retreat or a form of therapy. He advises interested people to live in one of the arks for a while before committing themselves to this way of life. As the director of L'Arche Homefires in Wolfville, Nova Scotia, put it:

"People who are profoundly handicapped sense the difference between someone who's involved because they want to be and someone who's paid to be there in a professional capacity."[221]

Vanier does not reject the advice of experts and professionals. He simply cautions that they should be on tap, not on top. As the son of a much-loved Governor General and his wife, Vanier served in the military and taught at universities. But he turned his back on power and prestige to work with the outcasts of society. Vanier has outlined the potential and limitations of living in community that make sense of the concept.

Paradoxically, the cultivation of community and collectiveness also involves the encouragement of diversity. Rollo May notes in *Power and Innocence*:

"I need my enemy in my community. He keeps me alert, vital...But beyond what we specifically learn from our enemies, we need them emotionally; our psychic economy cannot get along well without them...Our enemy is as necessary for us as our friend. Both together are part of authentic community."[222]

Community, far from being an escape from an oppressive world or a handy technology for overcoming problems of the poor, forces you to confront your being—and those of others—at the deepest levels. In our time, as throughout history, much of life consists of simply managing tensions, not avoiding or resolving them. From time to time, problems have to be quickly solved. If the human dynamics work well, this process can proceed smoothly and effectively. Or it can end in distrust and rancour. Jean Vanier recognized the problem of communities taking the musk-oxen stance:

"Communities need a sympathetic outsider who encourages them, takes the heat out of things, listens and asks questions. Members of a community are often so taken up in the immediate that they lose sight of the whole...This outsider or 'sponge' who absorbs the anguish must help communities to evaluate themselves."[223]

By an outsider, Vanier does not mean an expert, but "someone with common sense, and an understanding of people and human relationships who loves the community's fundamental goals."[224]

And he also writes of the way in which true community differs from communities of interest that operate as closed systems, its members believing themselves immune to criticism, as they cling to an ideology of exclusiveness.

"The other enemy of community can be human friendship and sympathy. It brings destruction if it means the grouping together of people of the same background and aspirations, to close themselves off from other members of the community. It brings destruction if it does not open the groups to all members of the community."[225]

Jean Vanier had no great vision, no belief that his ark would save the world. Since 1964, the initial venture in Trosly-Breuil has become "planetized" with one hundred similar centres in twenty-five countries.

Most of the L'Arche communities are small, housing ten to twelve handicapped people and "assistants." As Trosly, which now has several hundred people living in houses and apartments, became host to more and more social rejects, local residents became alarmed at their presence. Vanier learned the importance of local support for his arks. He saw Noah's boat as "the first covenant between God and Humanity." This concept of covenants, a mystical, spiritual relationship between people lies, at the root of L'Arche and of all successful community ventures.

Since the late Sixties, L'Arche communities have sprung up all over the world: Daybreak, in Richmond Hill, Ontario (1969); Asha Niketan, Bangalore, India (1970); Little Ewell, England (1974). In 1972 their founders met and worked on a charter. This process continues, with special attention to spiritual renewal sessions to sustain community development. Some communities centre on the handicapped, with government support and reliance on professionals and influential boards of governors. In others, assistants live with and like the poor, refusing state aid, welcoming all marginal peoples as well as the mentally handicapped.

The L'Arche communities have been called "The University of the Poor." For some who come to serve in them, living in community forms part of their pilgrimage through life. For others, it's a lifetime commitment. Some communities have closed. Vanier freely admits that his biggest challenge lies in finding people willing to commit themselves to life in a L'Arche community on a permanent basis.

Life in L'Arche can be very strenuous. Vanier writes about touching "the powers of darkness hidden within my heart" and feeling "more deeply my own poverty." Communities can be too well organized, too structured. Vanier notes that, "After sixteen years of responsibility in the community and on the international levels I had to let go of my desires for efficiency and learn to 'waste time' in simple, loving relationships." His venture began spontaneously, with compassion and concern, as a form of anti-structure, the polar opposite of acquisitive, competitive, organized structures.

Just how difficult life in L'Arche can be emerges from the story of a brain-damaged woman, abandoned by her parents. She lived for eighteen years in institutions before coming to L'Arche Daybreak. Here she crouched under a blanket, refused to dress and spat out any food: "It was almost as if she wanted to die."[226] After three years in an environment of loving kindness, Rose came back to life again and began to enjoy it.

In 1972, fifteen years after hearing about L'Arche, Debbie and Jeff Moore, two health professionals, created one in Nova Scotia. They had found themselves increasingly at odds with their peers, who saw their task as making the mentally handicapped "more like us" through "normalization." In 1979, the couple shocked family and professionals by welcoming a mute, handicapped young man into their family at Easter:

> "Having Keith live with us did not impress us as being a big deal although it did change our lives...We were...confronted with our own hypocrisy. We had our theories of normalization down to a tee; but to be confronted with 101 daily decisions for this young man! Keith had a lot of strengths but he had a lot of limitations as well. He needed a lot of respect and patience and sometimes our impatience and weakness showed in our relating to him...It was a struggle."

But the Moores went on to found a L'Arche community with local support.

The spirit embodied in L'Arche has spread throughout the world. A lawyer in a village in North Wales recalled that when he learned that his two and a half year old son was "subnormal," he was certain he would never smile again. At a conference in Dublin in 1971, he heard a speaker echo Jean Vanier's ideas: "We need these people amongst us to desophisticate, and de-intellectualize the rest of us—

and we may find in the final analysis that we need them more than they need us."

Pressure from interest groups forced the Secretary of State for Wales to develop a Strategy for the Development of Services for the Mentally Handicapped in 1983. It contained incentives for volunteer groups to try new approaches to dealing with them. This challenge revealed one of the problems of pressure group behaviour. Few of the advocates of a better way of treating the mentally handicapped came up with ideas for doing so: Nothing is impossible for the person who does not have to do it.

The lawyer from North Wales recognized that people who did not have mentally handicapped children or family members should be involved in integrating them into the community. He found a man who had worked in mental institutions and knew their limitations to head a new initiative. The village created Antur ("venture" or "adventure") Waunfawr.[228] Two hundred residents of Waunfawr became "shareholders," with limited personal liability, and the process of welcoming mentally handicapped individuals into the village began. Focusing on creating meaningful employment for them, the venture built stone walls, renovated old cottages, cut firewood, did landscaping, planted trees, started a garden centre, reopened the village store. Those once placed in institutions and rejected by mainstream society found their place in it again, doing useful work in a small community.

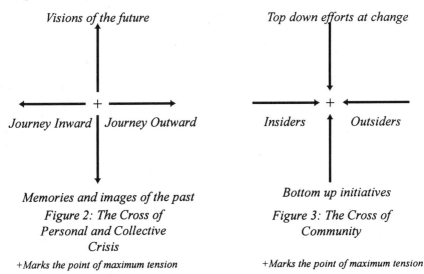

Visions of the future

Journey Inward | *Journey Outward*

Memories and images of the past

Figure 2: The Cross of Personal and Collective Crisis

+*Marks the point of maximum tension*

Top down efforts at change

Insiders | *Outsiders*

Bottom up initiatives

Figure 3: The Cross of Community

+*Marks the point of maximum tension*

205

Figures 2 and 3 show the dynamics of community, which lies at the centre of the cross, the point of maximum tension. The cross is not simply a Christian symbol. "Iceman," the lost traveller found in the Alps who died 4,400 years ago, had crosses tattooed on his knees. Early Christian representations of the cross show it with equilateral arms. The present one, which shows Christ nailed to the crossbar at the top, symbolizes his movement towards the father. The Romans reserved death on the cross for rebels and criminals who disturbed their orderly world. To Christians it has become a symbol of sacrifice and salvation, a reality and an image that touches them at their deepest levels, frightening and reassuring them about the present life—and their prospects in eternity.

As symbol and historical reality, the cross helps in understanding the sacred nature of community as a meeting point, a place in space and time where tensions can be confronted and resolved.

COMMUNITY REALITIES

"For every evil under the sun
There is a remedy or there is none.
If there be one, try to find it.
If there be none, never mind it."

Old Nursery Rhyme

THE SLUMBERING POTENTIAL

> "Everyone who has ever built anywhere
> a 'new heaven' first found the power
> thereto in his own hell."
>
> —Nietzsche

In the summer of 1997, Jean Vanier received the Vatican's Paul VI International Prize. He planned to use the $168,000 award to expand L'Arche into Eastern Europe. The fall of communism has plunged many people there into a liminal state, lost between the old rituals and ceremonies of a centralized, collectivized way of living and demands for the competitive individualism of capitalism. Under communism, everyone had a job—and identity—but not everyone had work. A Canadian academic visiting Russia recalled seeing a man in a booth in the Moscow subway, doing nothing, utterly idle, utterly bored.[229]

The change from communism to capitalism, described in Poland as "exchanging two dead cats for a dead dog", has been welcomed there by the Catholic Church. A Polish priest presided at the opening of a Coca-Cola plant, praising it as a symbol of capitalism and a new life.[230]

But serious doubts are being expressed about capitalism as the saviour of the economies of the former Soviet empire. George Soros, a financier, expressed his concerns in an article in the *Atlantic* of February, 1997. The sanest voice that has emerged from the rubble of collapsed communism is that of Václav Havel, a former outsider who became president of the Czech Republic. Cautioning against the lure of utopian theorists, he has presented a vision for his country with echoes of community development. It would be a pluralistic society with many small enterprises and a central government sensitive to, and knowledgeable about, what contributes to the common good—and what limits and destroys it.

Havel has publicly expressed his dismay at the way in which the worst excesses of capitalism have come to his country. Here many people live in limbo, lost between the security of a state run economy and society and the uncertainty that has come with the free market. Havel identifies "Our own main enemy today" as "our indifference to the common good; vanity; personal ambition, selfishness and rivalry."[231]

The opponents of communism in Czechoslovakia had a strong concern for the moral basis of society, an altruistic desire for the common good and the enduring human values on which it relies.

Jan Patocka, the first spokesman for Charter 77, the dissident group to which Havel belonged, died after eight hours in police custody. This philosopher cut to the heart of what community development is all about when he wrote:

"No society, no matter how good its technological foundations, can function without a moral foundation, without conviction that has nothing to do with opportunism, circumstances, and expected advantage. Morality...does not just allow society to function, it simply allows human beings to be human. Man does not define morality according to the caprice of his needs, wishes, tendencies, and cravings: it is morality that defines man."[232]

During the Eighties—the Greed Decade—the widespread abuse of power and privilege generated concern about ethics in the centres of power and among ordinary people. Business schools established courses on ethics. Politicians, aware of the widening gap between their promises and their performance, suddenly became interested in spiritual matters. In July, 1997, Premier Glen Clark of British Columbia held meetings with religious leaders to seek advice. Like many other politicians and civil servants, Clark had a sudden revelation as the British Columbia economy turned sour. He realized that governments make ethical and moral choices all the time. And that such choices involve spiritual values.

In the international field, the belief that the intended recipients of aid programmes have become victims of them has become stronger in recent years. In 1993 Canada's International Development Research Centre commissioned a study by Father William Ryan, a Jesuit with a doctorate in economics, into the links between culture, spirituality and development.[233] In his foreword to Ryan's report, Pierre Beemans, Vice-President of the Corporate Services at the Centre wrote:

"...mainstream development discourse [focuses] on the economic, social and political conditions that need to be changed, and [tries] to ascribe quantifiable indicators for the changes...This has led most of the conventional Western discourse to ignore or dismiss the cultural, moral, and spiritual dimensions of human well-being as either irrelevant to development or so intractably subjective as to be unamenable to a 'practical paradigm.'"[234]

Beemans adds that when societies and development theories and agencies ignore or undermine what he called "ontological needs"— the love of other, commitment, responsibility to family, clan, community, self-worth, roles and relationships, the sense of the sacred, relationships with nature, etc—the results are usually disastrous:

"When these needs are not met, societies, like individuals, can lose their inner bearings, and their sense of identity. Like individuals, some societies may rise above the resulting existential and social crises and wind up stronger and more creative communities...they may also lapse into behaviour patterns of aggression, stagnation and alienation...In Canada we have experienced the pernicious outcomes of development programs manufactured by government agencies for native peoples and impoverished residents of inner cities."[235]

Community development, so often seen by governments as a handy way to keep local people busy with trivial matters, requires a supportive public policy atmosphere in which to flourish, as Havel points out:

> "I have been persuaded time and time again that a huge potential of good will is slumbering within our society. It's just that it's incoherent, suppressed, confused, crippled, and perplexed—as though it does not know what to rely on, where or how to find meaningful outlets.
> In such a state of affairs, politicians have a duty to awaken this slumbering potential, to offer it direction, and ease its passage, to encourage and give it room, or simply hope. It is largely up to the politicians which social forces they choose to liberate and which they choose to suppress, whether they rely on the good in each citizen or the bad."[236]

This unprofessional politician notes:

> "A modern democratic state cannot consist merely of civil service, political parties, and private enterprises. It must offer citizens a colorful array of ways to become involved, both privately and publicly, and must develop very different types of civic coexistence, solidarity and participation."[237]

New social challenges spawn new languages.

The term "civil society" has slipped into the lexicon of local development to describe the sort of modern democratic state that Havel envisages.

One American scholar defines it as:

> "...the realm of organized social life that is voluntary, self-generating, (largely) self-supporting, autonomous from the state, and bound by a legal order or set of shared rules. It is distinct from society in general in that it involves citizens acting collectively in a public sphere to express their interests, passions, and ideas, exchange information, achieve mutual goals, make demands on the state, and hold state officials accountable."[238]

This American definition has limited applicability in Canada, although the essence of what mediating structures can do is relevant to life here. Most voluntary and interest groups in Canada are not "(largely) self-supporting, autonomous from the state." They rely heavily on government for funds, and this adds another dimension to civil society, especially in a time of government cutbacks and reduced commitments to social issues.

At one level, the concept of civil society focuses on good manners and respect for others. As Geothe put it: "There is no outward mark of courtesy that does not have a deep moral basis." In 1996, an anonymous New England family donated $35 million to establish The Institute for Civil Society. Pam Solo, its president, stated: "Civil society is more than civility and good manners. It is about rebuilding the very fabric of society."

Thus its focus is very much on what community development workers have been trying to do for a long time out of concern, compassion and a belief in democracy.

The interest in civil society, however, may be just another way of trying to do the right thing for the wrong reasons. It appears to reflect a feeling that society is breaking down, that things are not as they should be, that we tremble on the brink of chaos, disaster and disorder unless we change the way we think and behave. Unfortunately, the experts, analysts, policy wonks and symbol manipulators have already taken over the field of civil society and are submerging it in words. They are a trifle hazy about its reality. Inevitably, their conferences are dominated by linear thinkers, and shut out the voices of those from the grassroots.

Community development is civil society in action.

And we know a great deal about how to do it and how to restructure relationships to make ventures more open, democratic and accountable in the cause of creating better communities.

Throughout the world, communities—sometimes with political support, often against political opposition—have pioneered ways of making better lives for those who live in them. In times of rapid change, there's a tendency to neglect what remains stable and enduring as the pursuit of the new accelerates. But certain themes and concepts can be identified that underlie effective community development—if the essential mystery of the process is accepted. A few diagrams help to clarify what community development offers to those seeking stability and the capacity to handle change in creative ways.

THE BELL CURVE OF COMMUNITY

> "All excellent things are
> as difficult as they are rare."
> —Spinoza.

The residents of Judique on the west coast of Cape Breton once had a reputation for community spirit. The appearance of their dancers at any event gave rise to the cry: "Judique on the floor!" as they demonstrated their prowess.

In the Nineties the community was at war with itself. The Judique-on-the-Floor Historical and Cultural Society lobbied to preserve the old parish hall. St. Anselm's Parish Council and the Antigonish Diocese wanted to demolish it. The hall, built in 1929 with volunteer labour and donated materials, housed the collective memories of weddings, school graduations, bingos, the meeting and mingling of residents in warmth and community. Its construction embodied the old values of self-help, mutual aid and thrift. The new centre, which received a $956,712 government grant, had a debt of $400,000 on it. The preservationists wanted to turn the old hall into a tea room and a performance space for Celtic music. Many other residents sought the fullest use of the new building to pay off the debt. The historical society went to court in its efforts to save the building. In February, 1996, a judge of the Superior Court of Nova Scotia ruled that the decision about its future lay with the diocese and the community. Eventually the old hall was demolished.

The squabble over the old and the new in this village of one thousand reflects the tensions in all communities as its members seek to deal with change. Every nation, every province, every region, every collectivity includes those who seek to preserve the *status quo*, others who try to take everyone back to the past, and individuals and groups with their own particular (and peculiar) vision of the future.

Every community has geniuses and idiots with wonderful ideas on what it needs. Only too often, by the time you determine which is which, it's too late to stop some disastrous scheme. Even the smallest community has a complex network of relationships through which stability is maintained and innovation accepted or rejected. George Foster, an American anthropologist, developed his Theory of Limited Good after examining some stagnant communities in Italy.[239] Here the residents believed that resources were fixed and immutable. Those seen to have more goods, money, power or influence than anyone else must be taking more than their fair share. "Greedy" people were punished or ostracized. Appropriate technology can make the supply of goods, services and benefits larger. If properly introduced it can make the community cake larger and give everyone more resources. Sometimes local resources have to be rediscovered and at others there is a need to introduce new ideas and establish new linkages with the outside.

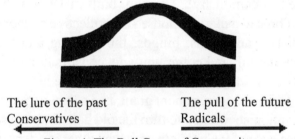

The lure of the past
Conservatives

The pull of the future
Radicals

Figure 4: The Bell Curve of Community

All communities have a bell curve of values and sentiments (Figure 4). Each contains "conservatives" who seek to pull residents into the past. Communities also harbour "radicals" at the other end of the bell curve who see themselves leading residents into the future. In Halifax, a mass of people opposing a government measure met another group supporting it in front of the provincial legislature, effectively cancelling each other out in the eyes of politicians.

One of the problems of political liberalism in our age of extremes revolves around the inability of its proponents to find the middle way, the golden mean between extremes. In Canada, Liberal parties struggle to deal with the conservatives in their ranks seeking to return to the good old days of patronage and privilege and those striving to create a more open and accessible society. Liberalism died in Britain when its leaders could not balance these competing demands. The cover of George Dangerfield's *The Strange Death of Liberal England* shows Liberal Prime Minister Asquith "Torn in Two." A red-shirted worker pulls him towards "Socialism" while a top-hatted capitalist drags him towards "Rich Radicalism." Asquith laments: "I wish I'd never had anything to do with either of them."[240]

Bell curves comes in a wide variety of forms. Some have long tails with few conservatives and radicals at either end. Others have more abrupt upward and downward curves at each end, with the middle squeezed between them. But most people in most communities live in the middle of the bell curve, seeking only a quiet life, desiring neither for a return to an imagined, better past nor a sudden leap into the future. The past is a nice place to visit, but few people in Canada would really like to live there. Most Canadians devote most of their time to trivial rounds and common tasks. Meals have to be bought and prepared, kids seen off to school, the car taken into the garage, the cat fed, the dog walked. The necessities of life demand a great deal of time. And family and friends visit, favourite TV programmes must be watched, sports events attended and analyzed.

Communities can be roused to fury and action by incursions that threaten them. But it takes a great deal of time, energy, enthusiasm and expertise to come up with constructive alternatives to threats and challenges—or to oppose them successfully. When Jack Granatstein set out to save his Toronto street, he soon discovered that the prevailing sentiment was: "Let Jack do it." The street housed eighty-five families. Only ten of them, about forty individuals, showed any interest or concern about the development he opposed. Granatstein found himself spending twenty hours a week, and his own money, protecting his community. And he alarmed his neighbours with suggestions about direct action. A lawyer helped him to defeat the development.

In co-housing projects, extremists at both ends of the bell curve—those favouring a highly individualistic lifestyle and those who tend to be *too* collectively minded—tend to leave. Those in the middle, who can balance the tensions between the two, usually stay in these intentional communities.

Understanding community development is made more difficult by the way that the media reflect society. The media don't mediate. They polarize people, concentrating on activities at the extreme ends of the bell curve of community. That's where the "news" is. There would be little point in the media describing the everyday activities of ordinary people: Its values are rooted in the need to jolt people. And to do this, they have to concentrate on the unusual, the heroes and villains in society, the rich and the famous, the poor and the depressed. Malcolm Muggeridge claimed that if the members of the modern media had been around at the time of Christ, they would not have bothered to cover the crucifixion. Reporters would have been trying to find scandal at Herod's court—or waiting for press handouts at Pilate's office. The resurrection might have caught their attention and received brief mention: "Today, a man executed last Friday appears to have survived his ordeal on the cross. And now, in other news."

Heroes, Saviours, Little Dutch Boys
and the Trinity of Social Action

> "...community work as an occupation never devel-
> oped the self-assurance to tolerate the scrutiny that
> systematic research would have thrown on it. It has
> an ambiguous and often insecure place in the minds
> of funders, policy-makers, politicians
> and its employing agencies..."
> —David N. Thomas,
> *The Making of Community Work* (1983)

Large corporate organizations, and especially government agencies, live or die by attention to numbers, to quantity. Community
development, on the other hand, is concerned with the quality of the
lives of people, with intangible factors that are difficult—sometimes
impossible—to measure. Invoked as a last resort by desperate people
who have seen every other instrumental way of solving problems fail
or falter, community development only too often becomes a means
to ends that its supposed beneficiaries have had no part in defining.
In the nineteenth century, the British devised a way of attacking for-
tresses held by those who resisted their rule. The Forlorn Hope
comprised a young officer and some soldiers who dashed forward
with a bag of gunpowder. Shot at by the defenders of the enemy strong-
hold, they dumped the explosive at its gates lit the fuse and retired
very quickly. If they survived, their feat became famous and promo-
tion followed. If they did not, their relatives received a splendid letter
from the commanding officer.

Community development has often been seen as a form of the
Forlorn Hope. It has not become professionalized in the way other
disciplines have, and remains a very open way of making a living,
developing oneself and serving others. On the frontier between theory
and practice, everyone is welcome if they can contribute something
of value to thought and action. This openness, however, has had some

liabilities. If others are intervening—or interfering—in the life of a community, with no clear mandate, and no idea of what they are doing, they tend to describe their activities as "Community Development."

Joseph Campbell wrote of the role of the hero-redeemer in times of trouble.[241] He or she sets out on a journey, suffers dangers, confronts evils, takes up a challenge. Then the hero returns, battered and bruised, telling tales of great daring and pointing out the perils of the journey. Since community development is so often invoked in times of crisis, it tends to attract people who see themselves as heroes or saviours, rescuing people from evil. And many communities are only too willing to be saved by individuals because they can then avoid confronting the sources of the ills that beset them.

The history of efforts to create community and to encourage community development offers many examples of individuals who were hailed as saviours being turned into scapegoats. In many places, community developers took over local leadership or weakened the ability of residents to solve their own problems by creating dependency. Others played power games:

> "One of the things we'd do was to go up to Faust [in northern Alberta], say, announce there's money for housing but the house would go to that guy or two who'd spoken the longest and hardest and strongest. Of course everybody else would get mad at him, jealous, resentful, and that's the end of his local base of support."[242]

A study examining the values of community development workers revealed confusion about their role.[243] The informants identified themselves as adult educators, planners, consultants, managers, community workers, human resource advisers. Most had no formal training in community development. All valued "self-determination" (i.e. doing their own thing, having control over their own lives) very highly. Thus an immediate value conflict in community development surfaced in their work. How can you do what you believe is right and serve the needs of others?

The recollections of the people interviewed reveal what happened when members of the middle class confronted the realities of life among the poor and marginalized. One woman wrote of arriving in a community believing she was "going to change this place and make it better." Then she realized how difficult this would be: "...you get angry and then go into withdrawal for a while; and then pick yourself back up and get going."[244] Wife battering, sexual exploitation, drug abuse and "armed truces" between married couples who did not particularly like each other shocked the idealistic interveners sent to "help" disadvantaged people. A community development worker trying to launch a health care programme and to nurture family values discovered that "pickup trucks and television sets" constituted the goals of the local people, not concerns about health. Another individual who went into a community to help with a housing project found that residents wanted "small CMHC cracker boxes" in a suburban landscape with everything else bulldozed flat. He quit.

Local people know who holds power over them—and how they use it. In one community, an American-owned mill poured toxins into a river. Everyone knew this: A local teacher had done a study on the pollution. A conspiracy of silence developed in the town because the mill employed 250 people. A community development worker sent there did not see his role as that of a political activist, so ignored the pollution. Another reported of local people:

"They look for the biggest pig at the trough and hope they can get what he sprinkles on the ground. So they go for the most worthless, the most unprincipled, the most rip-off politicians they can. If they get on their side, they'll get the most."[245]

And communities can be cruel to outsiders. On one northern reserve, people set their dogs on the school principal, a black woman.

Those involved in the study of values could come to terms intellectually with what was happening to them and in the community. They had trouble dealing with the practicalities of their assigned tasks. One worker reported that she had "a really good analysis of why people are small-minded and pull one another back...and do wretched, nasty, cruel things to each other." Despite her understanding, "There are days when I just rant and rave." Another respondent commented on the "Who-does-she-think-she-is?" syndrome: "Someone tries to take leadership or step ahead and others just rip her to shreds." In one community, a co-operative created a new power structure. Non-members resented it. But the co-op idea caught on. When the organizers of the fourth one went to those who had started the first one for a loan, they were told: "We pulled ourselves up by the bootstraps, you can, too."[246]

Determining whether a community is ready for change comes only from experience, from picking up those signs that indicate the mood of people as you decode the messages they give you. The history of the community's attitude towards outsiders can be instructive. Many communities in Canada have turned in on themselves and with good reason. Only too often they have been invaded by researchers who probed into their lives and rattled community skeletons. Seldom did these people bother to tell residents of the results of their studies. Communities have also had workers parachuted into them without any say in their selection, role or mandate. In *The Power to Make it Happen*, Donald Keating tells the story of a community development venture in Riverdale, a part of Toronto alleged to have generated more Ph.Ds than any other place in Canada, and how political manipulation ruined the best efforts to improve life there.[247] In *Fighting for Hope*, Joan Kuyek documents the difficulties she experienced in fostering change while serving on the Kingston, Ontario, city council.[248] The very titles of these books reveal the deep desire by their authors to sustain hope in others.

Jean Lagassé started Manitoba's community development programme just as the government began to flood large tracts of land for hydro schemes. At Grand Rapids, an Indian community would vanish under water when a dam was built. The government set up a committee which promised the local people an Indian Eden in a new location. The residents of Grand Rapids had little experience in dealing with outside agencies. Indian Affairs did nothing to keep them informed, involve them in their planned future or protect their interests. The various outside agencies involved in the hydro scheme did not co-operate, did not share information or present it in a way that local people could understand, did not co-ordinate their activities. Information in fragmentary form prevented the people of Grand Rapids from understanding what was happening to them. In 1962, Lagassé sent a community development worker to the settlement, noting that he "had been dropped into the community well after his services were really needed, and was forced to 'mop up.'"[249] Instead of mediating between the community and the outside forces affecting the lives of its people, the worker became an advocate and protector of it. The Indians eventually hired a lawyer to protect their interests. He worked for them for four years, but the case never came to court: "...the people failed to adequately direct him; they apparently assumed that once he had been hired, he would resolve the issue on his own." Shamattawa, the new community for the people of Grand Rapids, soon showed signs of social disintegration. Heavy drinking and solvent abuse increased. In 1992, a new chief, elected to clean up the community, died in a drunken brawl, stabbed to death by another resident.

As the efforts to bring about community change based on sending individuals to "help" residents failed, a new thrust appeared: Local people would be trained to do community development. A woman involved in these efforts wrote:

"I've been involved in any number of programmes that attempted to take people from the community and give them skills and put them back into their own communities. Their communities just destroy them—and destroy them very quickly. I don't know any programmes that have been successful in this. The community turns on them."[250]

This effort to train indigenous community workers validates the truth of an old axiom: You can't go home again.

"The field staff were subject to horrendous pressure from the community in which they worked. They experienced coercion by the organization's political leaders; harassment resulting from local affiliations and clan membership; role conflict due to political infighting and had totally unrealistic expectations placed upon them by the politicians and the communities [which] turned on them with a vengeance."[251]

The tensions, pressures, squabbles and intercine jealousies that mark any collective effort have to be considered in any community development venture. They are compounded by conflicts in agencies and organizations outside their boundaries which have responsibility for their residents.

Paradoxically, community developers have to be both blunt and direct—and patient. One of Lagassé's workers arrived on the Roseau River Reserve to be confronted by Indians who said: "You white guys shafted us a hundred years ago." The worker replied. "I wasn't there. You weren't there. We have to look at what we can do today to make a better life for our kids tomorrow." The band council asked him to arrange training for heavy equipment operators. This required few formal qualifications. Those who finished the course could apply what they learned very quickly on the reserve. If held in the winter, as planned, the training would offer an alternative to idleness. It took the worker eighteen months to arrange the course. The buck flew backwards and forwards in government bureaucracies. Instead of meeting the expressed needs of the people on the reserve, they offered to fund an upgrading programme. And they planned to start it right at the beginning of the period of seasonal employment.

The reflections of those involved in the study of the values of community workers include more questions than answers: "Does this make sense?", "Am I the right person for the task?"; "Does the community want something to happen, or should they be left undisturbed?" Some workers found themselves at the beck and call of everyone in their communities. People phoned one woman at all hours; she developed an ulcer.

The miracle of community development, and the mystery of it, is that some ventures do go well. With the aid of a worker, residents take control of their own destinies, learn to handle internal tensions and to deal fairly and openly with outsiders.

In a highly individualized society, the belief that one person can meet all the needs of a community while at the same time encouraging its members to take responsibility for their own lives dies hard. The image that appears on reviewing the efforts by single individuals to bring about change is that of the Little Dutch Boy or Girl (Figure 5). The stance looks heroic. But someone should be looking over the top of the dyke to estimate the water level—or downstream to determine what will happen if the water comes over the top of the dyke, the individual pulls out his or her finger, or the barrier collapses. Canada, like Britain, has institutionalized the Little Dutch Boy Syndrome through the establishment of royal commissions on pressing problems. While they take their time studying them, the bureaucrats work frantically to address the issues under scrutiny so that they can claim that they have already dealt with them when the commission's report is presented.

Figure 5: The Little Dutch Boy Syndrome

Effective community development requires three sets of skills. One person may possess all of them, but this combination of abilities and experience is very rare in a single individual. Canada's aboriginal peoples recognized that their communities needed different leaders at different times. A war chief would not make a good trade chief. The role of the shaman demonstrates that some people have an ability to communicate with the spirits and the unknown forces that affect the lives of a community. Among communities of interest the tendency has been to recruit like-minded people and to build mini-bureaucracies that become rigid, inflexible and unresponsive to new demands and social and economic change among those they have been set up to serve. The small business model best fits community development ventures. Such ventures require the skills of three people.

You need a thinker, an ideas person, a shaman if you will, someone aware of what is happening inside and outside the community boundaries, and can decode the local signals and those coming from a distance. The decisions that will affect any Canadian community in the future are made daily in Ottawa, London, New York, Washington, Tokyo and other places. In the same way, what people inside a community propose to do is already in their minds. In a small business, the ideas person looks for new niches and opportunities to supply goods and services. In a community development venture, he or she picks up the trends, forces and factors inside and outside the collectivity that will have an impact on the lives of people, serving as a radar screen to sort out signals from noise. On 5 October 1960, Air Marshal Roy Slemon was on the "hot seat" at the Colorado Springs headquarters of the North American Air Defence Command (NORAD). At 3:15 P.M., Thule radar reported forty incoming missiles. Slemon did not panic and order an immediate counterstrike against the Soviet Union. At 3:18 P.M., Thule contacted NORAD again. Its radar had "detected" the rising sun.

No small business can survive unless the owners learn how to read local and world trends. Nor can a community development venture last long if those involved close their ears, ignore what is happening around them, and deter strangers from questioning what they are doing. Like many small businesses, community development organizations have often suffered from poor management and organization. The business sector has to pay attention to the bottom line. The bottom line in community development, however, is often presented in altruistic terms—creating awareness, empowering people, helping the poor, etc. The community development literature contains numerous examples of individuals setting out to save the world—but proving themselves unable to keep a decent set of books. Official policies on funding non-governmental organizations have strengthened a hardy mythology about "arm's length" relationships. Too many NGOs want government funding—and to be allowed to do their own thing. In Britain, this is known as "the harlot's perquisite"—power without responsibility.

A small business can have a brilliant visionary, good management and organization, but end up in bankruptcy if it does not have good salespeople, and a good product or service. Enthusiasts only too often try to "sell" community development in packages as the answer to all the problems facing humans. The third member of a community development team is the animator, enabler, encourager, facilitator who helps others to make better decisions. There are a number of techniques for doing this, including strategic planning, social animation and what I have called the PAGE (Possible, Adoptable, Gainful, Ethical) matrix.

All the various techniques for handling change in creative ways demand hard work, intelligence, a measure of scepticism, and ongoing determination and dedication to the goals that communities set for themselves. Sometimes, strategic planning simply becomes a comforting ritual and you end up with SPOTS (Strategic Plans on the Top Shelf).

One of the numbing features of the western tradition of meetings and conferences is the way in which issues and problems are discussed in an abstract manner, as if they were outside the purview and responsibility of participants. At the local level, people want to know: What can we do tomorrow to make a better future for ourselves and our community? The social animation process seeks to blend thought and action. A group of dairy farmers in Quebec called in an animator.[252] They wanted to generate more money from the sale of their milk. The animator asked them where they sold it. To our own dairy, they told him. So there was no point in raising the price there. Where else did the farmers sell their milk? the animator asked. Some was sold to be made into dried milk. What was the market for dried milk? the animator asked. Nobody knew. Would the group like to hear from an economist who specialized in the marketing of dried milk? The farmers agreed to this suggestion.

The aim of an animator is to pose the right questions to people, and encourage them to think about solutions. In our professionalized, specialized world, communities tend to identify their problems in vague ways and call in an expert. If the problem is identified as a housing one, and a specialist in that subject arrives in a community, you can be very sure that all the problems will soon be blamed on the lack of proper accommodation. In many parts of Canada, the housing problem has its roots in poverty and the inability of poor people to pay market rents for a decent place to live. Habitat for Humanity does not lament or discuss the problem of poor housing. It builds houses for the poor, with their involvement and sweat equity. Social animation can be very useful in generating moments of truth for organizations which are bogged down in abstract discussion. If you can make a problem abstract enough then you don't really have to do anything about it. The naive questions of the animator forces groups to confront their problems and start finding what can be done in small and incremental ways. Social animation avoids the committee syndrome favoured by large organizations to suppress independent thought and action. Alfred North Whitehead described a committee as: "A group of the unwilling picked from the unfit to do the unnecessary." Social animation encourages people to think about what they can do, with what they've got, where they are—and to act.

The PAGE matrix helps groups and communities to define the limits of what is possible in a given place, at a given time, with the available resources. Community development has been much bedevilled by the concept of "felt needs." The community development worker goes into a community, gains the trust of local people, identifies their felt needs, then helps them to fill them. People in a community, given the worldwide impact of the media, especially TV, may feel they need all kinds of things. But what do they want? The PAGE matrix helps to identify the limits of the possible by asking questions about what is Possible, Adoptable, Gainful and Ethical, at the individual, organizational and community levels. As with social animation, the emphasis with this technique is upon asking questions—not providing answers. The Sprung Greenhouse in Newfoundland was technically possible. The provincial government, desperate for ways of increasing self-sufficiency and generating employment, adopted the idea. But the venture was not gainful, costing more to operate than it generated in profits. As to the ethics of the greenhouse, they have to be examined in light of what the proponent promised and what he delivered. Another ethical concern revolves around the possible alternative uses of the resources dedicated to the greenhouse. To the Jains of India the colour white is holy. An enterprising poultry farmer bought some white hens and they proved to be excellent producers. But his coreligionists began to shun him. While owning these hens was possible and gainful at the individual level, this innovation was not adoptable or ethical in Jain culture. The man's initiative was seen as exceeding holy limits through the misuse of the bearer of a sacred colour.

The three techniques for assisting groups and communities to make better decisions are summarized in the appendix.

The concept of teams of three as the key to effective community development has echoes in history.

Christianity originated with three men. John the Baptist, last of the Jewish prophets, called for repentance, urging the rulers of the world to serve God and their people. In his day, Roman and Greek culture had begun to undercut Jewish values. John urged a return to the old ways. The desert prophet claimed he was preparing the way for the messiah, the saviour of the Jews. His cousin Jesus (Joshua bar Joseph) wandered around a remote part of the Roman Empire, telling stories, healing the sick, performing miracles, organizing his followers. He presented a new ethic of love, of *agape*, in a society saturated with *eros* (sexual love). He sought to replace the old covenants, the old commandments, the relationship with the jealous, tribal god with new ones. Instead of telling his listeners what they could not do, Jesus told them how to gain eternal life through loving God and each other. Christianity might not have survived if St. Paul had not been converted and become its energetic proponent. He travelled far and wide, supporting the new Christian communities, bringing them money, news, ideas, advice and settling their quarrels.

First came the prophet, herald of a new life, crying in the wilderness. Then came the charismatic figure of Jesus who managed to do a great deal in his short ministry with few resources and a small staff. Then Paul, the animator, organizer, enabler took over, nurturing the seeds of the new faith, keeping the memory of Jesus alive while helping the new Christian communities to solve their problems and remain open to all seeking a new life.

The Holy Trinity of Father, Son and Holy Spirit, reflects a mystical fascination with threes. Hinduism has three main gods, Brahma, the Creator, Vishnu, the Preserver, and Shiva, the Destroyer, who preside over all life. In Teutonic mythology, the three Norns, Destiny, Present and Future, play similar roles.

Three men created modern Italy. Mazzini, the visionary, saw a new nation emerging from a patchwork quilt of states. Garibaldi, a charismatic figure, became the fighting arm of the nationalist movement. Cavour, statesman and diplomat, reassured the European powers about the new country's good intentions as Italy came into being.

The Riel Rebellion of 1885 might have ended differently had a third member of the Métis trinity emerged to explain their way of life to others. Riel had a vision of a better life for his people, but his experience reveals a conclusion that has emerged in community development—messiahs don't make good managers. Gabriel Dumont, a skilled, intelligent military leader, became the Garibaldi of the Métis. But they lacked the third leg of the stool, someone who knew how to negotiate with the holders of power in Ottawa.

The Soviet Union came into being through the activities of an unholy trinity. Lenin, prophet of Marxism, needed Trotsky, energetic, charismatic, ruthless, to save the revolution he led. When Lenin died in 1924, Stalin slowly extended his power, killing or exiling all who threatened his supremacy.

Three very different people played leadership roles in the Antigonish Movement. Father Jimmy Tompkins, its prophet, urged the university to take knowledge to the people. Sent into the wilderness, he put his ideas about adult education and co-operation into practice. Then his cousin, Moses Michael Coady, extended the movement he had begun, offering advice about how to achieve the good life through working together. The third member of the trinity, A.B. MacDonald, did the tough and difficult work of helping people to set up credit unions and co-operatives. The Antigonish Movement provided information from trustworthy sources, on an ongoing basis, to help people to make better decisions about their individual and collective futures.

That process lies at the core of community development.

Hourglasses and Spirals

"[The spiral] denotes eternity, since it may go on for
ever. But because we necessarily conceive infinity
in our own, and therefore finite, terms, we are
forced to limit the limitless."
—Jill Purce *The Mystic Spiral, 1974*

The three prime movers in community development cannot operate without some sort of organizational structure or financial backing. Another symbol-reality clarifies how effective community development ventures can link top-down efforts with those arising from the bottom-up for the betterment of all. Because top-down efforts at development have not been particularly effective, the cry has arisen for grassroots organizations to be given more power and resources. Efforts at bottom-up development can be just as futile and unsuccessful as those coming from the top down, as experience with community groups shows.

The hourglass symbolizes how top-down and bottom-up efforts in change can be linked: It works just as well upside down as downside up. Good ideas about human betterment can emerge from the centres of power—or from the edges. The hourglass only serves its purpose if sand is passing through the neck.

Our present polarized world can be represented by an hourglass. Figure 6 shows the hourglass. At its centre sit the team of community developers. The visionary scans upwards, downwards and sideways to determine what is happening in and around the hourglass. The manager/organizer ensures that everything is in working order, and that the neck of the hourglass does not become clogged. And the animator, facilitator, enabler moves through the neck of the hourglass, like sand, carrying information and messages that help those

Top down efforts

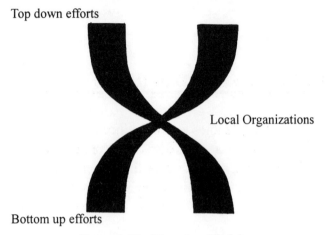

Local Organizations

Bottom up efforts

Figure 6: The Hourglass Model

in the top and the bottom sections to make sense of what is happening while identifying options for mutually beneficial actions.

The hourglass has a symbolic meaning at another level. Sand consists of silica, the basic material of computer chips. Fibre optic cables, which can transmit enormous amounts of information along slender threads, are made of glass.

People in traditional societies and many communities form a circle, facing inwards. Community development often hits a community like an arrow from the blue. It can stimulate upward spirals of activity, encouraging community members to make better use of existing resources and to identify and use anything of value from outside their boundaries to meet the needs of more and more people. If interveners or local residents cannot handle the tensions of change, a downward spiral can begin. More and more resources are expended for fewer and fewer results. In Cape Breton, Sydney Steel was about to be sold in 1998, thirty years after the provincial government took it over. About $2 billion has been spent on making the mill viable while the number of workers steadily decreased. On the other hand, New Dawn and similar community development ventures on Cape Breton have made good use of resources and opportunities that others had abandoned or ignored.

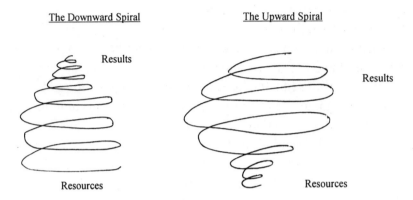

The Downward Spiral

Results

Resources

The Upward Spiral

Results

Resources

Figure 7: The Hourglass and the Spirals of Change

In a downward spiral, more and more resources generate fewer and fewer results for fewer and fewer people.
In an upward spiral, fewer and fewer resources generate more and more results for more and more people.

Spirals expand from a point, differentiating, contracting, then disappearing into the point again, growing towards wholeness—or disintegration. Spirals appear on ancient monuments and on jewellery from Troy. In the heavens, spiral galaxies have rotated for millennia. The double helix, two interwoven spirals, carries forward genetic information from one generation to the next. The spiral reveals both diversity and wholeness, the energy of linearity with the stability of the circle, the sense of moving into the future with an awareness of what can be done in the present. Figure 7 shows the spiral in the hourglass—how the two symbols are interrelated. Spirals in communities can begin their descent because of factors over which no one has any control—a disaster, the death of a leader, the absence of crucial resources at critical times. All seems lost, and a long slow, spiral slide into decay and disintegration begins. If the right interventions comes along at the right time, then an upward spiral can be encouraged, with the healing of divisions in the community, the resolution of simple problems, the better use of available resources. The idea of the spiral has echoes of Yeats' concept of gyres and of his figure of Accord and Discord. Community development seeks to strengthen the one, to limit the other. But in many places, the downward spiral into despair and dissolution has become too powerful and even the most skilled intervener can do nothing to arrest it.

Symbol-realities like the lichen, the bell curve, the hourglass and the spiral recognize the mystery of life, indicate what humans can control—and what they cannot. They point to possible ways forward, and are universal, found all over the world in creative ventures and in nature. They are not *answers* to problems, but simply guides and ways of making sense of a complex and confusing world.

The spiral process in community development depends for its upward thrust on the provision of accurate information from trustworthy sources on an ongoing basis. Information is to social change what oil is to war. If the right kind is not available in the right place, in the right quantity, at the right time and in usable form, everything bogs down and confusion and chaos ensue. The ability to collect information from inside and outside a community and to articulate it in plain and simple form are skills much needed in every field of human endeavour—and especially in community development. Civil society is rooted in civil communication. Informal settings allow people to express themselves freely and without restraint. A skilled listener can make sense of diverse viewpoints and opinions, always seeking to identify common concerns, and possibilities for consensus and co-operation. This enabling and mediating presence is vital in the maintenance of civil society. Every community has its wise men and women—and its blowhards. The media is structured towards listening to squeaky wheels and those who know how to manipulate information to press their own agendas.

These days, of course, no one believes what the government says and in this scepticism lies real dangers to democracy. In *To Empower People*, John Berger and Richard Neuhaus point to a persistent dilemma of the welfare state.[253] People want benefits from the state, but don't want to pay for them. While demanding services and rights from government, they dislike and distrust the agencies dispensing them. And people also mistrust large institutions like multinational corporations and banks while relying on them. Berger and Neuhaus present the concept of "mediating structures" as a way of handling these ambiguities. In a sense we're back to Archbishop Temple and his "intermediate groupings," that vast array of voluntary and non-governmental organizations in which people interact and learn from each other while serving larger needs than their own. Berger and Neuhaus define mediating structures as: "...those institutions standing between the individual in his private life and the larger institutions of public life."[254] Such bodies live in the shadowland between past and future, theory and practice, expectations about the good life and the possibility of realizing it. Belonging to them gives individuals meaning, fulfilment, identity, qualities difficult to experience in the megastructures that dominate our lives. Berger and Neuhaus believe that mediating structures can deliver services more effectively at the local level than can the state. This theory has gained increased credibility in the United States in light of the failure of the War on Poverty.[255] Neighbourhood, the family, churches and voluntary organizations can serve as mediating services, linking private and public life, insiders and outsiders. They can sit at the neck of the community development hourglass, offering spaces and places where different people can discuss ideas and options for action. Berger and Neuhaus don't indicate how mediating structures are created, strengthened, staffed and operated. But the community development experience in Canada and elsewhere in the world is rich in knowledge about their potential and limitations.

There's plenty of hope for the future when the pursuit and practice of community development in Canada is examined.

HOPE
FOR THE FUTURE

"That word Canada!—at the same time strong and sweet to hear would resound throughout the world like a rallying cry and an invitation to friendship."
—Gabrielle Roy, *Fragile Lights of Earth, 1982*

"Warmhearted, stable, fair to its many minorities, staunch in the cause of justice and democracy, Canada is one of the world's most highly respected countries."
—Murray Sayle,
The New Yorke, 13 November, 1995

CANADA'S CENTURY

"I think we can claim it is Canada
that shall fill the twentieth century."
—Sir Wilfrid Laurier, 1904

When he spoke these words, Canada's Prime Minister could never have imagined how awful the century he claimed for Canada would turn out to be. Laurier lived in an era of optimism and rising expectations. The steam turbine, the telegraph, electricity and other new technologies had conquered distance, made life easier, created new jobs, and offered the promise of more fruitful and rewarding lives for all.

At the end of the century, Canada has become a country of pessimism and declining expectations. An article in the 16 December, 1995, *Globe and Mail* asked "Are we better off now?" The piece compared the careers and lifestyles of two couples. The second daughter of the older one had been born in 1974, when the average weekly wage in Canada was $178. That of the younger couple had been born twenty years later, when the figure was $567.02. Between these births, the federal debt (in current dollars) rose from $21.2 billion to $503.8 billion. During the twenty-year period the average Canadian family income rose from $48,516 to $53,459 in constant dollars. The proportion of poor families went from 9.8 per cent to 14.5 per cent of Canada's population. The writer concluded that, economically, Canadians were barely better off than in 1974, but "socially, probably, we are, as roles shift and become more fluid."

Both families came from the professional middle class with its strong desire for individual freedom, stability and security. One of the problems confronting politicians is the belief among the middle class that they are falling into the working class—and the desire of the working class to live like members of the middle class. The older couple interviewed for the article expressed concern about the future of their children: "They are going to have to accept a lower standard than we did." The younger couple felt that their life was "filled with uncertainty" and concluded: "We just can't assume that we'll be looked after."

These concerns reflect a theme of this book. As the gap between the expectations that Canadians have of the good life and their ability to realize it widens, how do we react? Like caribou, banging heads with others over scarce resources? Like musk-oxen, forming a circle and looking only after our own? Or like the lichen, creating new relationships of mutual aid with others?

Canada has become a liminal state, hanging betwixt and between a safe and secure past and an uncertain future. The old rituals for keeping Canadians content, for running the country and managing the economy, for ensuring that Canada stays together, solving the unemployment problem and those of regional underdevelopment no longer work.

A survey of Canadian values in 1995 concluded that we believe in collective values, and don't want a country of haves and have nots. Only one in three Canadians surveyed trusted the government. We now have a "legitimation crisis" in Canada. This has followed upon a "rationality crisis" as governments find themselves unable to accomplish the economic goals they set for themselves. In August, 1997, the Department of Fisheries and Oceans discovered that ninety-one per cent of a surveyed group of fishermen in Shelburne County, Nova Scotia, had taken no training or attended workshops while participating in The Atlantic Groundfish Strategy (TAGS).[256] Its goal had been to wean fishermen away from their traditional way of life. But many of them still believe the fish will return, and have been quite happy to live on a federal dole until that happens. Shelburne County has been the site of some successful ventures in creating small businesses under the auspices of the Calmeadow Foundation. This approach to local, community development, however, is not going to generate a great deal of employment. Matthews writes about the identity crisis that pervades government these days, and the feelings of helplessness and exhaustion at the top of political and government structures:

"Those for whom plans are being made increasingly resist measures which often seem designed to undermine their local culture and way of life. On the other hand, the planners themselves are going through an identity crisis of their own, in which they question their own legitimacy and ability to make plans."[257]

Governments seek constantly to "re-invent" themselves, while the private sector "re-engineers" its activities to survive. And in this climate of fear and uncertainty, community development has only too often been invoked as a simple technique for improving life at the local level. As H.L. Mencken observed: "Every complex problem has a solution which is simple, direct, plausible—and wrong."

The rising interest in community development in Canada, and the increasing number of successful locally-based, locally-controlled ventures of all kinds in this field, point a way forward into the future. There's plenty of middle ground in this country for initiatives in those parts of society that are not dominated by the state or the private sector.

The successful efforts in community development originate with individuals who have a strong moral and ethical concern for change, but are not judgemental about what others do. They eschew the easy rhetoric of so many public figures who dominate the media with their worries about problems. Instead, they search quietly for solutions with others in a spirit of mutual trust and respect, rooting their efforts in mutual aid. Sometimes mutual aid emerges spontaneously in times of crisis. But, just as often, you need mediating, enabling, animating organizations to stimulate and support it.

Canada hangs suspended between two traditions—the British, who once ruled this land, and the Americans, who own large parts of our economy, directly and indirectly. The American genius for self-promotion hides feelings of self-doubt. And their individualism and love of liberty were cradled in an era of abundance and a belief in the infinite riches of their land, and bolstered by a faith in the ability of technology to exploit them. The British, more self-assured, have a genius for understatement and a strong class consciousness that contrasts with American egalitarianism. When Americans are good, they are very good. And when they are not, they tell you all about it, in great detail.

And this country is blessed with the presence of the Québécois and the Acadians and others who have adapted the ways of France to a new land. Immigrants from all over the world have come to Canada for a better life. Their traditions and experiences offer a rich source of ideas and information on how to survive and thrive in difficult times. Our aboriginal peoples have accumulated wisdom and knowledge on doing this in the past and the present.

What makes Canada truly unique can only be discovered by looking at our past and speaking to those people who are striving to make a better nation in the present. It is possible to avoid American hype and British understatement in doing so and to hear the authentic voices telling stories that inspire and offer hope for the future. The centres of power may no longer be able to hold. But there's plenty of evidence that things are not coming apart in Canada, and that Canadians are learning to ride the gyres of change and to create a better country. To appreciate how they are doing this involves turning our way of thinking on its head. The intellectualization of our times has encouraged people to think about problems. After all, that's where the money is for bureaucrats, social scientists, newspaper columnists and media commentators who pontificate about them and offer their solutions. By looking at what Canadians have actually done to solve problems and find solutions to them a different perspective emerges. By starting with solutions to problems and working back to what caused them, it's possible to determine how learning takes place. Canadians need not fall prey to the British style of fumbling through, or to the American mania for technology and managing the world.

The particular genius of Canadians has emerged very strongly, and paradoxically, for residents of the peaceable kingdom, during war time.

THE BIRTH OF A NATION

> "Perhaps...Canada is not so much a country as
> magnificent raw material for a country; and perhaps
> the question is not who are we but: what are we
> going to make of ourselves?"
> —Alden Nowlan (1971)

Alden Nowlan's life shows what can be done by effort and intelligence. Growing up on a hard scrabble farm in Nova Scotia, inspired by a dedicated teacher, he took to writing and produced poetry, essays and novels that caught the essence of life in the Maritimes. Nowlan became the much-loved friend of a provincial premier and of a senior military officer, among many other people. He also had a strong affection and respect for ordinary people.

Canadians have shown an incredible toughness, tenacity, dedication and initiative when led by the right kind of leaders. During the First World War, soldiers of the Canadian Corps, fighting together for the first time on Easter Monday, 9 April, 1917, took Vimy Ridge. The Canadians suffered ten thousand casualties, including 3,598 dead. But they did the job they were ordered to do—swiftly and efficiently, with thorough planning and preparation. On that day, Greg Clark, the Canadian writer who won the Military Cross during the battle, noted: "I have experienced my first full sense of nationhood." Our soldiers, led by Sir Arthur Currie, triumphed where French and British attackers had failed in previous years. Currie went on to lead the Canadian Corps in a series of brilliant actions that helped to end the war in 1918. One account describes his style of leadership:

> "No flashing genius but a capable administrator, cool headed
> and even tempered and sound of judgment. He has surrounded
> himself with a capable staff whose counsel he shares and

whose advice he takes. He is the last man to stick to his plan if a better one offers. So far as tactics go, he is first among equals for such is the way his staff work."[258]

Currie had been a rather unsuccessful real estate agent before the war. He joined the militia and learned quickly about war during the blood baths that bogged down armies on the Western Front. Currie preferred to expend shells rather than the lives of his men when assaulting enemy positions, and knew exactly what was happening on the battlefield.

Currie was not a professional warrior. His achievements point up a problem in Canada today. Until our present leaders give way to brighter, more competent people who know how the world really works, nothing much will change. During the Second World War, Canadians were handed the toughest and most difficult jobs—Hong Kong, Dieppe, Italy, the Normandy Landings, the Long Left Flank—and acquitted themselves well. But learning new ways proved painful—on land, on sea and in the air—and costly. At home, Canadians became incredibly efficient and productive in making the artifacts of war and death. And this country has an outstanding reputation for competence and efficiency in international peacekeeping, despite isolated incidents involving a few individuals.

In 1910, the American philosopher William James described war as "the strong life...life *in extremis*." War excuses every excess while nurturing courage and a sense of community. James identified the central issue of his time as "one of turning the individual and collective heroism and sacrifice demanded by war into more constructive channels."[259] How could nations identify and pursue "The Moral Equivalent of War?" he asked. James pointed out that militarism involves some important values—courage, comradeship, loyalty, hardihood, discipline, surrender of narrow interest, cohesiveness, contempt for softness, willingness to sacrifice oneself for others. He saw the need to stimulate these same values to defeat human suffering, poverty, disease and injustice: "The martial type of character can be bred without war. Strenuous honor and disinterestedness abound elsewhere." James called upon America's "gilded youth" to be conscripted into an army "enlisted against Nature." They would go to "coal and iron mines, to freight trains, to fishing in December...to road building and tunnel making..." James' vision is very American, with its idealistic, individualistic ring and its theme of overcoming nature. His aim was less to improve the lot of the poor than to build character and knock some practical sense into young men by doing hard, manual work. Then they would "come back into society with healthier sympathies and soberer ideas."[260]

By the time the American philosopher spoke these words, Canada had begun to put his ideas into action. Frontier College, founded in 1899, sends idealistic men and women to work and teach in remote communities. After the Second World War, the Americans set up the Peace Corps and VISTA (Volunteers in Service to America) to fight poverty and misery abroad and at home. If they had no special skills, the young people were assigned to community development. In Canada, the Company of Young Canadians and Canadian University Services Overseas (now CUSO) also recruited young idealists to help others. Federally funded youth programmes such as Katimavik and Canada World Youth stayed closer to James' individualistic view, offering young Canadians a chance to lose their childishness and return to society as better people. Much fumbling at the community level has been presented by these agencies as learning experiences in community development. Non-governmental bodies like Habitat for Humanity and Frontiers Foundation have been much more effective in encouraging both personal development and those of communities.

The true genius of Canadians lies in our ability to balance the tensions of individualism and collectivity and find middle ways between them that enhance personal, organizational and community development. The country offers possibilities for individual growth—and ways of coming together with others in mutually beneficial ways. The Acadians settled on the shores of the Bay of Fundy in homemade houses strung along rough roads. They co-operated to build dykes to create land, and then made it fruitful, celebrating their achievements, sorrows and culture in songs and dances. Brutally removed from the best lands by the British in 1755, some returned and once again built strong communities. Canadians reject the excessive individualism of Americans and don't much care for the tight, highly structured and entrenched ways of Europe and older civilizations that determine the fate of individuals before they are born.

Looking back at Canadian history, community development and mutual aid—rather than aggressive individualism or the glue of ancient tradition—has been an integral part of nation building. Barn raising, collective harvesting, neighbourliness and other forms of cooperation marked the life of the early Prairie settlers. They needed no government laws or regulations to assist each other. The Métis way of life, based on sharing, also allowed plenty of scope for individual enterprise in the service of others. The relationship between incomers and Canada's aboriginal peoples have been marked as much by mutual respect and benefit as by conflict and oppression.

Community development tends to attract a particular type of person, individuals seeking the moral equivalent of war. Like war, with its glory and its idealism, community development forces people to confront their fears and their capabilities at the deepest level, and to learn how to deal with their own internal needs and those of others in chaotic situations. There are plenty of people doing this in Canada. Increasingly, Canada's media has become centralized—you read the same thing in the daily newspapers as you hear on the radio and see on TV. Most of the interesting work in community development, in Canada, and throughout the world, is taking place in isolated areas and obscure corners. These places are not readily accessible to the media, and its style is unsuited to understanding and representing the complexity of the processes whereby people gain more control over their destinies.

The language of community development and the role of the key people in it does not fit neatly into media categories. Community developers work in that ambiguous, liminal land between past and future, idealism and realism, theory and practice. To be effective, they have to be realistic idealists—and idealistic realists. They are "conservative innovators." Such people achieve status and standing by adhering to the norms of their society—and introduce new ideas in specific areas for the benefit of others. John Bennett, in his study of Hutterites, writes of this communal people:

"The quickest route to innovation in a healthy colony is to work within the existing frame of cautions and sanctioned change—not to resist it. In most colonies, the most effective innovators are also the best Hutterian scholars...demonstrating their competence not only by efficiently managing their enterprises, [but by] cautiously suggesting improvements..."[261]

These conservative innovators also prepare themselves for governing roles in later life. Thus individualism and concern for community complement each other, rather than being in conflict.

One of the leaders in the post-communist world whose words have made a deep impression on people in high and low places is Václav Havel, president of the Czech Republic. Politics, often defined as the "art of the possible" has been recast by him as *The Art of the Impossible*, the title of his book of talks published in 1997. Subtitled "Politics and Morality in Practice," the book outlines Havel's ideas on the good society. The writer—which is the way he prefers to describe himself—does not duck the issues and problems that have arisen since his country gained its independence. Industry pollutes the environment, the utopia of communism bitterly divided Czechs and old hostilities still persist. Havel's life demonstrates the possibilities for hope in even the direst circumstances. He readily admits that he knows little about directing the fate of his new democracy. But there's a fundamental decency and honesty to Havel that is rare among politicians. He writes:

"A well-established network of local administrations should not complicate life for the central authorities, but on the contrary should make life easier, releasing them from the obligation to play the game of omniscience."[262]

247

Havel also notes that a flourishing non-profit sector is, "...another of the essential elements of a mature civil society."[263]

Communism was very good at shattering the traditional bonds and networks of mutual aid that bound people together.

Eric Hobsbawn, the Marxist historian, called his book on "The Short Twentieth Century " *Age of Extremes*. In this resolutely gloomy overview of events, he recognizes the role and value of symbiotic ventures that incorporate the Lichen Factor:

> "More serious than the evident breakdown of the two polar
> extremes was the disorientation of what might be called the
> intermediate or mixed programmes and policies which had
> presided over the most impressive miracles of the century.
> These had pragmatically combined public and private, mar-
> ket and planning, state and business, as the occasion and lo-
> cal ideology warranted. The problem here lay not in the ap-
> plication of some intellectually attractive or impressive theory,
> whether or not this was defensible in the abstract, for the
> strength of these programmes had been practical success rather
> than intellectual coherence."[264]

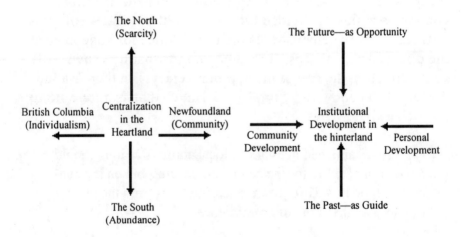

Figure 8: The Crosses and Gyres of Canada

Figure 8 shows the crosses and gyres of Canada, the tensions that have to be understood and properly handled if this country is to develop its potential. While the notion of civil society is proving increasingly attractive to politicians, none of them in Canada has seen fit to adopt the concept as a central plank of their electoral platform. This country has many outstanding examples of ways in which Canadians have shaped their own destinies and become participants in their own personal, institutional and community development. It also has some splendid examples of dependency and manipulation by both the powerful and the powerless as they attempt to hold on to what they have.

In the Czech Republic and the democracies of Europe, ancient hatreds and divisions continue to prevent people from working together for the common good. In the United States, rampant individualism limits what can be done to encourage a civil society. In the developing world, tribal anarchy and centralized bureaucracy stifle local initiative as people struggle to find enough to survive from day to day. Canada has a particularly privileged position in the world today, and is the envy of many nations. Despite our current ills and the laments of the alienated intellectuals and baffled politicians, this country still offers hope and opportunity for creating here a better, more democratic, more open society than prevails elsewhere.

Northern Realities

"The head does not hear anything
until the heart has listened."
—James Stephens

Canada, as the saying goes, has too much geography and not enough history. But we do have enough of a past, and ample knowledge of it, to sieve through what has happened in this country for the wisdom we need to move with confidence into the future.

And, as far as geography goes, much of our land is harsh, difficult, unbelievably hostile to the presence of humans.

You learn quickly in the North or you simply do not survive.

Community development resembles the Canadian North in being a frontier, a place where the known and the unknown meet and interact. Those who live beyond the settled southern belt of Canada recognize that the land, the bush, are the final arbiters of everything there. Chunks of the north have been despoiled. But its eternal silence remains, brooding, vast and unfathomable. If you spend any time there, you begin to experience feelings of humility. Any human arrogance is tempered by a sense of awe in this vast land. You seem to cling to the place by your very fingertips. Outside the settled areas, the land can swallow you without trace.

In the United States, the pioneers who headed west eventually reached the smiling land of California. In Canada if you keep going north on our frontier you will come to the Arctic Ocean. It looks solidly frozen, but in fact is in constant motion.

The American frontier created myths that are deeply etched into the national character of its people: individualism, the search for adventure and new experiences, expansiveness and possessiveness. Community development on the American model has been marked by some of these themes, as individuals set out to find new territories to conquer and control.

251

Things have been different in Canada.

It is less that certain people and groups choose community development, than that community development chooses them at a certain time in their lives. Riding the upward and downward gyres of change, struggling to handle both Accord and Discord at the community level, eschewing the simplistic division of the world into "right" and "left," those involved in community development seek to move forward on a steady course in a polarized world. To innovate while encouraging stability at the local level, to deal with those at both ends of the bell curve of a community demands stamina, skills of a peculiar kind and experience. Community development is no easy option, as the record shows. Those involved must quickly learn their own limits and those of others—and of the community—to separate the possible from the impossible. And sometimes only the impossible works.

In the Arctic, you have to do your job against a background of a constant struggle for existence. Even the best-equipped modern Arctic expeditions can only spend a limited time in this beautiful, barren land. Much of what can be achieved in the north—as in community development—depends on the individual. If you give less than your best, you are finished. And your failure may be fatal to everyone else in your group or organization, as disasters in the Arctic have shown.

One great advantage of being a Canadian lies in the unique opportunities that this country offers for personal and community development. Here, anyone can seek the Lichen Factor, develop themselves as individuals while coming together with others in mutually beneficial ways. Working together in ventures that generate a sense of joy and offer challenges, you can meet your own needs—and those of your community, however defined. Slowly but surely, the "Us" and the "Them" feeling vanishes, and the "I-Thou" relationship develops.

Lichens demonstrate vividly how vital co-operation is for survival on the harsh and difficult esges of Canada. By surviving and growing, lichens prepare the way for other forms of life and for a greater diversity and abundance of species of all kinds. And so, in human efforts embodying this kind of mysterious symbiosis, we too can work towards creating the conditions for a richer, fullt and rewarding life for future generations of Canadians.

If lichen, a humble form of God's creation, can develop mutually beneficial relationships under the harshest conditions on this planet, can not all we humans go forth and do likewise?

APPENDIX

Strategic Planning

The Social Animation Process

The PAGE Process

The PAGE Matrix

STRATEGIC PLANNING

"My idealistic schemes and plans of life, like those
of other people, are apt to be upset by the small
motives—of pique, ill-temper, nervous distate—
with which everyday decisions are often swayed."
M.Allerdale Grainger, *Woodsmen of the West*, 1908

Strategic planning has been much touted as a method of managing change, and has created its own vocabulary and definitions.

A Planning Team sets the direction of the process. It should be drawn from all sectors of the community. Through a process of consensus, the participants identify their personal interests. Then they work towards the common good, taking them into account. Priorities for action can then be established.

The Action Plan Team develops specific strategies for each priority area. The team should be made up of no more than seven members. Beyond that, you have a committee. The teams come back to the community group and determine where their suggestions complement and contradict each other. In one planning exercise, various teams came up with proposals for a certain part of Alberta. The final presentation showed that the whole area would disappear under water if it was initiated.

Mission Statement. This is aimed at answering the question: "What the hell are we really trying to do?" It can sometimes be developed at the beginning of the strategic planning process and should be no longer than twenty-five words. Beyond that, you stray into clichés and vague statements of good intent.

Belief Statement. This answers the question: "Why are we doing what we are doing?" It summarizes the community or group's values. This is another area prone to meaningless rhetoric, weasel words and obfuscation. If you express your values in print and in person you have to walk your talk.

External Analysis. What forces and factors outside your community or group will influence its future? Much of this analysis involves guesswork, but some trends—doing more with less—are abundantly obvious.

Internal Analysis. What are the strengths and weaknesses of the community or the group? How much can it do on its own? What does it require from outside sources? Sometimes this analysis is summarized as SWOT—Strengths, Weaknesses, Opportunities, Threats.

Objectives. What are the desired outcomes—the ends—of the planning process? Again, there is a need to be precise in stating these.

Strategies. What are the means to achieve the objectives of the group or the community?

Action Plan. Who will do what, when, how, with whom and with what resources—and for whom?

The strategic planning process moves from diffuseness to specificity. Many community development efforts have begun by trying to do everything for everyone, everywhere, and at once. In time, discussions became more specific.

Strategic planning, like social animation and the PAGE process, turns the usual approach to problem solving in our technique-worshipping, expert-reliant society on its head. Asking the right questions, rather than attempting to provide instant solutions lies at the heart of strategic planning, social animation and the PAGE process.

An outside facilitator, ignorant of the day-to-day life in a community, can often be more effective in identifying its underlying ethos, behavioural patterns, culture than a resident. He or she will have no vested interest in any specific solution and no personal friends or territory to protect. This approach worked well in Community Pride in British Columbia. Outsiders can also ask simple questions that residents refuse to confront. At a conference of social workers in Liverpool, England, that I attended in 1975, someone who was obviously not a member of that profession spoke out. He told of a social worker teaching poor people how to make soup from bones. One of them asked: "Who got the meat?"

Like any human tool or technique, strategic planning is only as good as those who engage in it. Well done, it can help communities and groups to become clear about their objectives and precise about the ways they will achieve them. It can speed up the decision making process. The overall goal is to initiate an upward process of reflection and action that uses fewer and fewer resources for the benefit of more and more people.

Strategic planning is an endless process—like life itself.

It can be used over an extended period for clarifying goals and objectives and determining how they can be achieved. Social animation and the PAGE process are directed at helping communities and groups to come to immediate decisions about meeting their needs. It requires skilled practitioners whose personal style does not antagonize participants in the processes.

The Social Animation Process

The process works like the lichen—two parallel trains of thought converge as a group works through the reasons for a problem, realizes its complexity, determines the options available and the rationale for them, and, moves into action.
Adapted from Jacques Beaucage, "La Participation".
Anthropologica, N.S. (2), 1967.

R: Pr. H --- S --- D --- R --- 0*
Att: Defr. --- Compl. --- R---A**

*Rational process (R)
Pr: What is the Problem?
H: What is the hypothesis
S: What are the possible solutions?
D: What decisions must be made?
R: Who should play which role?
0: What are the objectives?

**Attitudinal Change (Att.)
Defr: Defrustration.
Comp: Realization of the complexity of the problem
R: Rationale for action.
A: Action

The PAGE Matrix

	P.	O.	C.
Possible?			
Adoptable?			
Gainful?			
Ethical?			

P = Personal
O = Organization
C = Community

The PAGE Process

This simple matrix can speed up decision making. It determines whether a proposed action lies within the limits of each individual in a group, the organization with which they are involved, and the community in which it is located.

The matrix can be completed through a group process or by having each individual involved complete and submit it for tabulation.

NOTES AND REFERENCES

1. "The Earth's Hidden Light," *The Economist*, 21 Dec. 1996, p. 111.

2. Karen Casselman, *The Craft of the Dyer*, Toronto, University of Toronto Press, 1980.

3. John H. Bland, *Forests of Lilliput: The Realm of Mosses and Lichens*, Englewood Cliffs, N.J. Prentice-Hall, 1971, p. 3.

4. Vincent P. Miceli, S.J., *Ascent to Being: Gabriel Marcel's Philosophy of Communion*, New York, Desdee Co. 1965.

5. Max Hastings, *The Korean War*, London, Pan Books, 1988, p. 261.

6. George Orwell, "Politics and the English Language," in Sonia Orwell and Ian Angus, *The Collected Essays, Journalism and Letters of George Orwell, Vol. IV*, Harmondsworth, Penguin, 1970, p. 166.

7. *Ibid.*

8. *Ibid* p. 157.

9. Northrop Frye, *The Educated Imagination*, Toronto, CBC, 1963. p. 57.

10. *Ibid* pp. 62-63.

11. *Ibid* p. 61.

12. *Ibid.*

13. *Ibid* p. 68.

14. *Ibid.*

15. *The Last of Old Europe. A Grand Tour with A.J.P. Taylor*, New York, Quadrangle, 1976, p. 9.

16. Julien Benda, *The Treason of the Intellectuals (La trahison des clercs)*, New York, W.W. Norton, 1969, p. 9. (Originally published in 1928).

17. "Good Hope," *Destinations* magazine, Nov. 1993, p. 9.

18. Personal interview.

19. Tony German, *The Sea is at Our Gate: The History of the Canadian Navy*, Toronto, McClelland and Stewart, 1990, p. 202. See also Tony Keene, *The Ship that Voted No*, Hantsport, N.S., Lancelot Press, 1995.

20. Sir William Beveridge, *The Pillars of Security*, London, George Allen and Unwin, 1943, p. 104.

21. *Ibid* p. 77.

22. *Ibid* p. 76.

23. Beveridge, *The Pillars of Security* "Five Christian Standards," pp. 33-40.

24. Paul Addison, *Now The War Is Over*, London, BBC and Jonathan Cape, 1985, p. 199.

25. Noel Annan, *Our Age: The Generation That Made Modern Britain*, London, Fontana, 1991, p. 600.

26. Addison, *Now The War Is Over*, p. 202.

27. Quoted in Addison, *ibid.*

28. William Temple, *Christianity and Social Order*. Harmondsworth, Penguin, 1942, p. 46.

29. *Ibid* p. 47.

30. See Fernand Braudel's three volume work on "Civilization and Capitalism: 15-18th: Century" — *The Structures of Everyday Life* (1981), *The Wheels of Commerce* (1982) and *The Perspective of the World* (1984), published in New York by Harper and Row.

31. E.J. Hobsbawn, *Nations and Nationalism Since 1780: Programme, Myth, Reality*, Cambridge University Press, 1990, p. 5.

32. Paul Tellier, "It's Time to Re-engineer the Public Service, *Globe and Mail*, 25 February, 1994.

33. *Ibid.*

34. *Building on Our Strengths*. Final Report of the Royal Commission on Employment and Unemployment, St. John's, Newfoundland, 1986, p. 320.

35. *Ibid.*

36. Peter Evik, quoted in "Nunavut's Deadline Brings Reality Check." *Globe and Mail*, 7 July, 1997. A group of dedicated Inuit and non-Inuit people in the Keewatin are struggling to involve and inform local people in the decision making process, and encouraging them to take responsibility for running their communities.

37. "Nunavutians Build a Bureaucracy," *Globe and Mail*, 4 May, 1997.

38. The Uruguay examples come from V.S. Naipul, *The Return of Eva Peron,* New York, Alfred A. Knopf, 1980, pp. 136-137. Hernando de Soto's book, *The Other Path: The Invisible Revolution in the Third World,* New York, Harper and Row, 1989 describes the informal sector in Peru and its efficiency in meeting needs at the grassroots level. The rising interest in the underground economy in Canada and elsewhere in the world reflects the growing inability of bureaucracies to control local initiative and enterprise. See Owen Lippert and Michael Walker, *The Underground Economy: Global Evidence of its Size and Impact,* Vancouver, The Fraser Institute, 1997. The Karachi Development agency is mentioned in John Stackhouse "Elected government the obstacle for Pakistanis," *Globe and Mail* 28 September, 1993. On bureaucratic fear of local initiative, see Milton J. Esman and Norman T. Uphoff, *Local Organizations: Intermediaries in Rural Development,* Ithaca, Cornell University Press, 1984, p. 184.

39. Herschel Hardin, *The New Bureaucracy: Waste and Folly in the Private Sector* Toronto, McClelland & Stewart, 1991. The revelations about the inefficiency of Ontario Hydro Nuclear in August, 1997, revealed how management inertia and domination of its internal operations by certain unions had together created a somnolent system in which costs and consumer needs were ignored.

40. Laurence Surtees, *Pa Bell: A. Jean de Grandpré and the Meteoric Rise of Bell Canada Enterprise,* Toronto, Random House, 1992.

41. James Gleick, *Chaos: Making a New Science*, New York, Penguin, 1988.

42. Bertram Gross, *Friendly Fascism: The New Face of Power in America*, New York, M. Evans and Co. Ltd, 1980.

43. Simon Scharma, *Citizens*, Toronto, Vintage Books, 1990, p. 8.

43a. *The Acquisitive Society*, New York, Harcourt Brace, 1920, p.28

44. W. Bruce Lincoln, *Red Victory: A History of the Russian Civil War*, New York, Simon and Schuster, 1989, Chapter Fifteen. After the fall of communism, the Kronstadt "counter revolutionaries" were rehabilitated, achieving the secular equivalent of sainthood.

45. In late August, 1997, the Innu of Labrador again staged a sit-in to protest the building of a road and airstrip for the Voisey's Bay nickel mine that had not been subject to an environmental review. They were joined by the Labrador Inuit whose association succeeded in stopping work on the construction by using legal means and convincing the Supreme Court of Newfoundland and Labrador that it did not constitute "exploratory work," as the mining company claimed (*Globe and Mail*, Report on Business, "Court Blocks Inco Work at Voisey's Bay," 27 August, 1997.) The Canadian Inuit have traditionally been more interested in compromise than confrontation.

46. Robert Nisbet, "Victimology," p. 304 in *Prejudices: A Philosophical Dictionary*, Cambridge, Harvard Univ. Press, 1982.

47. "NB Micmac Community Sees Eighth Suicide in a Year," *Globe and Mail*, 28 July, 1993.

48. Guy Wright, *Sons and Seals: A Voyage to the Ice*, St. John's, Institute of Social and Economic Research, Memorial University, 1984.

49. Ottar Brox, *Newfoundland Fishermen in the Age of Industry: A Sociology of Economic Dualism*, St. John's. Institute of Social and Economic Research, Memorial Univ., 1972, p. 6.

50. The federal government expected about 26,000 people to qualify for TAGS, but the number totalled 40,000. An audit in 1996 showed that rules had been bent to enable some fishery workers to qualify for TAGS ("Fish bailout rules bent, audit finds," *Daily News* (Halifax), 21 November, 1996).

51. Ralph Surette, "Community Management versus ITQ," *Atlantic Cooperator*, June/July/August, 1997, p. 1.

52. Gerald L. Focius, *A Place to Belong: Community Order and Everyday Space in Calvert, Newfoundland*, Athens, University of Georgia Press, 1991.

53. *Community Matters*, p. 13.

54. Personal communication from the Hon. Shirley McClellan, Minister, Alberta Community Development, 14 March, 1997.

55. *Ibid.*

56. The research was undertaken by Dr. Grace Pretty, formerly of the Department of Psychology, Saint Mary's University, Halifax.

57. Address to the Character Education Conference, 14 May, 1995.

58. I visited the office of Business in the Community in London in 1989. See: Lotz, Jim, "Beyond the Bottom Line; business and the community in Britain," *Commerce* (Saint Mary's University, Halifax), 1 (1), May, 1990.

59. Stephen B. Clark, *Building Christian Communities: Strategy for Renewing the Church*, Notre Dame, Indiana, Ave Maria Press, 1972, pp. 183-84.

60. The newsletter is available from the Jesuit Basic Church Community Project, Box 1082, Depot #3, Victoria, B.C., V8W 2S6.

61. Robert Bellah, *Habits of the Heart: Individualism and Commitment in American Life*, New York, Harper and Row, Perennial Library, 1986. p. 72.

62. *Ibid* p. 206.

63. "Foreword," in Carolyn R. Shaffer and Kristin Anundsen, *Creating Community Anywhere*, New York, Jeremy P. Tarcher, 1991, p. vii.

64. *Ibid.*

65. The Foundation offers community building workshops—for a fee. One promoted in Canada, and held in Seattle, Washington in October, 1997, featured Gary Zukav, author of *The Seat of the Soul* and *The Dancing Wu Li Masters* and cost $345. Zukav defined community as "the vehicle through which we assist each other in spiritual growth. Spiritual growth is the conscious creation of harmony, sharing, cooperation, and reverence for life."

66. John McKnight, *Community and Its Counterfeits*, Toronto, CBC Radio Works, 1994.

67. Alexis de Tocqueville, *Democracy in America*, New York, Washington Square Press, p. 252.

68. Gordon Tullock, *The New Federalist*, Vancouver, The Fraser Institute, 1994, p. 9.

69. Joe Chidley, "The New Burbs," *Maclean's*, July 21,1997, pp. 16-25.

70. Amitai Etzioni, *The Spirit of Community: Rights, Responsibilities and the Communitarian Agenda*, New York, Crown, 1993.

71. Will Kymlicka, *Contemporary Political Philosophy*, Oxford, Clarendon Press, 1990, p. 199.

72. Federation of Egalitarian Communities, *Sharing the Dream*. Tecumesh, MO. n.d.

73. Carolyn R. Shaffer and Kristin Anundsen, *Creating Community Anywhere*, pp. 55-58.

73a. Warren Bennis, *On Becoming a Leader*, Reading, Mass., Addison Weslay, 1989.

74. Siegfried and Renata Ellwanger, "Our Christian Responsibility and the Radical Right," *The Plow* No.33, November/ December, 1992, p. 6.

75. *The Penguin Dictionary of Sociology*, 1988, p. 44.

76. G. Hillery, "Definitions of Community: Areas of Agreement," *Rural Sociology*, XX (2), 118-119, 1955.

77. Andrew Malcolm, *The Tyranny of the Group*, Toronto Clarke, Irwin, 1973.

78. Jack Quarter, "The Changing Kibbutz," *Together* 5 (1 & 2) Spring 1993, pp. 9-11.

79. Eliezer Ben-Rafael, "The Transformation of the Kibbutz," *Together*, 6 (3), Summer, 1994, pp. 6-9.

80. George Woodcock, "The Survival of the Kibbutzim," *Together* 6 (4), Fall, 1994, p. 2.

81. Paul Kaihla and Ross Laver, *Savage Messiah*, Toronto, McLelland-Bantam, 1993.

82. John Oliphant, *Brother Twelve*, Toronto, McClelland & Stewart, 1991.

83. Kathryn Marshall, *In the Combat Zone: An Oral History of American Women in Vietnam*, Boston, Little Brown 1987, p. 151.

84. "Michael Archangel: Encounter with a Doukhobor," pp. 292-263, in Woodcock, George, *Anarchism and Anarchists*, Kingston, Ont. Quarry Press, 1992.

85. Sharp, David, *Rochdale: The Runaway College*, Toronto Anansi, 1987, 137.

86. "The Lord is My Light" pp. 84-103 in Graham, Ron, *God's Dominion: A Sceptic's Quest*, Toronto, McClelland and Stewart, 1990.

87. Lord Martin Cecil, *On Eagle's Wings*, New York, Two Continents Publishing Group, 1977.

88. Martin Exeter, *Being in Community*, published by the Emissaries of Divine Light, P.O. Box 9, 100 Mile House, B.C. Canada, VOK 2RO.

89. Vivien Bowers, "Friends in Argenta, *Beautiful British Columbia*," 38 (3), Fall, 1996, pp. 34-39.

90. Reported in *Globe and Mail*, 30 October, 1992.

91. Reminiscence by poet Di Brandt in *Globe and Mail*, 24 December, 1993.

92. George Melnyk, *The Search for Community: From Utopia to a Co-operative Society*, Montreal, Black Rose Books, 1985, pp. 98-99. See also, Dietrick, Lorne, "Reflections on Matador," pp. 5-6 in *Together* 4 (4), Fall, 1992.

93. Molly Phillips, "Reminiscences of a Co-operative Rural Community," 1945-1947, 11 *Together*, 4 (l), Winter, 1992, p. 7-9.

94. Kathryn McCamant and Charles Durett, *Cohousing: A Contemporary Approach to Housing Ourselves*, Berkeley, Ca. Habitat Press/Ten Speed Press, 1988.

95. Pat Lorjé, "Reclaiming the NDP's Moral High Ground," *Globe and Mail* 16 August, 1994

96. James Laxer, *In Search of a New Left*, Toronto, Viking, 1996. p. 33-34.

97. *Ibid* p.188.

98. Northrop Frye, *The Educated Imagination*, Toronto, CBC, 1963 p. 62.

99. R.W. Southern, *Western Society and the Church in the Middle Ages*, Harmondsworth, Penguin Books, 1970, p. 237.

100. Catherine de Hueck Doherty, *Poustinia: Christian Spirituality of the East for Western Man*, Notre Dame, Indiana, Ave Maria Press, 1975, p. 30.

101. Quoted on p. 1, Landry, C. et al. *What a Way to Run a Railway: An Analysis of Radical Failure*, London, Comedia, 1985.

102. Spencer Klaw, *Without Sin: The Life and Death of the Oneida Community*, New York, Allen Lane, 1993. "Oneida Finds Silver Lining in Harsh Business Climate," *Globe and Mail*, 13 June, 1996.

103. Petr Kropotkin, *Mutual Aid: A Factor in Evolution*, Boston, Mass., Extending Horizons Books, 1955, p. vii.

104. *Ibid* ix.

105. Victor Turner, *The Ritual Process; Structure and Anti-Structure*, Chicago,

Aldine, 1969.

106. *Ibid* p. 95.

107. *Ibid* p. 126.

108. T.R. Batten, "The Major Issues and Future Directions of Community Development," pp. 27-43 in *Proceedings of the International Consultation on Community Development Education and Training*, September 17-19, 1973, University of Missouri-Columbia.

109. Turner, *The Ritual Process*, p. 127.

110. *Ibid*.

111. James A. Christenson and Jerry W. Robinson, Jr. (Ed), *Community Development in America*, Ames, Iowa, Iowa State University Press, 1980, pp. 8-11.

112. *Ibid* pp. 19-20.

113. Père Anselme Chiasson, *Chéticamp: Histoire et traditions acadiennes*, Moncton, Editions des Aboiteaux, 1972.

114. Central Office of Information, *Community Development: The British Contribution*, London, 1962, p. 3.

115. Kenneth Bradley, *Once a District Officer*, London, Macmillan, 1966, p. 96.

116. A "rough calculation suggests that between 1945 and 1951, Britain extracted some £140 millions from its colonies, putting in only about £40 million under the Colonial Development and Welfare Acts..." Basil Davidson, *The Black Man's Burden: Africa and the Curse of the Nation State*, New York, Random House, 1992, p. 219.

117. Central Office of Information, *Community Development*, p. 6.

118. T.R. Batten, "The Major Issues..." p. 31.

119. Kenneth Bradley, *Once a District Officer*, p. 100.

120. "Elton Mayo and the Hawthorne Investigations" pp. 126-130 in D.S. Pugh, D.J. Hickson, and C.R. Hinings, *Writers on Organizations*, Harmondsworth, Penguin, 1971.

121. *Ibid* "F.W. Taylor," pp. 97-101.

122. Quoted in Pugh *et al. Writers on Organizations*, p. 130.

123. Basil Davidson, *The Black Man's Burden*, p. 209.

124. Claude Ake, *West Africa*, 8 August, 1990 quoted in Davidson, *The Black Man's Burden*, p. 293-94.

125. Andrew Coulson, *Tanzania: A Political Economy*, Oxford, Clarendon Press, 1982: Freeman, Linda *CIDA, Wheat and Rural Development*, Halifax, Centre for Development Studies, 1980.

126. Robert Klitgaard, *Tropical Gangsters*, New York Basic Books, 1990, p. 12.

127. United Nations, *Popular Participation in Development: Emerging Trends in Community Development*, New York, 1971.

128. *Ibid* p. 1.

129. T.R. Batten, "The Major Issues..." p. 31.

130. "Nota Bene," *Globe and Mail* 7 May, 1994 citing *Mortgaging The Earth: The World Bank, Environmental Impoverishment and the Crisis of Development* by

Bruce Rich (Beacon Press).

131. Ivlonika Nikore, "The Oasis Makers," *World Monitor*, 46, February, 1993.

132. Jack Quarter, *Canada's Social Economy: Co-operatives, Non-profits, and Other Community Enterprises*, Toronto, Lorimer, 1992. The federal Co-operatives Secretariat in Ottawa issues an annual report. In 1995, this contained data on 5,412 non-financial cooperatives, with 4.5 million members. The report notes that community development co-operatives which "foster local-level leadership skills and full grassroots participation in problem-solving and innovation" had 11,742 members in 207 ventures, with assets of $12.2 million and revenues of $12.4 million.

133. Jim Lotz, "The Beginnings of Community Development in English-Speaking Canada," pp. 15-28 in Brian Wharf and Michael Clague, *Community Organizing: Canadian Experiences*, Toronto, Oxford University Press, 1997.

134. Jim Lotz and Michael R. Welton, *Father Jimmy*, Wreck Cove, NS, Breton Books, 1997.

135. Jim Lotz, and Michael R. Welton, "Knowledge for the People: The Origins and Development of the Antigonish Movement," pp. 97-111 in Michael R. Welton, (Ed.) *Knowledge for the People: The Struggle for Adult Education in English-Speaking Canada, 1892-1973*, Toronto, OISR Press, 1987.

136. "How FX Saved the Maritimes," *Maclean's*, 1 June, 1953, p. 25.

137. Dan MacInness, St. Francis Xavier University, quoted in *Atlantic Co-operator*, August, 1985.

138. J.T. Croteau, *Cradled in the Waves*, Toronto, The Ryerson Press, 1951.

139. *Ibid* p. 81.

140. A. Davis, "A Prairie Dust Devil: The Rise and Decline of a Research Institution," *Human Organization* 27(l), 1968, pp. 56-63.

141. Department of Agriculture and Immigration, *The People of Indian Ancestry*, Winnipeg, MB, February, 1959, Vol. 1, pp. 103-4.

142. Personal communication from Pat Dunphy, former community development officer, Manitoba.

143. Bert and Kaye Deveaux, "The Enemies Within Community Development," pp. 93-105 in Draper, James A. (Ed), *Citizen Participation: Canada*, Toronto, New Press, 1971.

144. Personal communication, Angus MacIntyre, former community development officer, Indian Affairs.

145. Sally Weaver, *Making Canadian Indian Policy: The Hidden Agenda 1968-70*, Toronto, University of Toronto Press, 1981. p. 28.

146. Stephen Brooks, *Maple Leaf Rag*, Don Mills, Ont. 1987, p. 201.

147. "Ottawa places Stoney Reserve in Trustee's Hands," *Globe and Mail*, 10 September, 1997.

148. "Reserve Headed Toward Trusteeship," *Globe and Mail*, 1 September, 1997.

149. "Sharon," quoted in Peter Duffy's column: "Hey, fair is fair, but what do you call this situation?" *Mail-Star* 28 November, 1995.

150. Dan Smith, *The Seventh Fire: The Struggle for Aboriginal Government*, To-

ronto, Key Porter Books, 1993, p. 2.

151. *Ibid* p. 116. The senator, Walter Twinn, led the challenge to Bill C-31. The band lost the case in 1995 but appealed the decision. Twinn died in 1997.

152. Edward C. Banfield, *The Moral Basis of a Backward Society* New York, The Free Press, 1954.

153. *Ibid* p. 116.

154. The video consists of two parts, one dealing with the descent into alcoholism and the other with the community development process at Alkali Lake that returned the people to sobriety. Available from: Alkali Lake Indian Band, Box 4479, Williams Lake, B.C., V2G 2V5.

155. On CESO, see Jim Lotz, *Sharing a Lifetime of Experience: The CESO Story*, Lawrencetown Beach, N.S. Pottersfield Press, 1997. On Habitat for Humanity, see Millard Fuller and Diane Scott, *Love in the Mortar Joints: The Story of Habitat for Humanity*, Piscatawy, N.J., Association Press, New Century Pubs. 1980.

156. Antony Lloyd, *Community Development in Canada*, Ottawa, Canadian Research Centre for Anthropology, Saint Paul University, 1967.

157. Dal Brodhead, Stewart Goodings, and Mary Brodhead, "The Company of Young Canadians," pp. 137-148 in Wharf, Brian and Michael Clague (Ed), *Community Organizing: Canadian Experiences*, Toronto, Oxford University Press, 1997. The National Film Board commissioned a film on the Company which apparently was never completed, for unexplained reasons.

158. Anne Alexander, *The Antigonish Movement: Moses Coady and Adult Education Today*, Toronto, Thompson Eucational Publishing, 1997, p. 188.

159. Michael Clague, "Thirty Turbulent Years: Community Development and the Organization of Health and Social Services in British Columbia," pp. 91-112 in Wharf, Michael and Michael Clague (Eds.) *Community Organizing: Canadian Experiences*, Toronto, Oxford University Press, 1997.

160. Deena White, "Contradictory Participation; Reflections on Community Action in Quebec," pp. 62-90 in Wharf and Clague, *Community Organizing*. Other provincial governments have shown little understanding of community development. New Brunswick held an inquiry into citizen participation, then set up regional development councils made up mainly of members of traditional elites. When poor people took over the councils after establishment people became bored, and began to confront government, the Hatfield government abolished them, claiming that they had outlived and overstepped their mandate. On Prince Edward Island, a Rural Development Council, founded by rural clergy in 1966, was independent of government. A federal agency provided some *ad hoc* funding for its operations. The provincial government viewed its activities at stimulating community development and public participation in decision making as hostile moves and terminated its funding. On the relationship between top down planning and bottom up initiatives, see Teresa MacNeil, "Assessing the Gap between Community Development Practice and Regional Development Policy," pp. 164-180 in Wharf and Clague op. cit.

161. Milton J. Esman, and Norman T. Uphoff, *Local Organizations: Intermediaries in Rural Development*, Ithaca, Cornell University Press, 1984, p. 185.

162. T.D. Regehr, (Ed) *The Possibilities of Canada are Truly Great!*, Toronto, Macmillan, 1971.

163. *Maclean's*, 2 April, 1966.

164. Human Resources Development Canada, Report to the Minister on Seasonal Work and Unemployment Insurance, Ottawa, March, 1995.

165. A. Paul Pross, *Group Politics and Public Policy*, Toronto, Oxford University Press, 1986, p. l.

166. See, for example, J. Lotz and D. Sewell, "The Process is the Product," pp. 61-165 in Sadler, Barry (Ed), *Public Participation in Environmental Decision Making*, Edmonton, Alberta, Environment Council of Alberta; 1980; Rosemarie Popham, David I. Hay and Colin Hughes, "Who Participates? Citizen participation in health Reform in BC," pp. 273-301 in Wharf, Brian and Michael Clague, *Community Organizing: Canadian Experiences*, Toronto, Oxford University Press, 1997. Dr. D. Connor issues a newsletter called *Constructive Citizen Participation* (Connor Development Services, 5096 Catalina Terr., Victoria, BC, V8Y 2A5).

167. J.L. Granatstein, *Marlborough Marathon: One Street Against A Developer*, Toronto, Hakkert and Samuel, 1971.

168. *Ibid* p. ii.

169. A. Paul Pross, *Group Politics and Public Policy*, p. 38.

170. Herbert Blumer, "Social Movements," pp. 8-29 in Barry McLaughlin, *Studies in Social Movements: A Social Psychological Perspective*, New York, The Free Press, 1969.

171. Quoted in "Groups playing hockey without skates, Charest told CEN (Canadian Environmental Network)" *National News*, February, 1992, p. 4.

172. "Lives Lived—Robert Broughton Bryce," *Globe and Mail*, 2 September, 1997.

173. Quoted in "Info Technology Translates into More Work for Consumers Association," *Mail-Star* (Halifax, N.S.), 11 July, 1994.

174. Peggy MacIsaac, "Women's War: Time to Level the Battlefield" *Mail-Star*, 29 January, 1996.

175. Letter from Diane Allen, *Globe and Mail*, 9 February, 1995.

176. Tennant, Deborah, "Fighting the Crisis of Infertility," *Globe and Mail*, 21 June, 1993.

177. Tzeporah Berman led the protest over the logging at Clayoquot Sound as a volunteer and was recruited by Greenpeace as a "true believer." In the summer of 1997, she led the organization's efforts to stop logging on the coast of British Columbia. Ms Berman was quoted as saying: "For us, compromise is impossible." *Globe and Mail*, 2 July, 1997, "Forest Companies Learn to Prepare."

178. John Bryden, MP (Hamilton-Wentworth), *Special Interest Group Funding: MP's Report*, November 1994.

179. Robert D. Putnam, *Making Democracy Work: Civic Traditions in Modern Italy*, Princeton, N.J., Princeton University Press, 1993.

180. Thomas J. Peters and Robert Waterman, *In Search of Excellence*, New York, Warner Books, p. 890.

181. Tim Brodhead, Brent Herbert-Copley and Anne-Marie Lambert, *Bridges of Hope? Canadian Voluntary Agencies and the Third World*, Ottawa, The North-South Institute, 1988. p. 44-45.

182. June Callwood, "Introduction," *A New Era for Voluntarism,* Toronto, United Way, 1986, p. 12.

183. On the organization of the craft sector in Nova Scotia, see Jim Lotz, *Head, Heart and Hands: Craftspeople in Nova Scotia*, Halifax, Braemar, 1986.

184. Kenneth Westhues, *The Working Centre: Experiment in Social Change*, Kitchener, Ont. Working Centre Publications, 1995.

185. Dave Conzani, "Miracle at Duke and Water," in Westhues, op. cit. p. 81.

186. Mary Douglas, *Purity and Danger*, Harmondsworth, Penguin, 1970, p. 17.

187. *Ibid* p. 12.

188. *Ibid.*

189. *Ibid* p. 193.

190. Milton J. Esman and Norman T. Uphoff, *Local Organizations*, Ithaca, Cornell Univ. Press, 1984, p. 229. In *Tropical Gangsters*, Robert Klitgaard writes of another problem with co-ops in new nations: "In each village a big man would be named president of the co-op and then would simply appropriate the lion's share of any inputs ordered or loans received or profits generated." (p. 164).

191. Charles Hampden-Turner, *From Poverty to Dignity*, Garden City, New York, Anchor Books, 1975, p. 128.

192. "Greg MacLeod, Founder of New Dawn, Cape Breton, Nova Scotia," pp. 70-71 in Report, Commission of Inquiry on Unemployment Insurance (the Forget Commission), Ottawa, 1986.

193. *Ibid.*

194. Economic Council of Canada, *From the Bottom Up: The Community Economic Development Approach*, Ottawa, 1990, p. 2-3.

195. Wayne MacKinnon, *The West Prince Industrial Commission*, Ottawa, Economic Council of Canada, October, 1989.

196. John Wickham, Richard Fuchs, and Janet Miller-Pitt, *Where Credit is Due: A Case Study of the Eagle River Credit Union*, Ottawa, Economic Council of Canada, October, 1989.

197. Michael B. Decter and Jeffrey A. Kowall, *A Case Study of the Kitsaki Development Corporation*, Ottawa, Economic Council of Canada, October, 1989.

198. Althea J. Tolliver and James A. Francois, *From Africville to New Road: How Four Communities Planned Their Development*, Dartmouth, N.S., Watershed Joint Action Committee/Black United Front, 1983.

199. Jim Lotz, "Eating an Elephant; The Community Pride Program in British Columbia," Halifax, Jim Lotz Assoc., December, 1989 (Mimeo.)

200. Personal communication, Catherine Campbell.

201. My wife and I met Karl Schutz on a visit to Chemainus on 12 October, 1995.

The Chemainus Festival of Murals Society has published a book on the murals, updated from time to time.

202. Quoted, in Stanley Meisler, "Take a Look at a Town that Wouldn't Lie Down and Die," pp. 54-64, *The Smithsonian*, May, 1994.

203. Susan Delacourt, "Rossland's Quiet Revolution," *Globe and Mail*, 21 May, 1994.

204. André Carrel, "Direct Democracy," Presentation at Canada West Foundation Annual General Meeting, 28 May, 1994.

205. The Corporation of the City of Rossland, *A Constitution For Local Government: A, Discussion Paper*, 21 August, 1991, p. 7.

206. David Bornstein, *The Price of a Dream*, New York, Simon and Schuster, 1996.

207. Andreas Fuglesang and Dale Chandler, *Participation as Process—What We Can Learn From Grameen Bank, Bangladesh*, Oslo, NORAD, n.d. p. 49.

208. Franz Kafka, *Stories 1904-1924*, London, Futura, 1983, pp. 194-195.

209. Hubert Campfens, *Community Development in Northern Manitoba*. A Research Report, University of Waterloo, 1972, p. 15.

210. R. Alexander Sim, *Intervention: The Ethics of Helping Others*, Paper prepared for the Special Secretariat of the Privy Council, Ottawa, June, 1969, p. 14.

211. Quoted in Environment Canada, Planning and Evaluation Directorate, *The Ark Project: Prince Edward Island: Evaluation Report*. 79-1(JB), 15 February, 1977, p. 1.

212. Fisheries and Environment Canada, *A Most Prudent Ark*, Ottawa, 1977, p. 4.

213. Environment Canada, *The Ark Project*, p. 4.

214. *Ibid.* Appendix A.

215. *Ibid.* Memo from Derek Lovejoy, Interregional Adviser for Non-conventional Energy, United Nations, New York, Mimeo. December, 1978.

216. H. Shirley Horne, "Spry Point Co-op Ark Thrives," *Atlantic Co-operator*. Dec. 96 - Jan. 97.

217. "Biosphere Was 'Bold' Experiment, But Doomed," *Mail-Star*, 30 November, 1996.

218. "The Hills Are Alive with Community Projects," *Coastal Communities News* l(l), December, 1995, p.11-13, and personal communication, Allan Andrews, EDM Design and Management, Halifax, which installed the system.

219. Jean Vanier, *Community and Growth: Our Pilgrimage Together*, Toronto, Griffin House, 1979, p. 35.

220. Jean Vanier, *An Ark for the Poor*, Toronto, Novalis, p. 12.

221. Jeff Moore, quoted in Mary Campbell, "Jean Vanier's Magnificent Ark," *Concordia University Magazine*, September, 1993, p. 12.

222. Rollo May, *Power and Innocence: A Search for the Sources of Violence*, New York, W.W. Norton, 1972, p. 248.

223. Jean Vanier, *Community and Growth: Our Pilgrimage Together*, Toronto, Griffin House, 1979, p. 70.

224. *Ibid.*

225. Jean Vanier, *Be Not Afraid.* Toronto, Griffin House, 1980, p. 79.

226. Deborah Cowley, "A Place of Small Miracles," *Reader's Digest*, October, 1988, pp. 102-106.

227. Debbie Moore, quoted in John Sumarah, *On Becoming a Community: A Married Couple's Journey to L'Arche*, Hantsport, N.S., 1989, p. 27, 29.

228. I visited Waunfawr in October, 1986, and spoke with key people involved in this venture. Those involved have carefully documented what is happening in this community. See *Antur Waunfawr*, published in 1987 by the organization.

229. Mary Anne White, "Difficult Times in a Changing Russia", *Dalhousie News*, 27 January, 1993.

230. John Huey, "The World's Best Brand," *Fortune*, 31 May, 1993, pp. 44-54.

231. Václav Havel, *The Art of the Impossible; Politics as Morality in Practice*, New York and Toronto, Knopf, 1997, p. 8.

232. Quoted in Jacques Rupnik, *The Other Europe*, London, Weidenfeld and Nicolson, 1988, p. 222.

233. William F. Ryan, S.J., *Culture, Spirituality and Economic Development*, Ottawa, International Development Research Centre, August, 1995.

234. *Ibid* p. vi.

235. *Ibid* p. vii.

236. Václav Havel, *Summer Meditations*, New York, Knopf, 1992 pp. 3-4.

237. Václav Havel, *The Art of the Impossible: Politics and Morality in Practice*, p. 146.

238. Larry Drummond, "Rethinking Civil Society: Toward Democratic Consolidation," in *Journal of Democracy* 5(3), July, 1994, p. 15.

239. George M. Foster, "Peasant Society and the Image of Limited Good," *American Anthropologist*, 67(2), 1965 reprinted in Yehudi Cohen (Ed), *Man in Adaptation: The Institutional Framework*, Chicago, Aldine, 1971, pp. 298-311.

240. George Dangerfield, *The Strange Death of Liberal England*, London, Paladin, 1970. Originally published in 1935.

241. Joseph Campbell, *The Hero with a Thousand Faces*, New York, Meridian Books, 1956.

242. Myrna Kostach, *Long Way from Home: The Story of the Sixties Generation in Canada*, Toronto, Lorimer, 1970, p.160. This is one of the few Canadian accounts of the Sixties and the rise of social activism in Canada based on first-hand accounts of those involved.

243. Jane Cruikshank, *Value Dilemmas in Community Development*, Ph.D. thesis, University of Toronto, 1987.

244. *Ibid* p. 131.

245. *Ibid* p. 191.

246. *Ibid* p. 98.

247. Donald Keating, *The Power to Make It Happen*, Toronto, Green Tree, 1975.

248. Joan Newman Kuyek, *Fighting for Hope: Organizing to Realize Our Dreams*,

Montreal, Black Rose Books, 1990.

249. James B. Waldram, *As Long as Rivers Run: Hydroelectric Development and Native Communities in Western Canada*, Winnipeg, University of Manitoba Press, 1988, p.95.

250. Cruikshank, *Value Dilemmas...*p. 103.

251. *Ibid.*

252. Jacques Beaucage, Personal communication.

253. Peter L. Berger, and Richard John Neuhaus, *To Empower People: The Role of Mediating Structures in Public Policy*, Washington. D.C., American Enterprise for Public Policy Research, 1977.

254. *Ibid* p. 2.

255. Joe Klein, "In God They Trust," *The New Yorker*, June 16, 1997, pp. 40-46.

256. "TAGS Run Aground in N.S.," *Mail-Star*, 8 August, 1997.

257. Ralph Matthews, *The Creation of Regional Dependency*, Toronto, University of Toronto Press, 1983, p. 220.

258. *Maclean's Journal*, quoted in Denis Winter, *Haig's Command: A Reassessment*, London, Penguin, Books, 1992, p. 271.

259. William James, "The Moral Equivalent of War," in Roth, John K. (Ed.) *The Moral Equivalent of War and Other Essays*, New York, Harper and Row, 1971, p. 4.

260. *Ibid* p. 14.

261. John W. Bennett, *Hutterian Brethren: The Agricultural Economy and Social Organization of a Communal People*, Stanford, University or California Press, 1967, p. 271.

262. Václav Havel, *The Art of the Impossible: Politics and Morality in Practice*, New York, Knopf, 1997, p. 146.

263. *Ibid* p. 147.

264. Eric Hobsbawn, *Age of Extremes: The Short Twentieth Century, 1914-1991*, London, Abacus, p. 565.

SELECT BIBLIOGRAPHY

Africville Genealogy Society, *The Spirit of Africville*, Halifax Formac/Maritext, 1992.

Alary, Jacques (Ed), *Community Care and Participatory Research*, Montreal, Nu-Age Editions, 1990.

Alinsky, Saul D, *Reveille for Radicals*, New York, Vintage Books, 1969.

_____ *Rules for Radicals: A Pragmatic Primer for Realistic Radicals,* New York,Vintage Books, 1972.

Arbuckle, Gerald, A.S.M., *Out of Chaos: Refounding Religious Congregations*, New York, Paulist Press, 1988.

Barth, Fredrik (Ed.), *Ethnic Groups and Boundaries: The Social Organization of Cultural Difference*, London, George Allen and Unwin, 1969.

Baxter, Joan, *Graveyard for Dreamers: One Woman's Odyssey in Africa*, West Lawrencetown, N.S. Pottersfield Press, 1994.

Bell, John (Comp.), *Key Trends in Communities and Community Development 1992/93*, London, Community Development Foundation, 1993

Bender, Sue, *Plain and Simple, A Woman's Journey to the Amish*, San Francisco, Harper, 1989.

Berger, Peter L., *A Rumor of Angels, Modern Society and the Rediscovery of the Supernatural*, Garden City, Doubleday Anchor, 1970.

_____ *Pyramids of Sacrifice: Political Ethics and Social Change*, Harmondsworth, Penguin, 1974.

Blau, Peter M., *Bureaucracy in Modern Society*, New York, Random House, 1956.

Boguslaw, Robert, *The New Utopians: A Study of System Design and Social Change*, Englewood Cliffs, N.J. Prentice-Hall, 1965.

Bonhoeffer, Dietrich, *Life Together*, San Francisco, Harper and Row, 1954.

Boucher, Douglas (Ed), *The Biology of Mutualism, Ecology and Evolution*, New York, Oxford University Press, 1995.

Bruce, Brendan, *Images of Power: How the Image Makers Shape Our Leaders*, London, Kegan Paul, 1992.

Brym, Robert J, and, R. James Sacoumen, *Underdevelopment and Social Movements in Atlantic Canada*, Toronto, New Hogtown Press, 1979.

Brzezinski, Zbigniew, *Out of Control: Global Turmoil on the Eve of the Twenty-First Century*, New York, Charles Scribner's Sons, 1992.

Cager, John G., *Kingdom and Community: The Social World of Early Christianity*, Englewood Cliffs, N.J. Prentice Hall, 1975.

Cain, Seymour, *Gabriel Marcel*, New York, Hillary House, 1963.

Calouste Gulbenkian Foundation, *Community Business Works*, London, 1982.

Canada, Employment and Immigration, *Community Economic Development in Rural Canada: A Handbook for Practitioners*, Ottawa, 1981.

Careless, Anthony, *Initiative and Response: The Adaptation of Canadian Federalism to Regional Economic Development*, Montreal, McGill-Queen's University Press, 1977.

Carpenter, Edmund, *Oh, What A Blow That Phantom Gave Me!* New York Holt, Rinehart and Winston, 1972.

Cayley, David, *Northrop Frye in Conversation*, Toronto, Anansi, 1992.

Chapin, Henry and Denis Deneau, *Access and the Policy-making Process*, Ottawa, Canadian Council on Social Development, 1978.

Clark, David, *Basic Christian Communities: Implications for Church and Society*, The Liverpool Institute for Socio-Religious Studies, Liverpool, 1978.

_____ *The Liberation of the Church*, Selly-Oak, Birmingham, National Centre for Christian Communities and Networks, 1984.

Clark, Samuel D., J.Paul Grayson, and Linda Grayson, *Prophecy and Protest: Social Movements in Twentieth Century Canada*, Toronto, Gage, 1975,

Clarke, Roger, *Our Own Resources: Co-operatives and Community Economic Development in Rural Canada*, Langholm, The Arkleton Trust, 1981.

Clarke, Tony, *Behind the Mitre: The Moral Leadership Crisis in the Canadian Catholic Church*, Toronto, HarperCollins, 1995.

Cleverly, Graham, *Managers and Magic*, Harmondsworth, Penguin, 1973.

Community Development Project, *The Costs of Industrial Change*, London, CDP Inter-Project Editorial Team, 1977.

Cooper, Matthew and Margaret Critchlow Rodman, *New Neighbours: A Case Study of Co-operative Housing*, Toronto, University of Toronto Press, 1992.

Cooper, Simon and Mike Farrant, *Fire in Our Hearts: The Story of the Jesus Fellowship*, Eastbourne, Kingsway Publications, 1991.

Coppin, Mike (Ed.), *Community Work: Solution of Illusion? Papers from the Second Australasian Conference on Rural Social Work Practice*, Perth, Western Australia, Kookynie Press, 1992.

Corbett, P.A., *We Have With Us Tonight*, Toronto, Ryerson, 1957.

Cowell, Raymond, *W.B. Yeats*, New York, Arco, 1970.

Craig, John G., *The Nature of Co-operation*, Montreal, Black Rose Books, 1993.

Daly, Margaret, *The Revolution Game*, Toronto, New Press, 1970.

Davies, Linda and Eric Schragge (Ed.), *Bureaucracy and Community*, Montreal, Black Rose Books, 1990.

Davis, Wade, *Shadows in the Sun: Essays on the Spirit of Place*, Edmonton, Lone Pine Publishing, 1992.

de Waal, Esther, *Seeking God: The Way of St. Benedict*, Collins, Fount Paperbacks, 1984.

D'Antonio, Michael, *Heaven on Earth: Dispatches from America's Spiritual Frontier*, New York, Crown, 1992.

Diggins, John Patrick, *The Rise and Fall of the American Left*, New York, W.W. Norton, 1992.

Dineen, Janice, *The Trouble with Co-ops*, Toronto, Green Tree, 1974.

Dorsey, Canada Jane and Ellen Ticoll (Eds.), *The Nuts and Bolts of Community Based Economic Development*, Edmonton, Social Planning Council, 1984.

Driver, John, *Community and Commitment*, Scottsdale, Pa, Herald Press, 1976.

Drucker, Peter F., *Innovation and Entrepreneurship: Practice and Principles*, Harper and Row, 1985.

Durran, Maggie, *The Wind at the Door: The Story of the Community of Celebration: Home of the Fisherfolk*, Aliquippa, Pa., Celebration, 1986.

Etzioni, Amitai, *The Moral Dimension: Towards a New Economics*, New York, The Free Press, 1988.

Eyerman, Ron and Andrew Jamison, *Social Movements: A Cognitive Approach*, University Park, Pa, Pennsylvania State University Press, 1991.

Ferguson, Ron, *Chasing the Wild Goose: The Iona Community*, London, Collins, 1988.

Firey, Walter, *Man, Mind and Land: A Theory of Resource Use*, Glencoe, Ill, The Free Press, 1960.

Fisher, Roger and William Ury, *Getting to Yes: Negotiating Without Giving In*, Harmondsworth, Penguin, 1983

Fitzgerald, George R., *Communes: Their Goals, Hopes, Problems*, New York, Paulist Press, 1971

Fleming, Berkeley (Ed.), *Beyond Anger and Longing: Community and Development in Atlantic Canada*, Fredericton, Acadiensis Press, 1988.

Fontan, Jean-Marc, *A Critical Review of Canadian, American and European Community Economic Development Literature*, Vancouver, Centre for Community Enterprise, 1993.

Fraser, Ian M., *Living a Countersign: From Iona to Basic Christian Communities*, Glasgow, Wild Goose, 1990.

Fuller, Millard, *Bokotola*, Piscataway, N.J., New Century Publishers, 1977.

Galanter, Marc, *Cults, Faith, Healing and Coercion*, New York, Oxford University Press, 1989.

Galaway, Burt and Joe Hudson (Eds.), *Community Economic Development: Perspectives on Research and Policy*, Toronto, Thompson Educational Publishing, 1994.

Goulet, Denis and Michael Hudson, *The Myth of Aid: The Hidden Agenda of the Development Reports*, New York, IDOC, 1971.

Government of Newfoundland and Labrador, *Change and Challenge: A Strategic Plan for Newfoundland and Labrador*, St. John's, June, 1992.

Government of Saskatchewan, *Public Involvement in Saskatchewan, A Guide for the Public Service*, Regina, 1994.

Hamilton, Ian, *The Children's Crusade*, Toronto, Peer Martin Assoc., 1970.

Hammond, Herb, *Seeing the Forest Among the Trees: The Case for Wholistic For-*

est Use, Vancouver, Polestar Press, 1991.

Hancock, Graham, *Lords of Poverty*, London, Macmillam, 1989.

Harper, Michael, *A New Way of Living*, Plainfield, N.J., Logos International, 1973.

Hardy, Dennis, *Alternative Communities in Nineteenth Century England*, London, Longman, 1979.

Havel, Václav, *Living in Truth*, London, Faber and Faber, 1987.

Helman, Claire, *The Milton-Park Affair: Canada's Largest Citizen-Developer Confrontation*, Montreal, Véhicule Press, 1987.

Hill, Karen, *Helping You Helps Me: A Guide Book for Self-Help Groups*, Ottawa, Canadian Council on Social Development, 1983.

Hostetler, John A. and Gertrude Enders Huntington, *Hutterites in North America*, New York, Holt, Rinehart and Winston, 1967.

Hug, James E., S.J., *Tracing the Spirit: Communities, Social Action and Theological Reflection*, New York, Paulist Press, 1983.

Jacobs, Jane, *Systems of Survival: A Dialogue on the Moral Foundation of Commerce and Politics*, New York, Random House, 1992.

Jones, Maxwell, *Social Psychiatry in Practice: The Idea of the Therapeutic Community*, Harmondsworth, Penguin, 1968.

Kilgour, David, *Inside Outer Canada*, Edmonton, Lone Pine, 1990.

Korten, David C., *Getting to the 21st Century: Voluntary Action and the Global Agenda*, West Hartford, Conn., Kumarian Press, 1960.

Krohn, Roger G., Berkeley Fleming, and Marilyn Manzur, *The Other Economy: The Internal Logic of Local Rental Housing*, Toronto, Peter Martin Assoc., 1977.

Laidlaw, Alexander Fraser, *The Campus and the Community: The Global Impact of the Antigonish Movement*, Montreal, Harvest House, 1961.

_____ *The Man from Margaree: Writings and Speeches of M.M. Coady*, Toronto, McLelland and Stewart, 1971.

_____ *Housing You Can Afford*, Toronto, Green Tree, 1977.

Lasch, Christopher, *The Culture of Narcissism: American Life in an Age of Diminishing Expectations*, New York, Warner Books, 1977.

Lee, Bill, *Pragmatics of Community Organization*, Mississauga, Ont. 2nd. ed. 1992.

Lockley, Andrew, *Christian Communes,* London, SCM Press, 1976.

Lotz, Jim (Ed.), "Développement Communautaire, Community Development," Special Issue, *Anthropologica*, 9(2), 1967.

Lotz, Patricia A., *New Patterns for Christian Life*, Unpublished MTS thesis, Atlantic School of Theology, 1995.

MacIntyre, Gertrude Anne, *Active Partners: Education and Local Development*, Sydney, N.S., University College of Cape Breton Press, 1995.

MacLeod, Greg, *New Age Business: Community Corporations That Work,* Ottawa, Canadian Council on Social Development, 1986.

_____ *From Mondragon to America: Experiments in Community Economic Development,* Sydney, N.S., University College of Cape Breton Press, 1997.

_____ *Chéticamp*, Sydney, N.S., The Tompkins Ins., University College of Cape Breton, 1991.

MacDonald, J.D. Nelson, *Memoirs of an Unorthodox Clergyman*, Truro, N.S., Co-operative Resources, 1996.

MacPherson, Ian, *Each for All: A History of the Co-operative Movement in English Canada, 1900-1945*,Toronto, Macmillan, 1979.

Mathews, Robin, *Canadian Identity: Major Forces Shaping the Life of a People*, Ottawa, Steel Rail, 1988.

Mathias, Philip, *Forced Growth*, Toronto, James Lewis and Samuel, 1971.

Matthews, Ralph, *"There's No Better Place Than Here: Social Change in Three Newfoundland Communities,"* Toronto, Peter Martin Assoc., 1976.

McCann, Larry (Ed.), *People and Places*, Fredericton, Acadiensis Press, 1987.

McCormack, Cathy, "From the Fourth to the Third World - A Common Vision of Health," *Community Development Jnl.* 28(2): 206-217, July, 1993.

McCuaig, Linda, *Shooting the Hippo*, Toronto, Viking, 1995.

McGill Michael, *American Business and the Quick Fix*, New York, Henry Holt, 1988.

McGuiness, Fred, *Bootstrap Two: Stories of Rural Manitoba Entrepreneurs*, Winnipeg, Manitoba Department or Rural Development, 1989.

Melnyk, George, *Radical Regionalism*, Edmonton, NeWest Press, 1981.

Melville, Keith, *Communes in the Counter Culture: Origins, Theories, Styles of Life*, New York, William Morrow, 1972.

Meštrovi , Stjepan with Miroslav Goreta and Slavin Letica, *The Road from Paradise: Prospects for Democracy in Eastern Europe*, Lexington, University of Kentucky Press, 1993.

Morton, Ralph T., *The Iona Community: Personal Impressions of the Early Years*, Edinburgh, The Saint Andrews Press, 1977.

Moynihan, Daniel P., *Maximum Feasible Misunderstanding*, New York, The Free Press, 1970.

Mungall, Constance, *More Than Just a Job: Worker Cooperatives in Canada*, Ottawa, Steel Rail, 1986.

Negodaeff, Margaret, "Alkali Lake celebrates triumph over alcohol," *Intercom* (Indian Affairs and Northern Development, Ottawa.) August, 1986, p. 1.

Ng, Roxana, Gillian Walker and Jacob Muller (Eds.), *Community Organization and the Canadian State*, Toronto, Garamond Press, 1990.

Nisbet, Robert, *The Social Philosophers: Community and Conflict in Western Thought*, New York, Thomas Crowell, 1973.

Novak, Michael (Ed.), *Democracy and Mediating Structures*, Washington, American Enterprise Institute for Public Policy Research, 1980.

Nozick, Marcia, *No Place Like Home: Building Sustainable Communities*, Ottawa, Canadian Council on Social Development, 1992.

O'Connor, Elizabeth, *The New Community*, New York, Harper and Row, 1976.

Osborn, Fairfield, *Our Plundered Planet*, New York, Pyramid Books, 1968.

Osborne, David and Ted Gaebler, *Reinventing Government: How the Entrepreneurial Spirit is Transforming America*, New York, Plume/Penguin, 1992.

Overy, Richard, *Why the Allies Won the War*, London, Jonathan Cape, 1995.

Pardy, William, *Recreating Community—New Perspectives, New Directions*, Halifax, Saint Mary's University, 1996.

Peck, Scott, *The Different Drum: Community Making and Peace*, New York, Simon and Schuster, 1987.

Perry, Stewart E., *Communities on the Way: Rebuilding Local Economies in the United States and Canada*, Albany, State University of New York, 1987.

Perry, Stewart, Mike Lewis, and Jean-Marc Fontan, *Revitalizing Canada's Neighbourhoods: A Research Report on Urban Community Economic Development*, Vancouver, Centre for Community Enterprise, 1993.

Perry, Stewart, and Mike Lewis, *Reinventing the Local Economy*, Vernon, B.C., The Centre for Community Enterprise, 1994.

Pierce, Neal and Carol F. Steinbach, *Corrective Capitalism: The Rise of America's Community Development Corporations*, New York, Ford Foundation, 1987.

Ponting, J. Rick (Ed.), *Arduous Journey: Canadian Indians and Decolonization*, Toronto, McClelland and Stewart, 1986.

Pross, A. Paul, *Planning and Development: A Case of Two Nova Scotia Communities*, Halifax, Institute of Public Affairs, 1975.

Putnam, Robert D., *Making Democracy Work: Civic Traditions in Modern Italy*, Princeton, N.J., Princeton University Press, 1993.

Purce, Jill, *The Mystic Spiral: Journey of the Soul*, London, Thames and Hudson, 1974.

Quarter, Jack and George Melnyk (Ed.), *Partners in Enterprise: The Worker Ownership Phenomenon*, Montreal, Black Rose Books, 1989.

Redekop, Paul, "The Grain of Wheat Community is much more than an Experiment in Creating Community," *Mennonite Mirror*, 17: 19-20, Dec. 1988.

Reynolds, Charles H. and Ralph V. Norman, *Community in America: The Challenge of 'Habits of the Heart,'* Berkeley, University of California Press, 1968.

Rigby, Andrew, *Communes in Britain*, London, Routledge and Kegan Paul, 1974.

Robinson, Michael P, *Sea Otter Chiefs*, Calgary, Bayeux Arts, 1996.

Rossland, Mark, *Towards Sustainable Communities: A Resource Book for Municipal and Local Governments*, Ottawa, National Roundtable on the Environment and the Economy, 1992.

Ross, David P. and Peter J.Usher, *From the Roots Up: Economic Development as if Community Mattered*, Ottawa, Canadian Council on Social Development/James Lorimer, 1986.

Ross, Rupert, *Dancing with a Ghost: Exploring Indian Reality*, Markham, Ont., Octopus, 1992.

Royal Commission on Aboriginal Peoples, *Sharing the Harvest: The Road to Self-Reliance*, Ottawa, Canadian Communications Group, 1993.

Ruskin College, *Communities in Crisis: A Resource Programme for Local Organizations and Leaders*, Oxford, William Temple Foundation/Ruskin College, 1985.

Sacouman, R. James, "Underdevelopment and the Structural Origins of Antigonish Movement Co-operatives in Eastern Nova Scotia," *Acadiensis* 7(1): 66-85, Autumn, 1977.

Sanders, Marion K., *The Professional Radical: Conversations with Saul Alinsky*, New York, The Perennial Library, 1970.

Sarlo, Christopher A., *Poverty in Canada*, Vancouver, The Fraser Institute, 2nd ed. 1996.

Saul, John Ralston, *Voltaire's Bastards: The Dictatorship of Reason in the West*, Toronto, Viking, 1992.

Schon, Donald A., *Beyond the Stable State: Public and Private Learning in a Changing Society*, Harmondsworth, Penguin, 1973.

Seabrook, Jeremy, *Pioneers of Change: Experiments in Creating a Humane Society*, Philadelphia, New Society, 1993.

Schutz, Karl (Ed), *The Chemainus Murals*, Chemainus, B.C. Festival of Murals, 1993.

Sheehan, Thomas, *The First Coming: How the Kingdom of God Became Christianity*, New York, Random House, 1986.

Siegel, Daniel, and Jenny Yancey, *The Rebirth of Civil Society*, New York, Rockefeller Brothers Fund, 1992.

Siggins, Maggie, *Revenge of the Land: A Century of Greed, Tragedy and Murder on a Saskatchewan Farm*, Toronto, McClelland and Stewart, 1991.

Sim, R. Alex, and Jane Gurr, *Where the Grass Thrusts Through The Concrete: A Survey of Rural Innovations in Canada*, Ottawa, Voluntary Action Directorate, Canadian Heritage, 1994.

_____ *Land and Community: The Crisis in Canada's Countryside*, Guelph, University of Guelph, 1989.

Smillie, Ian, *The Land of Lost Content: A History of CUSO*, Toronto, Deneau, 1985.

Steele, Harvey, S.F.M., *Winds of Change: Social Justice through Co-operatives*, Truro, N.S., Co-operative Resources, 1986.

_____ *Dear Old Rebel; A Priest's Battle for Social Justice*, Lawrencetown Beach, N.S., Pottersfield Press, 1993.

Sviridoff, Michael, "The Seeds of Urban Renewal," *The Public Interest*, Winter, 1994; 82-103.

Tawney, R.H., *The Radical Tradition*, Harmondsworth, Penguin, 1966.

Taylor, Charles, *The Malaise of Modernity*, Toronto, Anansi, 1991.

Taylor, Marilyn, *Signposts to Community Development*, London, Community Development Foundation, 1992.

Thompson, Rollie, *People do it All the Time*, Ottawa, Ministry of State for Urban Affairs, 1976.

Turner, Victor, *Dramas, Fields and Metaphors: Symbolic Action in Human Society*, Ithaca, Cornell University Press, 1974.

Van de Weyer, Robert, *Guru Jesus*, London, SPCK, 1975.

_____ *The Little Gidding Way: Christian Community for Ordinary People*, London, Dartman, Longman and Todd, 1988.

_____ *Little Gidding: Story and Guide*, London, Lamp Press, 1989.

van Rees, Wim et al, *A Survey of Contemporary Community Development*, The Hague, Dr. Gradus Hendriks-stichting, October, 1991.

Vanier, Jean, *An Ark for the Poor: The Story of L'Arche*, Toronto, Novalis, 1995.

Vesey, Laurence, *The Communal Experience: Anarchist and Mystical Counterculture in America*, New York, Harper and Row, 1973.

Vickers, Sir Geoffrey, *The Art of Judgement: A Study of Policy*, London, Methuen, University Paperbacks, 1968.

_____ *Value Systems and Social Progress*, Harmondsworth, Penguin, 1970.

_____ *Freedom in a Rocking Boat: Changing Values in an Unstable Society*, Harmondsworth, 1972.

Vogt, William, *The Road to Survival*, New York, William Sloane, 1948.

Wharf, Brian, *Communities and Social Policy in Canada*, Toronto, McClelland and Stewart, 1992.

Wilkinson, Paul and Jack Quarter, *Building a Community-Controlled Economy*, University of Toronto Press, 1996.

Wismer, Susan and David Pell, *Community Profit: Community-based Economic Development in Canada*, Toronto, Is Five Press, 1981.

Wright, Richard, "Financing native dreams," *Canadian Banker* Jan.-Feb., 1994, pp. 16-20.

York, Geoffrey, *The Dispossessed: Life and Death in Native Canada*, Toronto, Lester and Orpen Denys, 1989.

Zablocki, Benjamin, *The Joyful Community*, Baltimore, Penguin, 1971.

Index